Simple to Spectacular

Simple to Spectacular

HOW TO TAKE ONE BASIC RECIPE TO FOUR LEVELS OF SOPHISTICATION

JEAN-GEORGES VONGERICHTEN
and MARK BITTMAN

BROADWAY BOOKS NEW YORK

Broadway Books titles may be purchased for business or promotional use or for special sales. For information, please write to: Special Markets Department, Random House, Inc., 1540 Broadway, New York, NY 10036.

BROADWAY BOOKS and its logo, a letter B bisected on the diagonal, are trademarks of Broadway Books, a division of Random House, Inc.

Visit our website at www.broadwaybooks.com

Library of Congress Cataloging-in-Publication Data

Vongerichten, Jean-Georges.

Simple to spectacular : how to take one basic recipe to four levels of sophistication / Jean-Georges Vongerichten and Mark Bittman.—1st ed.

    p. cm.

Includes index.

    1. Cookery. I. Bittman, Mark. II. Title.

TX714.V66 2000

641.5—dc21   00-036055

FIRST EDITION

Designed by Vertigo Design, NYC

Photographs by Gentl & Hyers

ISBN 0-7679-0360-9

00 01 02 03 04 10 9 8 7 6 5 4 3 2 1

For our children

No book of this size and ambition is accomplished by its authors alone. Many people helped us, but chief among them was Daniel Del Vecchio, who was with us the entire way, and contributed not only his formidable skills but wonderfully creative ideas throughout the process. If it were not for Danny, this book would be a long time coming.

You can see for yourselves the beautiful work that Andrea Gentl and Marty Hyers did in shooting *Simple to Spectacular*. Their photographs perfectly embody the spirit of the book. We have art directors Mario Pulice and Roberto de Vicq de Cumptich and the folks at Vertigo design to thank for the book's great overall look.

We were fortunate enough to have not one but two top editors to work with: Harriet Bell and Jennifer Josephy. Jennifer Griffin and Judith Sutton also played key roles in smoothing the text. Less readily apparent but extremely important work was done by Anne Resnik, Luisa Francavilla, and Rebecca Holland. Jackie Everly-Warren, Gerry Howard, and Tammy Blake were and continue to be extremely supportive, and Broadway/Doubleday president Steve Rubin is, to put it mildly, a prince. Thanks, too, to his predecessor Bill Shinker for seeing value in our idea.

We'd also both like to thank Angela Miller, our indefatigable agent, for everything.

Jean-Georges Vongerichten and Mark Bittman

I am fortunate enough to work with the greatest people in the restaurant business, and many of them were extremely helpful to me in putting together this book. So thanks to Christian Carrere, Phillipe Gouze, Alicia Fitzgerald, Sue Kim, Bertrand Pierson, Steve Lahhaie, Lois Freedman, Roy Saunders, Suzanne Phillips, Connor Coffey, and Mohammed Kahn; Philippe Vongerichten, David Pogrebin, Kurt Eckert, Denis Bouron, Danny Valentin; Agnes Deshayes, Marie Marco, Ana Marie Mormando, Kerry Simon, Rudy Tauscher, and Geralyn Dalaney; Ron Gallo, Keith Williams, Pierre Shutz, Mike Ramos, Pierre Roubul, Lee Tak Sum, Tim Tolley, Sandrine Zimnol, Geoff Felsenthal, John Grubb, Mohammed Islam, Jonathan Snyder, Chris Beischer, Alex Powell, Heather Clark, Lynn Bound, Guy Rabarijaona, Josh Eden, Creseciano Torres, Eric Hubertt, Gabriel Kreuther, and Jacques Qualin.

Special thanks to my partners, Bob Giraldi and Phil Suarex, my co-author and friend Mark, my parents Jeanine and Georges, and my kids, Louise and Cedric.

Jean-Georges Vongerichten

I, too, owe a debt to all of the great people who work for and with Jean-Georges, and would like to add my thanks to Phil and Bob; the energetic and good-spirited Josh Eden; Eric Hubert; and Pierre Shutz and Keith Williams.

For their support and love, I am in deep debt to David Paskin, Pamela Hort, Angela Miller, John H. Willoughby, and Karen Baar. Special wishes to Kate and Emma Baar-Bittman, who will not soon forget all that this partnership has given us. And finally, thanks and love to Jean-Georges, whose incredible skills and imagination shine on every page of this book.

Mark Bittman

Contents

The idea for *Simple to Spectacular* came to us while we worked on our first book, *Jean-Georges: Cooking at Home with a Four-Star Chef.* I have always liked the recipe-and-variation format, and have used it in all of my other books. But I always kept all of the variations on a simple level, which is natural because I'm a self-trained home cook, not a chef.

Nevertheless, it has long seemed appealing to begin with a basic recipe and prepare progressively more sophisticated variations. Using this "system," a book could serve all levels of people interested in cooking, especially newcomers but even those with experience—assuming, of course, that the variations were truly spectacular. With Jean-Georges as a partner, this was guaranteed, because not only is he capable of preparing the most astonishing four-star dishes, he completely understands simplicity and the challenges facing the home cook.

When, in 1998, I mentioned the simple-to-spectacular concept to Jean-Georges, his instant response was enthusiastic: Not only did he want to join me in this venture, he saw it as the logical departure from our first book. During that project, a collection of his best and best-known recipes, we explored the ways in which a basic dish could be easily transformed into a creation worthy of a four-star restaurant. We'd work in reverse, too, breaking down a menu item from Restaurant Jean Georges and tracing it back to its often simple roots.

Whenever we cooked together we discussed ways in which recipes could be stripped to make them easier or enhanced to make them more spectacular. And we have found that our skills and working styles complement each other perfectly—Jean-Georges is always looking to make dishes more worthy of a four-star restaurant, and I to make them simple enough to prepare by a single cook in a minimally equipped kitchen. Our first book resulted in a happy compromise—some of the world's best restaurant recipes made accessible to home cooks.

Simple to Spectacular is different, comprising fifty different groupings of five recipes. Each grouping begins with a basic recipe and proceeds to four increasingly sophisticated variations, all based on the same techniques. We think it will give you a real understanding of the methods by which chefs and advanced cooks use the basics as springboards for creating recipes—the best way to cook.

For example, we show how a simple poaching technique for fish leads to Halibut with Mustard-Nut Crust, one of the more popular lunch dishes at Jean Georges; we turn Steamed Sticky Rice into Sticky Rice Salad with Scallions; we take a bare-bones tapenade and create Tapenade with Moroccan Spices—an exotic, all-purpose sauce for grilled foods. We prepare and analyze many of our favorite simple dishes—roast stuffed tomato, Sautéed and Roasted Chicken with Natural Juices, and Short Ribs Braised in Red Wine, for example—and let our joint creativity (and Jean-Georges' incomparable skills) build them into spectacular ones like Roast Tomato with Tomato Confit and Basil Oil, Curried Chicken with Dried Fruit and Yogurt, and Short Ribs Braised with Citrus.

Happily, although we welcomed the opportunity to use less common ingredients and more advanced techniques in the complex recipes, we quickly found that most cooks would find even those dishes readily achievable. In fact, we soon came to believe that *Simple to Spectacular* would not only introduce novices to solid, basic recipes but also demonstrate that four-star recipes are often little more than elaborate versions of those basics. By building on simple techniques, we could transform basic dishes into those worthy of a great restaurant; yet they could still be cooked at home.

Jean-Georges has been building on the classics since the 1980s. His rigorous formal training was one-dimensional, and it wasn't until his move from France to Asia that he was exposed to new techniques and ingredients. That done, his openness and ability to integrate foreign components into his once-classic style took over. His career was built upon that ability, and it is a talent and a craft that has become second nature; when you watch him develop a new dish (or a new menu), you see him build on what came before. Furthermore, Jean-Georges has developed an uncanny ability to keep most of his recipes easy to execute.

Underlying his cooking, my cooking, and this book in general is the belief that almost all recipes proceed from the basics, and that once a home cook or a chef becomes comfortable with a given recipe, taking it another step is not difficult. (Most cookbooks, which simply lump all recipes together as if they were all equally challenging, fail to recognize this point.) Therefore, mastery of basic recipes and an idea of how to vary them lead to almost limitless options, as we hope we've demonstrated here.

Mark Bittman
FALL 2000

Introduction   xi

After much work, Jean-Georges has produced a line of sauces and spice mixes, the recipes for some of which are duplicated in this book. They're sold at various specialty stores and online. For more information, call 1-888-622-VONG or visit Jean-Georges.com. Of special interest are the Jean-Georges Passionfruit, Honey-Balsamic, Lemon-Thyme, and Truffle vinaigrettes; Vong Rosemary-Ginger and other sauces; and Vong Curry, Asian, and Fisherman's spice mixes. Worth noting, too, is that Jean-Georges bottles and sells top quality grapeseed oil, the oil of choice in many of our recipes.

soups

Chicken stock

STOCKS are said to be the *fond*—foundation—of great cuisine, but they are really more than that. Once made, they are among the best flavor enhancers, a wonderful addition to countless dishes. We rely primarily on the first two given here. The first of these is traditional chicken stock, a combination of chicken and vegetables that is simmered for just about an hour. Most people think stock takes forever, but it need not, and, as Jean-Georges says, "The best stock tastes of meat, not bones. Shorter cooking times, with lots of meat and not many bones, produces the best stock."

The other is *jus rôti*, a dark stock of intensely roasted chicken and vegetables, which, when reduced, makes a fine sauce. We use it throughout the book, and I recommend that you try making it at least once; you will understand why we like it so much.

KEYS TO SUCCESS

We prefer chicken wings. They have the right balance of gelatin and meat and produce a full-bodied, rich stock quickly. They're also easy to handle. But you can use any chicken parts you like, as long as you include meat and bones, not just bones.

All of these recipes can be multiplied as desired, since those given here make relatively small amounts.

Store stock in the refrigerator; if you bring it to a boil every three days it will keep nearly indefinitely. Or freeze for up to several months.

From there, we offer an Asian-flavored stock, great as a basis for Asian-style soups and stews, as you might expect; a super-enriched jus rôti, which needs only a few noodles or vegetables to become a meal; and consommé, a nearly forgotten classic that looks like chicken broth and tastes like . . . heaven.

One-hour chicken stock

½ large onion

4 cloves

2 pounds chicken wings, cut into 3 or 4 pieces each

1 medium carrot, peeled and chopped

½ stalk celery, chopped

½ leek, trimmed, well washed and chopped

4 cloves garlic

1 bay leaf

10 peppercorns

3 sprigs thyme

Our basic stock, quick and easy enough to make while you're doing something else. It's so flavorful that you may find yourself regretting using canned stock when this runs out.

1 Stud the onion with the cloves and combine all the ingredients with 6 cups water in a large saucepan. Bring to a boil, then lower the heat so that the mixture bubbles steadily but not rapidly. Cook, skimming any foam that accumulates, for about 1 hour.

2 Cool slightly, then strain. Refrigerate (you can skim off the fat after the stock cools completely) and use within 3 days; or see Keys to Success, page 2, for storage suggestions.

MAKES ABOUT 6 CUPS   TIME: 1¼ HOURS, LARGELY UNATTENDED

Dark chicken stock (jus rôti)

2 pounds chicken wings, cut into 3 or 4 pieces each

2 tablespoons extra-virgin olive oil

½ onion, peeled and chopped

1 carrot, peeled and chopped

4 cloves garlic, peeled

½ stalk celery, chopped

3 sprigs thyme

This takes a little time and a little care: the chicken must be fully browned before you add the vegetables, or their liquid will stop the browning process. If you like, you can strain the stock and reduce it, over high heat, to a cup or two of shiny glaze, enough to make a flavorful sauce for meat, chicken, fish, or vegetables. Store the sauce as you would the stock.

1 Place an oven rack in the lowest possible position (if you can roast on the floor of the oven, so much the better) and preheat the oven to its maximum (550°F is ideal).

2 Combine the chicken and olive oil in a roasting pan just large enough to hold the chicken in one layer. Roast for about 45 minutes, stirring and scraping occasionally, until the meat is nicely browned. Add the vegetables and seasonings and stir once or twice, scraping the bottom of the pan, then return to the oven for about 20 minutes more, stirring once or twice.

3 Place the pan on top of the stove (careful—it is very hot) and add 6 cups water. Bring to a boil over medium heat and cook for another 30 minutes, stirring and scraping occasionally. Cool slightly, then strain. Refrigerate (you can skim off the fat after the stock cools completely) and use within 3 days; or see Keys to Success, page 2, for storage suggestions.

MAKES ABOUT 6 CUPS   TIME: 1½ HOURS, LARGELY UNATTENDED

Simple to Spectacular

Asian jus rôti

2 pounds chicken wings, cut into 3 or 4 pieces each

2 tablespoons peanut oil

2 stalks lemongrass, trimmed, roughly chopped, and bruised with the back of a knife

½ onion, peeled and chopped

1 carrot, peeled and chopped

6 scallions, trimmed and roughly chopped

4 ounces ginger, peeled and roughly chopped

½ head garlic, cut in half

1 tablespoon Szechwan peppercorns

This is dark chicken stock with Asian seasonings. It makes a lovely broth—garnished with some chopped scallions—or a base for a noodle soup with lightly cooked vegetables.

1 Place an oven rack in the lowest possible position (if you can roast on the floor of the oven, so much the better) and preheat the oven to its maximum (550°F is ideal).

2 Combine the chicken wings and peanut oil in a roasting pan just large enough to hold the chicken in one layer. Roast for about 45 minutes, stirring and scraping the bottom of the pan occasionally, until the meat is nicely browned. Add the vegetables and seasonings and stir once or twice, scraping, then return to the oven for about 20 minutes more, stirring once or twice.

3 Place the pan on top of the stove (careful—it is very hot) and add 6 cups of water. Bring to a boil over medium heat and cook for another 30 minutes, stirring and scraping occasionally. Cool slightly, then strain. Refrigerate (you can skim off the fat after the stock cools completely) and use within 3 days; or see Keys to Success, page 2, for storage suggestions.

MAKES ABOUT 6 CUPS   TIME: ABOUT 1½ HOURS, LARGELY UNATTENDED

Ultra-rich dark stock (fond riche)

2 tablespoons extra-virgin olive oil

One 8-ounce piece prosciutto or other dry-cured ham, cut into chunks

2 pounds chicken wings, cut into 3 or 4 pieces each

½ onion, peeled and chopped

1 carrot, peeled and chopped

4 cloves garlic, peeled

½ stalk celery, chopped

3 sprigs thyme

1 recipe One-Hour Chicken Stock (page 3)

Simple chicken stock turned into jus rôti, with the addition of ham: a powerful combination. After cooking, this can be reduced to a glaze of just about 2 cups, and can then serve as a wonderful sauce, especially for simply steamed vegetables. But it is so flavorful that it can just be used without reduction as a light sauce, or as part of other sauces. Really delicious.

1 Place a rack in the lowest possible position (if you can roast on the floor of the oven, so much the better) and preheat the oven to its maximum (550°F is ideal).

2 Combine the olive oil, prosciutto, and chicken in a roasting pan just large enough to hold the chicken in one layer. Roast for about 45 minutes, stirring and scraping the bottom of the pan occasionally, until the meat is nicely browned. Add the vegetables and seasonings and stir once or twice, scraping, then return to the oven for about 20 minutes more, stirring once or twice.

3 Place the pan on top of the stove (careful—it is very hot) and add the stock. Bring to a boil over medium heat and cook for another 30 minutes, stirring and scraping occasionally. Cool slightly, then strain. Refrigerate (you can skim off the fat after the stock cools completely) and use within 3 days; or see Keys to Success, page 2, for storage suggestions.

Simple to Spectacular

MAKES ABOUT 6 CUPS   TIME: ABOUT 1½ HOURS, LARGELY UNATTENDED

Consommé

1 recipe One-Hour Chicken Stock (page 3)

10 to 12 ounces boneless, skinless chicken meat, preferably from the leg

½ onion, peeled and chopped

1 medium carrot, peeled and chopped

1 stalk celery, chopped

½ leek, trimmed, well washed, and chopped

1 tomato, cut into quarters

Salt and freshly ground black pepper

4 egg whites

1 cup ice cubes

You might think consommé, a crystal-clear broth, is for sick people, but you'll change your mind after you try it. It's deceptively addictive, a rich, clear soup that makes you wonder where all its intense flavor comes from. There is some time and patience involved here, mostly after adding the egg whites, which act as a magnet to clarify the broth.

1 Place the stock in a large saucepan, turn the heat to medium-high, and bring to a boil. Adjust the heat so that the mixture bubbles steadily but not too rapidly.

2 Meanwhile, chop the chicken, onion, carrot, celery, leek, and tomato into ¼-inch pieces; or put them in a food processor and grind all together, but not too fine. Season the mixture well; season the simmering stock too.

3 Stir the egg whites and ice cubes into the chicken mixture and add it all at once to the simmering stock. Whisk once or twice and bring back to a boil. Adjust the heat so that the liquid bubbles steadily but not too rapidly; the solids will form a "raft" on top of the liquid. Create a "chimney," a hole in one side of the raft, simply by spooning some of the solids out of the way. Let cook for about 10 minutes, gradually enlarging the chimney by scooping the solids from the edge of the raft onto the middle.

4 Ladle the liquid through a strainer lined with cheesecloth. Refrigerate (you can skim off the fat after the stock cools completely) and use within 3 days; or see Keys to Success, page 2, for storage suggestions. Serve hot, garnished with diced tomatoes, thin noodles, and/or pieces of meat, or completely naked.

MAKES ABOUT 6 CUPS   TIME: ABOUT 30 MINUTES

SOUPS like these are the easiest, quickest way to combine a variety of different ingredients in one dish—and it's almost impossible to find someone who doesn't like soup. Start with good chicken stock, like that on page 3, or even decent canned stock, add a few ingredients, and you have a great starter or centerpiece of a fine meal.

We first shock the broth with a load of flavor and just a little body with a parsley puree, then go on to a thick, healthy, big-tasting vegetable soup. After that we add wontons and raviolis—there's little difference between the two—to a couple of appropriately flavored broths, and finally create a rather grand soup garnished with lentils and a rich flan based on chicken liver.

KEYS TO SUCCESS

Good broth makes a huge difference here. If you can't use our One-Hour Chicken Stock (page 3), you might consider this quick fix for canned broth: Simmer it for about 15 minutes with a roughly chopped carrot, celery stalk, an onion, and a little garlic and thyme or parsley before proceeding with the recipe.

Keep the heat moderate and don't overcook soup ingredients—they should be tender, of course, but not mushy.

If you're making soup in advance, hold off cooking starchy ingredients—like our wontons and raviolis—until you reheat the broth. Otherwise, they'll become pasty and make the broth too thick.

Chicken soup with parsley puree

6 cups One-Hour Chicken Stock (page 3) or other stock

Salt and freshly ground black pepper

2 cups parsley leaves, rinsed but not dried

1 clove garlic, peeled

2 tablespoons extra-virgin olive oil

If, when you make stock, you know that it is destined for this quick soup, add some parsley stems to the simmering broth. And feel free to make this quick puree with any tender herb you like—basil, chives, chervil, dill, or a combination.

1 Heat the stock over medium-high heat and season it with salt and pepper. Meanwhile, combine the parsley, garlic, olive oil, and salt to taste in a blender and turn on the machine. Add a little of the stock if necessary to allow the machine to do its work, and blend the mixture until it is a smooth puree.

2 Serve the soup, spooning a dollop of the puree into each bowl.

MAKES 4 SERVINGS   TIME: 20 MINUTES

Fresh vegetable soup

6 cups One-Hour Chicken Stock (page 3) or other stock

4 to 6 cups chopped vegetables, such as onion, leek, carrot, cabbage, and celery

2 to 3 large cloves garlic, peeled and thinly sliced

Salt and freshly ground black pepper

1 cup orzo

With the exception of the slices of garlic, our vegetable assortment here is pretty much classic (and really quite terrific), but almost any combination you can imagine will work well. In place of orzo, you can use pastina or other "soup" pasta.

1 Put the stock in a large saucepan and turn the heat to medium-high. Add the vegetables, garlic, and salt and pepper to taste. Cook at a slow boil, stirring occasionally, until the vegetables are beginning to become tender, about 10 minutes. Season to taste.

2 Add the orzo and continue to cook, stirring occasionally, until the orzo and vegetables are tender but not mushy. Taste and adjust the seasoning—this is good with plenty of black pepper—then serve.

MAKES 4 TO 6 SERVINGS   TIME: 40 MINUTES

Chicken soup with chicken wontons

6 cups One-Hour Chicken Stock (page 3) or other stock

5 stalks lemongrass, trimmed and roughly chopped

2 ounces ginger, roughly chopped (don't bother to peel)

½ small chile (optional)

1 clove garlic

2 tablespoons peeled and julienned ginger

1 boneless, skinless chicken breast, about 12 ounces

½ small chile, minced (optional)

1 tablespoon peeled and minced ginger

¼ cup minced scallions

2 tablespoons minced cilantro

Twelve 2-inch-square wonton wrappers

½ cup chopped scallions or chives

Wonton wrappers are sold in virtually every supermarket in the country and are easy to handle.

1 Combine the stock, lemongrass, chopped ginger, ½ chile, if using, and garlic in a saucepan and bring to a boil. Simmer for 15 minutes, then strain the stock. Reheat to a simmer with the julienned ginger.

2 While the stock is simmering, chop the chicken breast into ¼-inch dice (you can use a food processor for this, but be careful not to grind the meat too fine). Combine with the minced chile, if using, minced ginger, scallions, and cilantro.

3 Put a tablespoon or so of the chicken mixture in the center of each of the wontons; rub the edges of the dough with a little water, then fold over and seal to make a triangle. (If you like, you can dampen the two opposite corners of each triangle and fold over onto the center to make an attractive package rather like a large tortellini.)

4 Poach the wontons in the simmering broth for 5 minutes, then add the scallions or chives; cook for another 5 minutes and serve.

MAKES 4 SERVINGS   TIME: 40 MINUTES

Rich chicken soup with chestnuts and mushroom ravioli

1½ pounds chicken wings, each cut into 3 or 4 pieces

2 stalks celery, roughly chopped

2 carrots, peeled and roughly chopped

½ cup peeled and chopped celeriac (celery root)

1 onion, peeled and roughly chopped

1 leek, trimmed, well washed, and roughly chopped

25 chestnuts, peeled (see page 98) and roughly chopped

1 tablespoon extra-virgin olive oil

1 bay leaf

1 sprig thyme

Salt and freshly ground black pepper

8 cups One-Hour Chicken Stock (page 3) or other stock

2 tablespoons butter

8 ounces assorted mushrooms, trimmed, washed, and roughly chopped

2 tablespoons minced shallots

½ cup chopped parsley

¼ cup freshly grated Parmesan

Twelve 2-inch round ravioli or wonton wrappers

Think of this broth as chicken stock squared—it's really intense, even more so thanks to the addition of the strong flavors of celery root and chestnuts. With the mushroom ravioli, this becomes a super-soup.

---

1 Preheat the oven to 450°F. Put the chicken in a roasting pan on top of the stove and turn the heat to high; cook the wings, stirring occasionally, until they start to brown, about 5 minutes. Add the vegetables, chestnuts, olive oil, bay leaf, and thyme, along with salt and pepper to taste, and cook, stirring occasionally, until the vegetables begin to release their liquid, about 5 minutes.

2 Put the pan in the oven and roast, stirring occasionally, until the mixture begins to darken, about 20 minutes—don't let it get too brown. Add the stock and cook for about 1 hour, until the liquid is reduced by about one-quarter. Remove and reserve a few of the chestnut pieces for garnish. Put the remaining mixture into a food mill and puree, removing the bones as they get in the way. Press the resulting puree through a fine sieve and reheat gently in a saucepan.

3 While the stock is roasting, make the ravioli: Put 1 tablespoon of the butter in a skillet over medium-high heat and add the mushrooms and shallots. Cook, stirring occasionally, for about 10 minutes, or until softened. Remove from the heat

and cool slightly, then combine with the parsley, Parmesan, and salt and pepper to taste. Put a tablespoon or so of this mixture in the center of each of the ravioli wrappers; moisten the edges of the dough with water and fold over to seal.

4 Bring a medium saucepan of water to a boil. Cook the ravioli for about 3 to 4 minutes, just until tender.

5 Stir the remaining 1 tablespoon butter into the broth, then taste and adjust the seasoning. Put 2 or 3 ravioli and a few chestnut pieces into the bottom of each of four to six bowls, ladle the broth over all, and serve.

MAKES 4 TO 6 SERVINGS   TIME: ABOUT 2 HOURS, SOMEWHAT UNATTENDED

Chicken soup with lentils and chicken liver flan

2 ounces chicken liver

1 tablespoon marrow (optional)

1 small clove garlic

½ cup milk

1 egg

Salt and freshly ground black pepper

6 cups One-Hour Chicken Stock (page 3) or other stock

1 tablespoon sherry vinegar, or to taste

1 cup cooked lentils (you can use the recipe on page 160, or simply poach ½ cup dried lentils in water until tender), gently warmed

½ cup crumbled crisp-cooked bacon, about 4 strips

¼ cup chopped chives

A meltingly tender flan of chicken liver and seasonings makes this soup quite swank, and the lentils provide a perfect textural foil.

1 Preheat the oven to 350°F. Combine the liver, marrow, if using, garlic, milk, egg, and salt and pepper to taste in a blender and puree.

2 Lightly butter 4 small ramekins (ideally, they'll be 3- or 4-ounce ramekins, but if yours are larger, just don't fill them as full). Pour one-quarter of the puree into each, then put the dishes in a small baking pan and add hot water to come about halfway up their sides. Bake for 20 to 25 minutes, until barely set; they should still be quite jiggly.

3 Meanwhile, heat the stock in a saucepan; add the vinegar, then taste and adjust the seasoning.

4 Gently overturn a flan into each of four bowls; surround with a couple of spoonfuls of the lentils, then garnish with the bacon and chives. Spoon the broth over all and serve.

MAKES 4 SERVINGS   TIME: 45 MINUTES

PERHAPS the most amazing recipe here is the first one, which demonstrates just how easy it is to make a creamy, velvety soup without cream. The secret ingredient? Butternut squash, which, when pureed, creates a soup as silky as one laden with cream.

Not that this can't be improved upon. We do so by browning the squash first and adding herbs; by garnishing the soup with chestnuts and making it even creamier with the addition of crème fraîche; by adding coconut milk, Thai spices, and shrimp; and by making a quick dumpling for added elegance and flavor.

KEYS TO SUCCESS

Note that a 2-pound squash yields just about 1 pound of flesh, which is the right amount for all of these recipes.

To peel, cut the squash in half right where it begins to bulge. Peel with a paring knife, and don't worry too much about precision. Cut the bottom section in half and scoop out the seeds before cubing; the top section can usually just be cut into chunks. The smaller the chunks, the faster the squash will be soft enough to puree.

Creamy **butternut squash soup**

2 pounds butternut squash, peeled, seeded, and cut into chunks

4 cups One-Hour Chicken Stock (page 3) or other stock

Salt and freshly ground black pepper

One of the simplest soups imaginable, yet surprisingly wonderful.

1 Combine the squash, stock, and salt and pepper to taste in a saucepan. Bring to a boil, turn the heat to medium-low, and cook, covered, until the squash is very tender, 15 to 30 minutes (depending on the size of your chunks).

2 Carefully puree the squash in a blender with enough of the stock to allow the machine to do its work. The mixture should be very smooth. Combine with the stock remaining in the saucepan and whisk until smooth. Taste and season again with salt, if necessary, and lots of black pepper. Reheat if necessary and serve.

MAKES 4 SERVINGS   TIME: 30 TO 40 MINUTES

Simple to Spectacular

Roasted butternut squash soup

2 tablespoons extra-virgin olive oil

1 teaspoon minced garlic

2 pounds butternut squash, peeled, seeded, and cut into 1-inch chunks

½ teaspoon red pepper flakes

1 teaspoon thyme leaves

Salt and freshly ground black pepper

4 cups One-Hour Chicken Stock (page 3) or other stock

3 tablespoons freshly grated Parmesan

Here, the squash is pan- and then oven-roasted before adding the stock, intensifying both flavor and color.

1 Preheat the oven to 450°F. Place the olive oil in a large ovenproof skillet, preferably nonstick, and turn the heat to high. Add the garlic and squash, then the red pepper flakes, thyme, and salt and pepper to taste. Cook, stirring frequently, until the squash begins to brown, about 10 minutes.

2 Transfer to the oven and cook for another 15 minutes, shaking the pan once or twice.

3 Return the skillet to the top of the stove over medium heat and add the stock. Cook until the squash is very tender, another 15 minutes or so; carefully puree in a blender. Reheat, garnish with the Parmesan, and serve.

MAKES 4 SERVINGS   TIME: 45 MINUTES

Creamy butternut squash soup with glazed chestnuts

2 pounds butternut squash, peeled, seeded, and cut into chunks

4½ cups One-Hour Chicken Stock (page 3) or other stock

Salt and freshly ground black pepper

12 chestnuts

Neutral oil, such as canola or grapeseed, as needed

1 tablespoon butter

1¼ cups crème fraîche, sour cream, or yogurt, plus 4 teaspoons for garnish

Minced chives for garnish

Chestnuts add their distinctive flavor to this soup, and crème fraîche makes it supremely creamy.

1 Combine the squash, 4 cups of the stock, and salt and pepper to taste in a saucepan. Bring to a boil, turn the heat to medium-low, and cook, covered, until the squash is very tender, 15 to 30 minutes (depending on the size of your chunks).

2 Meanwhile, use a paring knife to cut a circle around the equator of each of the chestnuts. Put enough oil to come to about ¼ inch deep in a 10-inch skillet with high sides; turn the heat to high. After a few minutes (the oil should be at least 350°F), add the chestnuts and cook, stirring them (or shaking the pan) until they begin to pop open, 3 to 4 minutes. As they do, drain them briefly on a towel, then peel off the skins, using a towel to protect your hands.

3 Put the peeled chestnuts in a small saucepan with ¼ cup of the stock, butter, and salt and pepper to taste and cook over medium heat, covered, until the liquid is just about gone, about 10 minutes. Add the remaining ¼ cup stock and cook until the chestnuts are glazed and tender, about 20 minutes total; turn off heat and let them rest while you puree the soup.

4 Carefully puree the squash in a blender with enough of the stock to allow the machine to do its work. The mixture should be very smooth. Combine with the stock remaining in the saucepan and whisk until smooth. Taste and season again with salt, if necessary, and lots of black pepper. Whisk in the crème fraîche and reheat.

5 Put 3 chestnuts in each of four bowls. Cover with a portion of the soup, then garnish with a small dollop of crème fraîche and some chives.

MAKES 4 SERVINGS   TIME: 40 MINUTES

Curried butternut squash soup with shrimp

4 tablespoons butter

2 teaspoons Thai yellow curry paste or curry powder

2 pounds butternut squash, peeled, seeded, and cut into chunks

3 cups One-Hour Chicken Stock (page 3) or other stock

1 can (about 14 ounces) unsweetened coconut milk

1 tablespoon nam pla (Thai fish sauce), or to taste

Juice of 1 lime, or to taste

12 medium to large shrimp, peeled

Minced cilantro for garnish

Lime wedges

An unexpected departure and, with the shrimp, very much main-course material.

1 Place 3 tablespoons of the butter in a medium saucepan and turn the heat to medium-high. When it melts, add the curry paste or curry powder and cook, stirring, for 1 minute. Add the squash and cook for about 5 minutes, stirring, just until it begins to brown.

2 Add the stock and cover; cook until the squash is just about tender, 15 minutes or so. Stir in the coconut milk and cook for about 5 minutes more, until the squash is very tender. Carefully puree the squash in a blender with enough of the stock to allow the machine to do its work. The mixture should be very smooth. Combine with the stock remaining in the saucepan and whisk until smooth. Season with the nam pla and lime juice. Keep warm.

3 Meanwhile, place the remaining 1 tablespoon butter in a 10-inch skillet and turn the heat to medium-high. When the butter melts, cook the shrimp for about 2 minutes per side, until pink.

4 Put 3 shrimp in each of four bowls. Cover each with a portion of the soup, then garnish with some minced cilantro. Serve with lime wedges.

MAKES 4 SERVINGS   TIME: 40 MINUTES

Simple to Spectacular

Butternut squash soup with herbed cheese dumplings

2 pounds butternut squash, peeled, seeded, and cut into chunks

4 cups One-Hour Chicken Stock (page 3) or other stock

Salt and freshly ground black pepper

1 teaspoon minced tarragon

2 tablespoons minced chervil

1 tablespoon minced parsley

1 tablespoon minced chives

4 ounces fresh goat cheese or 4 ounces ricotta, drained in a strainer for a few minutes

1 egg

¼ cup flour

⅛ teaspoon grated nutmeg

¼ cup freshly grated Parmesan

Small fresh dumplings, made from cheese and seasonings—you can call them gnocchi if you prefer—add a light, special touch to this basic soup.

1 Combine the squash, stock, and salt and pepper to taste in a saucepan. Bring to a boil, turn the heat to medium-low, and cook, covered, until the squash is very tender, 15 to 30 minutes (depending on the size of your chunks).

2 While the squash is cooking, combine the herbs with the goat cheese or ricotta, egg, flour, nutmeg, Parmesan, and salt and pepper to taste. Refrigerate.

3 Carefully puree the squash in a blender with enough of the stock to allow the machine to do its work. The mixture should be very smooth. Combine with the stock remaining in the saucepan and whisk until smooth. Taste and season again with salt, if necessary, and lots of black pepper.

4 Reheat the soup until it is just steaming, then drop teaspoons of the dumpling mixture into it. Cook for about 2 minutes from the time of the final addition, or until the dumplings are hot; they will remain quite delicate. Serve immediately.

MAKES 4 SERVINGS   TIME: 40 MINUTES

Gazpacho

WHAT makes a gazpacho? Is it pureed tomatoes? Is it cold? Is it vinegary? Does it contain bread? Ask five different people familiar with Spanish food and you'll get five different answers. We've decided to define it this way: It's a cold, refreshing soup with a fairly high level of acid that comes from vinegar, tomatoes, or lemon or lime juice.

We've come up with a super-fast uncooked tomato-based gazpacho; a smooth gazpacho with quickly sautéed cantaloupe; another made with cucumbers, coconut milk, and Thai flavors; an almond gazpacho Jean-Georges learned in Portugal half a lifetime ago; and a gorgeous gazpacho consommé.

KEYS TO SUCCESS

Keep the cooking time short in all of these—maintaining the fresh flavor of the vegetables is key.

If you choose to peel tomatoes—not absolutely necessary, although we prefer to take this extra step—cut a small X in the smooth ends and drop them into boiling water for about 10 seconds. Plunge into ice water, then peel. You can seed them by cutting them in half through their equators and squeezing and shaking out the seeds.

To chill the cooked mixtures quickly, put them in a wide bowl inside an even wider bowl that has been filled with ice and water. Whisk occasionally until cooled.

Fast gazpacho

1 medium cucumber, peeled

4 tomatoes (about 1½ pounds), cut into chunks

1 red bell pepper, cored, seeded, and cut into chunks

1 small onion, peeled and cut into chunks

Salt and freshly ground black pepper

Tabasco sauce to taste

3 tablespoons extra-virgin olive oil, or to taste

3 tablespoons sherry vinegar, or to taste

Nothing faster, and quite good, especially when made with high-quality vegetables. Be sure to taste and adjust the seasoning before serving.

1 Cut the cucumber lengthwise in half and scrape out the seeds.

2 Combine the cucumber, tomatoes, red pepper, onion, and salt and pepper to taste in the container of a blender. Blend, but don't make it too smooth; the soup is better with a coarser texture.

3 Add more salt, if necessary, and the Tabasco, olive oil, and vinegar. Serve, or cover and refrigerate for up to 2 hours.

MAKES 4 SERVINGS   TIME: 10 MINUTES

Tomato-melon **gazpacho**

One 3-pound cantaloupe

5 tablespoons extra-virgin olive oil

4 tomatoes (about 1½ pounds), cored, peeled, seeded, and cut into 1-inch chunks

1½ cups water, or 1 cup water and ½ cup ice cubes

10 leaves basil

Salt and freshly ground black pepper

Juice of 1 lemon, or to taste

We love this dish, which is smooth and creamy, with just enough acidity to make it sing. To turn it into a meal, grill some shrimp and serve them in or alongside the soup.

1 Halve and seed the melon. Remove the flesh from the rind; cut into chunks. Place 1 tablespoon of the olive oil in each of two 10- or 12-inch skillets and turn the heat under both to high (you can do this sequentially if you prefer). Add the melon to one and the tomatoes to the other and cook, stirring, until they both become juicy, no longer than 2 minutes.

2 Put the melon, tomato, water (and ice cubes), and basil in a blender, along with the remaining 3 tablespoons oil, and salt and pepper to taste, and puree until smooth. Chill.

3 Add the lemon juice and adjust the seasoning. Serve.

MAKES 4 SERVINGS   TIME: 20 MINUTES, PLUS TIME TO CHILL

Simple to Spectacular

Cucumber-coconut **gazpacho**

1 medium onion, peeled and chopped

2 cloves garlic, peeled and chopped

2 tablespoons extra-virgin olive oil

1 pound cucumbers, peeled

Salt and freshly ground black pepper

1¼ cups One-Hour Chicken Stock (page 3) or other stock

1 cup canned unsweetened coconut milk

½ cup mint leaves

Tabasco sauce to taste

Juice of 1 lime, or to taste

1 to 2 tablespoons nam pla (Thai fish sauce), or to taste

Minced cilantro for garnish

This Thai-flavored gazpacho, rich and delicious, is a surprising and delightful change from the Spanish standard.

1 Combine the onion and garlic in a skillet with the olive oil and turn the heat to medium. Cook, stirring occasionally, until the onion softens, about 5 minutes. Meanwhile, cut the cucumbers lengthwise in half and scoop out the seeds. Cut the cucumbers into chunks.

2 Add the cucumbers, along with a little salt and pepper to taste, to the onion. Cook for 2 minutes, stirring occasionally, then add the chicken stock and cook for 5 minutes until the cucumbers just begin to become tender.

3 Add the coconut milk and cook for 3 minutes, then add the mint, Tabasco, lime juice, and 1 tablespoon of the nam pla. Remove from the heat.

4 Put the mixture in the container of a blender and puree until smooth. Taste and add more nam pla, lime juice, and/or Tabasco to taste. Chill.

5 Serve garnished with cilantro.

MAKES 4 SERVINGS   TIME: 20 MINUTES, PLUS TIME TO CHILL

Simple to Spectacular

Rice, almond, and apple **gazpacho**

2 medium cucumbers, peeled

1 cup cooked rice

1 Granny Smith apple, unpeeled, cored and chopped

1 green bell pepper, cored, seeded, and chopped

1 medium onion, peeled and chopped

2 tablespoons red wine vinegar

¾ cup extra-virgin olive oil

1 cup almond powder (sold at many supermarkets and all pastry supply stores, or see page 407)

Tabasco sauce to taste

Salt and freshly ground black pepper

1 large or 2 small slices bread, cut into ½-inch cubes

1 hard-boiled egg, chopped

1 tomato, peeled, seeded, and finely chopped

2 ounces Gruyère, Manchego, or other flavorful semi-hard cheese, minced

Thanks to the rice and almond powder, this is a thicker, sweeter gazpacho than most. The flavors, which include apple, are subtle but distinctive. Feel free to play with the garnishes, which can be varied at will.

1 Cut the cucumbers lengthwise in half and scoop out the seeds. Chop one and mince the other; set the minced cucumber aside.

2 Combine the chopped cucumber, rice, apple, green pepper, onion, and vinegar in a bowl with 2½ cups water and let sit for 15 minutes. Put into the container of a blender and carefully puree until smooth.

3 Transfer to a bowl and add all but 3 tablespoons of the olive oil, along with the almond powder, Tabasco, and salt and pepper to taste. Whisk until smooth, then chill.

4 Put 2 tablespoons of the remaining olive oil in a medium skillet and turn the heat to medium. Cook the bread cubes, shaking the skillet occasionally, until nicely browned, 5 to 10 minutes.

5 Divide the gazpacho among four bowls and garnish each with the croutons, egg, tomato, minced cucumber, and cheese. Drizzle with the remaining 1 tablespoon olive oil and serve.

MAKES 4 SERVINGS   TIME: 40 MINUTES

Soups

Cold gazpacho consommé with crab

1 medium cucumber, peeled

5 large tomatoes (about 2 pounds), chopped

1 green bell pepper, seeded, cored, and chopped

1 red bell pepper, seeded, cored, and chopped

1 small beet (about 4 ounces), peeled and chopped

6 egg whites, beaten lightly

2 tablespoons extra-virgin olive oil

1 tablespoon red wine vinegar

1 cup ice cubes

Salt and freshly ground black pepper

Tabasco sauce to taste

2 cups crabmeat, about 1 pound, picked over for shells and cartilage

1 cup peeled, seeded, and diced tomato

1 cup peeled, seeded, and diced cucumber

½ cup minced basil

You can use any cooked seafood of your choosing in this lovely red consommé, or serve it as a plain chilled broth. As a small starter, it will serve eight. The flavor is intense—and delicious.

1 Cut the cucumber in half lengthwise and scoop out the seeds; chop it. Combine the cucumber, chopped tomatoes, peppers, and beet in a large saucepan with water to cover (4 to 5 cups). Bring to a boil over high heat; turn the heat to medium and cook until the vegetables are tender, about 20 minutes.

2 Combine the egg whites with the oil and vinegar and stir into the simmering liquid, along with the ice cubes. Bring to a boil, stirring, then turn the heat down so that just a few bubbles appear at different spots on the surface. As the egg white "raft" solidifies, poke a hole in it with a spoon so that the bubbling liquid has a place to escape. Cook for 15 minutes.

3 Line a strainer with a cloth napkin. Ladle out the liquid through the hole— don't worry if some of the solids come along with it—and pour it through the strainer; it will be red and clear. Chill for up to a day.

4 Season the consommé with salt and pepper and Tabasco to taste. Serve it garnished with the crabmeat, tomato, cucumber, and basil.

MAKES 4 TO 8 SERVINGS   TIME: ABOUT 1 HOUR, PLUS TIME TO CHILL

Salads

FRISÉE is an ultra-curly lettuce (actually a chicory, but who cares?) that has two benefits: Its shape traps lots of dressing, and its flavor is fairly bitter and strong, though still quite pleasant. Of course, you can make these salads with any greens you like.

A very simple, basic vinaigrette starts us off, then we move to three French classics—greens with blue cheese and nuts, greens with bacon and poached eggs, and greens with gizzard confit and lentils. Finally, the coup de grâce: a superb salad of greens, scallops, white truffles, and Parmesan.

KEYS TO SUCCESS

Figure 2 ounces of frisée per person, about half of a small head.

Frisée is tastier and less bitter when pale yellow than when dark green.

To clean frisée, cut out the core with a paring knife, then separate the leaves, wash, and spin dry.

Frisée salad with simple vinaigrette

2 heads frisée or other lettuce, or a mixture
(about 8 ounces total)

2 tablespoons peeled and minced shallots

¼ cup sherry vinegar

2 tablespoons hazelnut or walnut oil

2 tablespoons grapeseed or canola oil

Salt and freshly ground black pepper to taste

One of the most basic of all salads, yet, when done right, near perfection.
Using nut oil makes a huge difference; just make sure it is fresh.

1 Trim, wash, and dry the lettuce. Whisk together the remaining ingredients. *(The dressing can be prepared in advance and allowed to sit, covered and refrigerated, overnight. Whisk again before serving.)*

2 Dress and toss the lettuce, season again if necessary, and serve.

MAKES 4 SERVINGS   TIME: 15 MINUTES

Frisée salad with Roquefort and walnuts

20 walnut halves

2 heads frisée or other lettuce, or a mixture (about 8 ounces total)

2 tablespoons minced shallots

¼ cup sherry vinegar

2 tablespoons hazelnut or walnut oil

2 tablespoons grapeseed or canola oil

Salt and freshly ground black pepper

4 ounces Roquefort or other ripe, soft blue cheese

Minced chives for garnish

The walnuts and Roquefort make this substantial enough to serve as a light lunch dish or a serious first course.

1 Toast the walnuts in a dry skillet over medium heat, shaking the pan occasionally, until they are fragrant, about 3 minutes. Set aside.

2 Trim, wash, and dry the lettuce. Whisk together the shallots, vinegar, oils, and salt and pepper to taste. *(The dressing can be prepared in advance and allowed to sit, covered and refrigerated, overnight. Whisk again before serving.)*

3 Dress and toss the lettuce; season again if necessary. Crumble the walnuts and Roquefort over the salad and toss lightly. Garnish with chives and serve.

MAKES 4 SERVINGS   TIME: 15 MINUTES

Simple to Spectacular

Frisée salad Lyonnaise-style

4 ounces good bacon, cut into strips
¼ inch thick and 1 inch long

2 tablespoons extra-virgin olive oil

2 ounces good bread (1 or 2 slices), cut into ½-inch cubes

1 tablespoon any white vinegar

4 eggs

2 heads frisée or other lettuce, or a mixture (about 8 ounces total)

2 tablespoons minced shallots

¼ cup sherry vinegar

2 tablespoons hazelnut or walnut oil

2 tablespoons grapeseed or canola oil

Salt and freshly ground black pepper to taste

Everything here can be done in advance—even the poached eggs, which only need to be reheated at the last moment. Don't be intimidated by the idea of poaching eggs; you're just boiling them without their shells. The fresher the eggs, the better they will hold together. This is a classic lunch dish in Lyon, and a very filling one. Serve it at home for lunch, brunch, or even dinner.

1 Cook the bacon in a dry skillet over medium-high heat, stirring occasionally, until crisp, 5 to 10 minutes. Set aside.

2 Place the olive oil in a small skillet and turn the heat to medium. Cook the bread cubes, turning occasionally, until crisp and brown on all sides, 5 to 10 minutes. Set aside.

3 Bring a medium pot of water to a boil, turn the heat to medium-low (the water should be bubbling, but just barely), and add the white vinegar. One by one, crack the eggs and slip them into the water (it's easier if you break each one into a small bowl or cup first, then use that to transfer the egg into the water). Cook

for about 4 minutes, just until the whites are set. Use a slotted spoon to transfer the eggs to a cloth towel. To make them look nicer, trim the wisps of egg white with scissors. *(The eggs can be poached an hour or two in advance; rewarm in simmering water for a minute before serving. They are not quite as fragile as they look.)*

4 Trim, wash, and dry the lettuce. Whisk together the remaining ingredients. *(The dressing can be prepared in advance and allowed to sit, covered and refrigerated, overnight. Whisk again before serving.)*

5 Dress the lettuce and toss it with the bacon and croutons; season again if necessary. Place a portion of the salad in each of four bowls, top with a poached egg, and serve.

MAKES 4 SERVINGS   TIME: 30 MINUTES

Frisée salad with gizzard confit and lentils

12 ounces chicken gizzards

16 cloves garlic, peeled

3 branches thyme

Salt and freshly ground black pepper

1½ to 2 cups extra-virgin olive oil or duck fat

½ cup lentils, rinsed and picked over

1 small carrot, peeled

1 small onion, peeled

1 clove garlic, crushed

2 heads frisée or other lettuce, or a mixture (about 8 ounces total)

2 tablespoons minced shallots

¼ cup sherry vinegar

2 tablespoons hazelnut or walnut oil

2 tablespoons grapeseed or canola oil

Chopped parsley for garnish

Tiny dark green French lentils, usually called lentilles du Puy, are best here if you can find them. Don't be put off by the idea of cooked gizzards; many people can't get enough of them.

There is some time involved in this recipe—it's not a super-simple dish—but it is among the best salads we know. And the time-consuming part, the confit, can be done in advance.

1 Combine the gizzards with the whole garlic cloves, 2 branches of the thyme, 2 teaspoons salt, and ¼ teaspoon pepper. Cover and marinate overnight in the refrigerator.

2 Drain the gizzards of any accumulated juices and combine them, along with the garlic and thyme, in a small heavy pot with olive oil or duck fat to cover. Cook at a slow simmer (if you have a thermometer, about 190°F is ideal) for about 2 hours, or until tender. When cool, remove the gizzards and cut them in half. Reserve the garlic and the oil.

3 Meanwhile, combine the remaining branch of thyme with the lentils, carrot, onion, and crushed garlic in a small saucepan and add water to cover. Bring to a boil over medium-high heat, then lower the heat and cook until the lentils are tender, about 30 minutes. Season to taste and keep warm. *(You can cook the lentils a day or two in advance if you like; refrigerate and just rewarm the lentils before serving.)*

4 Put 2 tablespoons of the reserved olive oil or duck fat in a medium skillet and turn the heat to medium-high. Add the gizzards and the reserved garlic cloves and sauté until nicely browned, turning occasionally, about 10 minutes.

5 Meanwhile, trim, wash, and dry the lettuce. Whisk together the ingredients for the dressing, along with salt and pepper to taste. *(The dressing can be prepared in advance and allowed to sit, covered and refrigerated, overnight. Whisk again before serving.)*

6 Toss the frisée with most of the dressing; toss the lentils with the rest. Top the lettuce with the lentils and the gizzards and garlic. Drizzle with the little bit of the fat you used for sautéing the gizzards, sprinkle with parsley, and serve.

MAKES 4 SERVINGS   TIME: OVERNIGHT, LARGELY UNATTENDED

Frisée salad with scallops, white truffles, and Parmesan

4 tablespoons butter

1 tablespoon minced white truffle

1 tablespoon balsamic vinegar

1 tablespoon sherry vinegar

Salt and freshly ground black pepper

8 sea scallops, cut in half through their equator

Cayenne pepper

3 tablespoons extra-virgin olive oil

2 heads frisée or other lettuce, or a mixture (about 8 ounces total)

8 to 12 thin slices white truffle (use a mandoline or vegetable peeler)

8 to 12 thin slices Parmesan

Coarse salt or fleur de sel

This is a fairly easy dish—it just costs a lot of money. If you're lucky enough to have a white truffle, it is, however, really amazing. And if you double the quantities, it will serve as a main course for a special occasion.

You can use extra-virgin olive oil in place of the beurre noirsette; you can also omit the truffle, though, of course, the dish will not be the same. In any case, use only good Parmigiano-Reggiano here, the real thing.

1 Prepare a bowl of ice water and set aside. Place the butter in a small heavy saucepan and turn the heat to high. Cook, swirling the butter in the pan occasionally, until it turns nut-brown. Plunge the bottom of the pan into the bowl of ice water to stop the cooking and prevent the butter from burning. Combine the butter in a small dish with the minced truffle, vinegars, and salt and pepper to taste.

2 Place a large nonstick skillet over medium-high heat. Sprinkle the scallops with salt and a little cayenne. When the skillet is hot, add 2 tablespoons of the oil, followed by half the scallops; you don't want to crowd these, so cook them in two batches, using the remaining tablespoon of olive oil for the second batch. Cook until nicely browned on one side, about 2 minutes, then turn and cook for about 1 minute on the other side. (The scallops should not be cooked all the way through.)

3 Trim, wash, and dry the lettuce. Place a portion of the lettuce in the center of each of four plates, then put 4 scallop slices around it. Top the lettuce with the truffle and Parmesan slices, then drizzle with the vinaigrette and sprinkle with coarse salt.

Simple to Spectacular

MAKES 4 SERVINGS   TIME: 30 MINUTES

MESCLUN, a Niçoise word for mixture, describes any combination of young, tender greens, sometimes, but not always, mixed with edible flowers. Generally, the more varieties of greens, the better the salad, so you have a combination of flavors and textures, from sweet to bitter, from tender to tough. A few herbs thrown in add interest as well.

More than any other salad greens, when you start with a good mesclun mix, you really are guaranteed a good salad. And there are so many directions it can go that we found it hard to limit ourselves to five variations. What we have here are a straightforward salad spiked with herbs; a grilled chicken salad; the classic *salade Niçoise*, but made with fresh rather than canned tuna; a salad featuring scallops and a creamy orange sauce; and, finally, one of Jean-Georges' signature salads, mesclun with porcini, artichokes, and foie gras—the ultimate main-course salad.

KEYS TO SUCCESS

Not all mesclun is the same; see if you can find a mix with a great variety of greens, including some herbs.

Always wash mesclun well but, equally important, dry it well. Soak it in several changes of water, then spin it dry.

Note that many of these dressings can (and should) be made in a blender.

Mesclun and herb salad

10 leaves basil

2 sprigs chervil or parsley

10 chives

1 teaspoon thyme leaves

6 to 10 leaves tarragon

6 cups mesclun, washed and dried

2 tablespoons fresh lemon juice

2 tablespoons extra-virgin olive oil

Salt and freshly ground black pepper

You can use any assortment of herbs here—consider this recipe no more than a list of suggestions. The dressing is as simple as can be, so as not to overwhelm the greens.

1 Coarsely chop the herbs, cut them with scissors, or just tear them; don't make the pieces too small. Toss them with the greens.

2 Combine the lemon juice and olive oil in a small bowl and whisk briefly with a fork or wire whisk. Dress the salad, season to taste, toss, and serve.

MAKES 4 SERVINGS   TIME: 15 MINUTES

Simple to Spectacular

Mesclun salad with grilled lemon chicken

2 boneless chicken breasts, cut in half

3 tablespoons extra-virgin olive oil

2 teaspoons rosemary leaves

2 lemons

1 tablespoon fresh lemon juice

1 teaspoon honey

6 cups mesclun, washed and dried

Salt and freshly ground black pepper

A fine lunch or dinner dish, nicely flavored, well balanced, and very, very fast.

1 Prepare a grill fire or preheat a broiler. The fire need only be moderately hot, and the rack should be 4 to 6 inches from the heat source. Brush the chicken breasts with 1 tablespoon of the olive oil and sprinkle with half the rosemary.

2 Cut the lemons in half and section them as you would a grapefruit, discarding the seeds and reserving any juice.

3 Grill the chicken breasts until they are cooked through, about 3 minutes per side.

4 Combine the lemon pulp and any juice, the 1 tablespoon lemon juice, and the honey, along with the remaining 2 tablespoons olive oil; beat or whisk briefly. Dress and toss the greens, then season them to taste. Top with the chicken and the remaining rosemary.

MAKES 4 SERVINGS   TIME: 15 MINUTES

Salade Niçoise

12 small potatoes (about 8 ounces)

Salt and freshly ground black pepper

8 ounces green beans, preferably haricots verts, trimmed

24 fresh fava, lima, or other shell beans

8 quail eggs or 4 large eggs

12 ounces fresh tuna

3 tablespoons fresh lemon juice

3 tablespoons extra-virgin olive oil

4 anchovy fillets, minced

6 cups mesclun, washed and dried

1 pound tomatoes, cut into eighths

24 Niçoise olives, pitted

This is a flexible recipe, and many substitutions are possible—use whatever vegetables you like and, of course, substitute canned tuna for fresh if it's more convenient (Niçoise salads are in fact made with canned tuna packed in olive oil). Note that much of the cooking for this can be done in advance.

1 Cook the potatoes in boiling salted water until tender, 15 to 30 minutes; remove with a slotted spoon, then run them under cold water to stop the cooking. Blanch the green beans in the same water for about 2 minutes, or until bright green and crisp-tender; remove and run under cold water. Now blanch the beans for about 2 minutes, remove, and cool; peel if necessary, as it will be with favas. Finally, reduce the heat and simmer the eggs—1 minute for quail eggs, 6 to 7 minutes for chicken eggs—run under cold water, and let sit in the water.

2 Season the tuna with salt and pepper and sear in a hot skillet or grill until medium-rare; cut into chunks.

3 Peel the eggs; if they are chicken eggs, cut them into slices or quarters; halve quail eggs.

4 Combine the lemon juice and olive oil in a small bowl and whisk briefly with a fork or wire whisk; stir in the anchovies. Assemble the salad: Put the greens on a platter and top and/or surround them with the potatoes, beans, tuna, tomatoes, olives, and eggs. Drizzle the vinaigrette over all and serve.

MAKES 4 SERVINGS   TIME: ABOUT 1 HOUR

Simple to Spectacular

Mesclun with scallops Maltaise

Zest of 1 orange

½ cup orange juice, preferably fresh

2 egg yolks

4 tablespoons butter, or 2 tablespoons each butter and extra-virgin olive oil

Salt and cayenne pepper

1 pound sea scallops

2 tablespoons fresh lemon juice, plus more to taste if needed

2 tablespoons extra-virgin olive oil

6 cups mesclun, washed and dried

1 orange, sectioned

4 ounces fennel, trimmed, fronds (if any) reserved, and thinly sliced

This orange-based sauce—essentially a hollandaise with orange in place of lemon—is extremely subtle, so be sure to season it well. It will hold at room temperature for about an hour.

1 Combine the zest and orange juice in a small saucepan and cook over medium-high heat, stirring and scraping down the sides occasionally (a rubber spatula is best for this), until reduced to about a tablespoon—this will take 15 minutes or so.

2 Mix the egg yolks with 3 tablespoons water and place in the top section of a double boiler over simmering water. Beat with a whisk until foamy and thick, about 5 minutes. Add 2 tablespoons of the butter, a little bit at a time, whisking after each addition to incorporate. Season with salt and cayenne, add the reduced orange juice, and set aside.

3 Split the scallops horizontally and season with salt and cayenne. Place the remaining 2 tablespoons butter or the olive oil in a large skillet and turn the heat to medium-high; sear the scallops for about 1 minute per side, until lightly browned (you may have to do this in batches).

4 Combine the lemon juice and extra-virgin olive oil in a small bowl and whisk briefly with a fork or wire whisk. Dress the salad, season to taste, and toss. Reheat the sauce briefly, just until warm; taste and adjust the seasoning, adding a bit of lemon juice if necessary. Top the mesclun with the orange sections, fennel, and scallops. Spoon the sauce over all, top with the fennel fronds, and serve.

MAKES 4 SERVINGS   TIME: 45 MINUTES

Salads

Mesclun salad with porcini, artichokes, and foie gras

2 tablespoons canned truffle juice, available at specialty food shops

2 tablespoons soy sauce

2 tablespoons fresh lemon juice

½ cup plus 1 teaspoon extra-virgin olive oil

Salt and freshly ground black pepper

2 tablespoons walnuts or pecans

4 fresh porcini (about 8 ounces), trimmed and cut into ¼-inch-thick slices, or 8 ounces shiitakes, stems removed, and sliced

4 large artichokes, choke and tough leaves removed, trimmed to the heart and cut into thin slices, or 12 baby artichokes, trimmed and cut into thin slices

4 (½-inch-thick) slices raw foie gras (about 8 ounces)

6 cups mesclun, washed and dried

Coarse salt

Chives cut into 1-inch sections for garnish

What can you say about a dish that combines what Jean-Georges calls "the best salad dressing ever" with some of the best possible ingredients? It's an amazingly superior salad—expensive, but not at all difficult.

1 Preheat the oven to 450°F. Combine the truffle juice, soy sauce, lemon juice, 6 tablespoons of the olive oil, and ¼ teaspoon pepper in the container of a blender and blend; or combine in a bowl and whisk with a fork. Set aside.

2 Toast the nuts in a dry skillet over medium heat, tossing occasionally, until fragrant, 1 to 2 minutes. When they're cool, mince them.

3 Place 1 tablespoon of the olive oil in a skillet and turn the heat to high. Sear the mushrooms, sprinkling them with salt and pepper and tossing or turning occasionally, until tender and nicely browned, 5 to 10 minutes. Set aside. Place another tablespoon of olive oil in the skillet and turn the heat to high. Sear the artichoke slices, sprinkling with salt and pepper and tossing or turning occasionally, until tender and nicely browned, 5 to 10 minutes. Set aside.

4 Season the foie gras with salt and pepper, then sear it over medium-high heat in an ovenproof skillet with the remaining 1 teaspoon olive oil for about 1 minute per side. Place the skillet in the oven and roast for 5 minutes; remove and set aside.

45

5 Put the greens in a bowl and toss with salt and pepper to taste and about half the dressing. Portion the greens onto four plates. Top each portion with some of the artichokes and mushrooms, and a slice of foie gras. Sprinkle with a little coarse salt, then drizzle with the remaining dressing (and a little of the foie gras fat if you like). Top with the nuts and chives and serve.

MAKES 4 SERVINGS   TIME: 40 MINUTES

Simple to Spectacular

Eggs, crepes, and savory tarts

JEAN-GEORGES' Oeufs au Caviar were, for a time, the talk of the town. And, although the dish is undeniably spectacular—with its vodka-flavored whipped cream and dollop of beluga caviar—the key to it is his simple but perfect scrambled eggs.

These are a brilliant lesson in technique. They're made in a different fashion from any other scrambled eggs, though the results are very similar to the very slow cooked—40 minutes—eggs popularized by James Beard years ago. Yet they take just 5 minutes to cook.

KEYS TO SUCCESS

The best pans for these recipes are saucepans or skillets with sloping sides; they should hold the eggs at a depth of ¼ to ½ inch. These recipes are for two; you can double them, but use a larger pan.

You can use a nonstick pan, but switch to a wooden spoon instead of a whisk. The results will be fine.

The technique requires practice. Our suggestion: Buy a couple dozen eggs (they're cheap) and have at it. Within a half hour, you will nail the method.

Make sure to stop the cooking when the mixture is very loose; these eggs should be eaten with a spoon.

Best scrambled eggs

5 eggs

1½ tablespoons butter

Salt and freshly ground black pepper

A revelation. You'll never go back to hard-cooked scrambled eggs.

1 Combine the eggs, butter, and salt and pepper to taste in a saucepan or skillet, preferably one with sloping sides. Turn the heat to medium-high and begin to beat the egg mixture with a whisk, stirring almost constantly but not too fast; you do not want it to become foamy.

2 After the butter melts, the mixture will begin to thicken, and then to lump up in small curds; this will take between 3 and 8 minutes, depending on the thickness of your pan and the heat level. If the mixture begins to stick on the bottom, remove the pan from the heat for a moment and continue to whisk, then return to the heat.

3 When the eggs become creamy, with small curds all over—not unlike loose oatmeal—they are ready; do not overcook. Add more salt and pepper if necessary and serve.

MAKES 2 SERVINGS   TIME: 10 MINUTES

Scrambled eggs with tomato and basil

5 eggs

1½ tablespoons butter

Salt and freshly ground black pepper

1 medium tomato, peeled, seeded, and chopped into ¼-inch cubes

½ cup roughly chopped basil

Slightly more flavor than the first version, and no more difficult, this begins to give you an idea of the possibilities. Serve at brunch, lunch, or dinner.

1 Combine the eggs, butter, and salt and pepper to taste in a saucepan or skillet, preferably one with sloping sides. Turn the heat to medium-high and begin to beat the egg mixture with a whisk, stirring almost constantly but not too fast; you do not want it to become foamy.

2 After the butter melts, the mixture will begin to thicken, and then to lump up in small curds; this will take between 3 and 8 minutes, depending on the thickness of your pan and the heat level. If the mixture begins to stick on the bottom, remove the pan from the heat for a moment and continue to whisk, then return to the heat.

3 When the eggs are very creamy, with small curds all over—not unlike very loose oatmeal—they are just about ready. Immediately stir in the tomato and cook for another minute, just to warm the tomato. Stir in the basil, along with more salt and pepper if necessary, and serve.

MAKES 2 SERVINGS   TIME: 10 MINUTES

Scrambled eggs with cream cheese, smoked salmon, and sorrel

5 eggs

1½ tablespoons butter

Salt and freshly ground black pepper

3 ounces smoked salmon, cut into ½-inch dice

4 ounces cream cheese, cut into ½-inch dice

½ cup shredded sorrel

Minced chives for garnish

You can substitute spinach for the sorrel here, although it will not "melt" as sorrel does (and of course will taste different too). The cream cheese gains an especially lovely texture in this dish.

1 Combine the eggs, butter, and salt and pepper to taste in a saucepan or skillet, preferably one with sloping sides. Turn the heat to medium-high and begin to beat the egg mixture with a whisk, stirring almost constantly but not too fast; you do not want it to become foamy.

2 After the butter melts, the mixture will begin to thicken, and then to lump up in small curds; this will take between 3 and 8 minutes, depending on the thickness of your pan and the heat level. If the mixture begins to stick on the bottom, remove the pan from the heat for a moment and continue to whisk, then return to the heat.

3 When the eggs are very creamy, with small curds all over—not unlike very loose oatmeal—they are just about ready. Immediately stir in the smoked salmon and cook for another minute, just to warm it. Stir in the cream cheese and sorrel, along with more salt and pepper if necessary. Garnish with the chives and serve.

MAKES 2 SERVINGS   TIME: 10 MINUTES

Scrambled eggs with crispy potatoes and prosciutto

1 large baking potato (about 12 ounces)

¼ cup extra-virgin olive oil

Salt and freshly ground black pepper

2 ounces prosciutto or other dry-cured ham

5 eggs

1½ tablespoons butter

Minced chives for garnish

Crisp potatoes make this dish a real contrast in textures, and prosciutto adds a great flavor kick.

1 Peel the potato, then cut it into ⅛-inch dice (about 1½ cups); rinse and dry. Put the oil in a 10- or 12-inch skillet and turn the heat to high. A minute later, add the potatoes, along with salt and pepper to taste, and turn the heat to medium-high. At first the potatoes will stick together, but as you stir and shake the pan occasionally, they will separate as they brown.

2 When the potatoes are brown and crisp, add the ham and cook for 1 minute. Remove the potatoes with a slotted spoon and drain on paper towels. Drain any remaining fat from the pan and return the potato-ham mixture to it, but keep it off the heat for now.

3 Combine the eggs, butter, and salt and pepper to taste in a saucepan or skillet, preferably one with sloping sides. Turn the heat to medium-high and begin to beat the egg mixture with a whisk, stirring almost constantly but not too fast; you do not want it to become foamy.

4 After the butter melts, the mixture will begin to thicken, and then to lump up in small curds; this will take between 3 and 8 minutes, depending on the thickness of your pan and the heat level. If the mixture begins to stick on the bottom, remove the pan from the heat for a moment and continue to whisk, then return to the heat.

5 When the eggs become creamy, with small curds all over—not unlike loose oatmeal—they are ready; do not overcook. Add more salt and pepper if necessary and place in two warmed bowls. Reheat the potatoes quickly—30 seconds should be enough—and garnish the eggs with them. Top with chives and serve.

MAKES 2 SERVINGS   TIME: 30 MINUTES

Simple to Spectacular

Oeufs au caviar

½ cup heavy cream

Salt and cayenne pepper

2 teaspoons fresh lemon juice, or to taste

2 teaspoons vodka

4 eggs

1½ tablespoons butter

2 to 4 teaspoons caviar

This is a rich, luxurious dish, soothing to the eye and the palate, and a perfect appetizer for four. The contrast between hot, cold, salty, sweet, creamy, and slightly crunchy is amazing.

1 Whip the cream until it holds stiff peaks, then beat in salt and cayenne to taste, along with the lemon juice and vodka. Taste and adjust the seasoning; it should really sing. Whip the cream again until stiff.

2 For a really dramatic presentation, remove the tops from the eggshells, pour the eggs into the saucepan, and set the bottoms of the shells in egg cups. (Or, you can do what one of us does and serve these in a bowl; they'll taste just as good and still look great.)

3 Combine the eggs, butter, and salt and cayenne to taste in a saucepan or skillet, preferably one with sloping sides. Turn the heat to medium-high and begin to beat the egg mixture with a whisk, stirring almost constantly but not too fast; you do not want it to become foamy.

4 After the butter melts, the mixture will begin to thicken, and then to lump up in small curds; this will take between 3 and 8 minutes, depending on the thickness of your pan and the heat level. If the mixture begins to stick on the bottom, remove the pan from the heat for a moment and continue to whisk, then return to the heat.

5 When the eggs become creamy, with small curds all over—not unlike loose oatmeal—they are ready; do not overcook. Add more salt and cayenne if necessary and place in the eggshells (or two warmed bowls). Use a spoon or a pastry bag to pipe the whipped cream on top of the eggs (or in a small circle around the top if the eggs are in bowls). Top each with a spoonful of caviar and serve.

MAKES 4 SMALL OR 2 LARGE SERVINGS   TIME: 20 MINUTES

Eggs, Crepes, and Savory Tarts

THE TRADITIONAL CREPE of Brittany has more flavor than any other wrapper, thanks to buckwheat's characteristic earthiness. Essentially, these are extremely thin buckwheat pancakes. There's no reason you couldn't top them with butter and sugar, or butter and syrup, but they're designed to be served with other savory foods. The well-known buckwheat blini of Russian cooking, often served with caviar, is closely related.

We put them through a cross-cultural gamut, starting with smoked salmon and cream cheese, then filling them with ham and cheese before crisping them in butter (a typical Bretagne preparation). We then move to two dishes that have been popular in Jean-Georges' restaurants, crabmeat-filled crepes, and crepes refried as chips, served here with scallops. Finally, we use them in a kind of moo shu duck dish, where the combination of buckwheat and plum sauce is memorable.

KEYS TO SUCCESS

Crepe batter, especially that made with buckwheat, needs time to rest: An hour is the minimum, but you can make the batter the day before you cook it; cover and refrigerate.

You need a medium (10-inch) skillet for these, preferably nonstick and unmarred. It will make your life markedly easier (if you find yourself making crepes often, you might reserve this skillet for crepe making so it stays in good shape).

Keep the heat fairly high and the cooking time short. You will not need a lot of oil, since the pan is nonstick.

Bear in mind that the first crepe (or two) is always a failure. Don't start worrying. These are easy, and you'll quickly get the hang of it.

Buckwheat crepes with smoked salmon and cream cheese

¼ cup flour

1 cup buckwheat flour

2 eggs

½ cup milk

Neutral oil, such as canola or grapeseed, as needed

4 ounces cream cheese, softened

8 ounces thinly sliced smoked salmon

Salt and freshly ground black pepper

32 chives

An unexpected and sensational brunch item.

1 Combine the first 4 ingredients and 1 cup water in a bowl; whisk until smooth and let sit for at least an hour, refrigerated.

2 Heat a 10-inch nonstick skillet over high heat for about 2 minutes. Add a thin layer of oil and wipe it out, leaving just a trace behind. Pour in ¼ cup of the batter and swirl it around so that it coats the bottom of the pan completely; pour the excess back into the remaining batter. Adjust the heat so that the batter dries on top before it burns on the bottom; it will be ready to turn in 1 to 2 minutes. Turn and cook the second side for about 30 seconds, then remove. Repeat to use up the batter, adding more oil to the pan if necessary (it may not be); you need 8 near-perfect crepes for this recipe. Let cool to room temperature.

3 Spread each of the 8 crepes with a thin layer of cream cheese—it need not cover the crepe perfectly, but try to get some out to the left and right edges. Make a layer of salmon on top of the cheese; again, try to get the salmon out to the left and right edges. Top each crepe with salt and pepper and 4 chives.

4 Roll up the crepes from the bottom edge, cut into 1- or 2-inch sections, and serve.

MAKES 4 SERVINGS   TIME: ABOUT 1½ HOURS, LARGELY UNATTENDED

Simple to Spectacular

Buckwheat crepes with ham and cheese

¼ cup flour

1 cup buckwheat flour

2 eggs

½ cup milk

Neutral oil, such as canola or grape-seed, as needed

8 to 16 thin slices cheese, such as Gruyère, Emmenthaler, or Cheddar

8 to 16 thin slices ham

4 tablespoons butter, more or less

In this recipe, the cooked crepes are sautéed with ham and cheese and become alluringly fragrant and slightly crisp.

1 Combine the first 4 ingredients and 1 cup water in a bowl; whisk until smooth and let sit for at least an hour, refrigerated.

2 Heat a 10-inch nonstick skillet over high heat for about 2 minutes. Add a thin layer of oil and wipe it out, leaving just a trace behind. Pour in ¼ cup of the batter and swirl it around so that it coats the bottom of the pan completely; pour the excess back into the remaining batter. Adjust the heat so that the batter dries on top before it burns on the bottom; it will be ready to turn in 1 to 2 minutes. Turn and cook the second side for about 30 seconds, then remove. Repeat to use up the batter, adding more oil to the pan if necessary (it may not be); you need 8 near-perfect crepes for this recipe. Let cool to room temperature.

3 Place 1 or 2 slices each of cheese and ham on top of each crepe. Fold the bottom edge one-third of the way toward the center. Fold the sides and then the top over; it's okay if some of the ham remains exposed.

4 Preheat the oven to 200°F. Put a tablespoon of the butter in a large skillet and turn the heat to medium. When the butter melts, add as many crepes as will fit without crowding, open side down, and turn the heat to high. Cook for just a minute on the open side, then turn, turn the heat to medium-low, and cook the other side until nicely browned, about 3 minutes. Remove and keep warm in the oven while you cook the remaining crepes, adding butter to the skillet as needed.

5 Serve open side up.

MAKES 4 SERVINGS   TIME: ABOUT 1½ HOURS, LARGELY UNATTENDED

Simple to Spectacular

Crabmeat **crepes**

¼ cup flour

1 cup buckwheat flour

2 eggs

½ cup milk

Neutral oil, such as canola or grapeseed, as needed

2 cups crabmeat, picked over for shells and cartilage

2 tablespoons Mayonnaise (page 362), or use bottled mayonnaise

2 teaspoons fresh lemon juice

1 tablespoon minced tarragon, plus a few sprigs for garnish

Salt and cayenne pepper

2 egg yolks, beaten

4 tablespoons butter, preferably salted

4 lemon wedges

These filled crepes are quite satisfying, so one per person is enough. Of course, you can make 8 crepes and simply double the other ingredients.

1 Combine the first 4 ingredients and 1 cup water in a bowl; whisk until smooth and let sit for at least an hour, refrigerated.

2 Heat a 10-inch nonstick skillet over high heat for about 2 minutes. Add a thin layer of oil and wipe it out, leaving just a trace behind. Pour in ¼ cup of the batter and swirl it around so that it coats the bottom of the pan completely; pour the excess back into the remaining batter. Adjust the heat so that the batter dries on top before it burns on the bottom; it will be ready to turn in 1 to 2 minutes. Turn and cook the second side for about 30 seconds, then remove. Repeat, adding more oil to the pan if necessary (it may not be); you need 4 near-perfect crepes for this recipe. Let cool to room temperature.

3 Mix the crabmeat with the mayonnaise, lemon juice, and tarragon. Season with salt and cayenne. Put one-quarter of the crab mixture in the center of each crepe. Brush the edge of the top half of the crepe with egg yolk, then fold the crepe over onto itself like an apple turnover.

4 Put half the butter in a 10-inch skillet and turn the heat to medium. When the butter melts, add 2 of the crepes to the pan. Cook for 3 to 4 minutes, until nicely browned, then turn and cook the other side. Repeat with the remaining 2 crepes, using the remaining butter. Serve with lemon wedges, garnished with tarragon sprigs.

MAKES 4 SERVINGS   TIME: ABOUT 1½ HOURS, LARGELY UNATTENDED

Eggs, Crepes, and Savory Tarts

Buckwheat crepe chips with scallops

¼ cup flour

1 cup buckwheat flour

2 eggs

½ cup milk

Neutral oil, such as canola or grapeseed, as needed

1 tablespoon Dijon mustard

2 tablespoons cider vinegar

4 tablespoons salted butter, or more as needed

Salt and freshly ground black pepper

24 medium or 12 large scallops (about 1½ pounds), large ones cut horizontally in half

Minced parsley for garnish

These crepes become chips. You only need 4 to complete the recipe, but we recommend that you make crepes and then crepe-chips from the entire batch of batter, because they're addictive.

1 Combine the first 4 ingredients and 1 cup water in a bowl; whisk until smooth and let sit for at least an hour, refrigerated. Heat a 10-inch nonstick skillet over high heat for about 2 minutes. Add a thin layer of oil and wipe it out, leaving just a trace behind. Pour in ¼ cup of the batter and swirl it around so that it coats the bottom of the pan completely; pour the excess back into the remaining batter. Adjust the heat so that the batter dries on top before it burns on the bottom; it will be ready to turn in 1 to 2 minutes. Turn and cook the second side for about 30 seconds, then remove. Repeat, adding more oil to the pan if necessary (it may not be). You need 4 crepes for this recipe; they need not be perfect. Cut them into chip-sized diamonds or squares.

2 In a small bowl, combine the mustard, vinegar, and 2 tablespoons oil; set aside. Put 2 tablespoons of the butter in a 10- or 12-inch skillet and turn the heat to medium. When the butter melts, cook the chips, in batches, until crisp on both sides, adding more butter if necessary; they'll only need a couple of minutes each. Drain on paper towels and sprinkle with salt.

3 Wipe out the skillet and add the remaining 2 tablespoons butter to it. Turn the heat to medium-high. When the butter melts, add the scallops, season them with salt and pepper, and cook until browned on both sides, 5 minutes at most (scallops are at their best when rare in the center). Divide the chips among four plates; add the scallops and drizzle them with their pan juices. Garnish with parsley and pass the dressing at the table.

Simple to Spectacular

MAKES 4 SERVINGS   TIME: ABOUT 1½ HOURS, LARGELY UNATTENDED

Buckwheat crepes with duck breast and plum sauce

½ cup sugar

½ cup white vinegar

1 small chile, stemmed

½ cup pitted dried prunes, dates, or apricots

¼ cup flour

1 cup buckwheat flour

2 eggs

½ cup milk

¼ cup neutral oil, such as canola or grapeseed, plus more as needed

1 small daikon radish or white turnip (about 4 ounces)

1 medium cucumber

8 scallions

2 tablespoons sesame seeds

1 medium onion, peeled and chopped

1 tablespoon chopped cilantro root (optional)

Pinch of coriander

¼ teaspoon freshly ground black pepper

1 tablespoon tomato paste

1 tablespoon chile paste or 1 teaspoon red pepper flakes

1 tablespoon chopped garlic

2 tablespoons fresh lime juice

Salt

1½ pounds boneless duck or chicken breasts

4 leaves romaine lettuce, cut in half lengthwise

As you can see from the ingredients list, this is a bit of work, but the payoff is very filling, big-flavored, rather magnificent crepes.

Note the inclusion of cilantro root: often you can buy cilantro with the roots attached. After washing well, these are perfectly edible—and powerfully flavored.

1 Combine the first 4 ingredients in a small saucepan with ½ cup water. Bring to a boil over medium-high heat, then turn the heat down and simmer for 1 hour.

2 Meanwhile, combine the next 4 ingredients and 1 cup water in a bowl; whisk until smooth and let sit for at least an hour refrigerated.

3 Heat a 10-inch nonstick skillet over high heat for about 2 minutes. Add a thin layer of oil and wipe it out, leaving just a trace behind. Pour in ¼ cup of the batter and swirl it around so that it coats the bottom of the pan completely; pour

the excess back into the remaining batter. Adjust the heat so that the batter dries on top before it burns on the bottom; it will be ready to turn in 1 to 2 minutes. Turn and cook the second side for about 30 seconds, then remove. Repeat to use up the batter, adding more oil to the pan if necessary (it may not be); you need 8 near-perfect crepes for this recipe. Let cool to room temperature.

4 Peel and shred or grate the daikon or turnip, and the cucumber. Trim the scallions and cut them into long strips. Put the sesame seeds in a small dry skillet and turn the heat to medium. Toast, shaking the pan occasionally, until the seeds begin to pop, just a minute or two. Set aside.

5 Put 2 tablespoons of the oil in a medium skillet and turn the heat to medium-high. Add the onion and cook, stirring occasionally, until it begins to brown, 5 to 10 minutes. Add the cilantro root, if using, coriander, pepper, tomato paste, chile paste or red pepper flakes, and garlic. Cook until the onion is soft, about 10 minutes. Combine with the simmered fruit mixture and puree in a blender. Add the lime juice and salt to taste. Set aside.

6 Put the remaining 2 tablespoons oil in a skillet and turn the heat to medium-high. Add the duck (or chicken) breasts and cook, turning once or twice, until done (duck is best medium-rare; chicken should be cooked just until white in the center), about 10 minutes. Let cool slightly, then shred the meat with your hands or cut it into thin strips. Mix the meat with enough of the plum sauce to hold it together, ½ cup or so.

7 Divide the lettuce among the 8 crepes, laying it from left to right. Top each with some of the duck (or chicken), then the grated daikon and cucumber, some scallion strips, and a piece of lettuce. Roll up, but not too tightly, cut into 1- to 2-inch sections, and arrange on plates, cut sides up. Sprinkle with the sesame seeds and serve, passing the remaining plum sauce at the table.

MAKES 4 SERVINGS   TIME: ABOUT 1½ HOURS, LARGELY UNATTENDED

THESE are pies—pizza being the simplest—that can be made with puff pastry, pizza dough, pie crust (especially one made with olive oil), or phyllo dough. All are treated similarly, though there are differences based on the thickness and moisture content of the dough (see Keys to Success).

The pizza has a simple combination of tomato, basil, and garlic as its topping. From there we go to two traditional French "pizzas," pissaladière and tarte flambée, both of which feature onions, though in markedly different forms. Jean-Georges' tuna-wasabi tart—which was inspired by Barry Wine—is a lovely creation akin to sushi, and the leek and truffle tart is sheer heaven. None of these take much time, and all are baked in small rounds perfect for appetizers.

KEYS TO SUCCESS

The best doughs for this are puff pastry and phyllo. The latter can be bought in any freezer case, and is generally a good product. Most frozen puff pastry, unfortunately, is made with margarine, not butter, and is not a great alternative. So we've included a recipe for real puff pastry here too. But feel free to use pizza dough or a good pie crust. (Or try to find puff pastry made with butter.)

Oven temperatures vary, so be sure to cook the tarts until the crust is nice and brown, regardless of the kind of crust you use. Lining ovens with unglazed quarry tiles or a pizza stone really helps.

Puff pastry

4 cups flour, plus some for working the dough

1 tablespoon salt

1¼ pounds (5 sticks) butter, 1 stick softened

Making puff pastry is not at all difficult—just remember to chill the pastry well between turns, and to let it warm up a bit if it's difficult to work—but it is time-consuming. The work, however, takes place at easily varied intervals, so it's a nice project for a day when you're around the house.

1 Toss together the flour and salt in a bowl, then mix in the softened butter, rubbing it gently between your fingers until incorporated. Add 1 cup cold water and quickly gather the mixture into a ball. Wrap in plastic and refrigerate for at least 30 minutes. Place the remaining butter between two sheets of foil or plastic wrap and pound it into a 6 × 8-inch rectangle with a rolling pin or the bottom of a pot.

2 Remove the dough from the refrigerator, flatten it into a disk, and make a shallow X in the middle. Roll each of the segments you've just created out from the center making a cloverleaf pattern, sprinkling with flour as necessary and leaving the dough slightly higher in the middle. Fold the butter so that it is about the same size as the central square, and place it there. One at a time, fold the petals over the butter, stretching them slightly so as to encase the butter and overlap each other.

3 Pound the dough package lightly with the rolling pin, square off the sides, and then pound again, but not so hard that butter begins to leak out the sides. Roll it out into a 9 × 18-inch rectangle, sprinkling with flour as necessary and sealing the seams with your fingers so the butter does not leak out. Fold it into thirds from the short ends. Sprinkle with flour and roll again, repeating the process (it will be easier this time). After the second turn and fold, wrap the dough in plastic or a towel and let rest in a cool place or the refrigerator for at least 30 minutes.

4 After the dough has chilled, do two more turns. (If the dough is stubborn at first because it is too cold, let it sit at room temperature for 10 minutes before trying again.) Refrigerate for at least 30 minutes again, then do two more turns. When you're finished, you will have more than 2 pounds of puff pastry; cut it into halves or quarters and refrigerate or freeze for a week or two.

Simple to Spectacular

MAKES ABOUT 2½ POUNDS (ENOUGH FOR SEVERAL USES)   TIME: 3 HOURS, LARGELY UNATTENDED

Puff pastry pizza

4 rounds puff pastry or other dough, each 5 to 6 inches across and about ¼ inch thick

1 tomato, cored and cut into 8 thin slices

Salt and freshly ground black pepper

2 tablespoons extra-virgin olive oil

1 teaspoon minced garlic

¼ cup roughly chopped basil

You've never had a pizza with such flaky, rich, and delicious dough. But even with ordinary dough, these fresh ingredients make for a wonderful pie.

1 Preheat the oven to 400°F. Use a nonstick baking sheet, or cover any baking sheet with a piece of parchment paper. Arrange the disks of pastry on the sheet. Cover each with a couple of slices of tomato, sprinkle with salt and pepper, and top with a portion of the olive oil, garlic, and basil.

2 Bake for about 15 minutes, or until the tomato slices are bubbly and the pastry nicely browned. Serve hot or at room temperature.

MAKES 4 SERVINGS   TIME: 20 MINUTES, WITH PREMADE PASTRY

Pissaladière (onion pizza)

3 tablespoons extra-virgin olive oil

3 large onions, peeled and thinly sliced

Salt and freshly ground black pepper

4 rounds puff pastry or other dough, each 5 to 6 inches across and about $\frac{1}{4}$ inch thick

24 good black olives, pitted

8 anchovy fillets, cut into long slivers

The classic pizza of Nice, essentially sautéed sweet onions with salty olives and anchovies. Sliced tomatoes are a good addition here, too, as are a few sprigs of thyme or some basil leaves.

1 Preheat the oven to 400°F. Put the olive oil in a large skillet, turn the heat to medium, and add the onions, along with a big pinch of salt and pepper to taste. Cook, stirring occasionally, until the onions are tender and golden, about 15 minutes.

2 Use a nonstick baking sheet or cover any baking sheet with a piece of parchment paper. Arrange the disks of pastry on the sheet and cover each with a portion of the onions, 6 olives, and some anchovy slivers (it's nice to arrange the anchovies like spokes radiating from a hub, with the olives in between).

3 Bake for about 15 minutes, or until the onions begin to brown and the pastry is nicely browned. Serve hot or at room temperature.

MAKES 4 SERVINGS   TIME: 40 MINUTES, WITH PREMADE PASTRY

Simple to Spectacular

Tarte flambée

1 medium onion, peeled and very thinly sliced

Salt and freshly ground black pepper

4 ounces good bacon, cut into ⅛ × ⅛ × 1-inch strips

1 cup fromage blanc or sour cream

¼ teaspoon grated nutmeg

1 egg yolk

4 rounds puff pastry or other dough, each 5 to 6 inches across and about ¼ inch thick

Minced chives for garnish

This is Alsatian—Jean-Georges is from Alsace—although he says, "They'll kill you if you use chives as a garnish there." It's a simple and unusual pizza-like tart.

1 Preheat the oven to 400°F. Sprinkle the onion slices with salt; set aside. Put the bacon in a small saucepan and cover with cold water; bring to a boil, drain, and rinse. Mix the fromage blanc or sour cream with salt and pepper to taste, add the nutmeg, and beat in the yolk.

2 Use a nonstick baking sheet or cover any baking sheet with a piece of parchment paper. Arrange the disks of pastry on the sheet and cover each with a portion of the fromage blanc, then some of the bacon, onions, and salt and pepper to taste. Bake until the pastry is nicely browned, about 15 minutes. Garnish with chives and serve.

MAKES 4 SERVINGS   TIME: 30 MINUTES, WITH PREMADE PASTRY

Simple to Spectacular

Tuna-wasabi **tart**

4 rounds puff pastry or other dough, each 5 to 6 inches across and about ¼ inch thick

½ cup ricotta

4 ounces cream cheese, softened

2 teaspoons prepared wasabi paste

2 teaspoons mirin

Salt and freshly ground black pepper

2 teaspoons dry white wine

4 teaspoons sesame seeds

4 leaves shiso, shredded, or 2 leaves each basil and mint, shredded

12 ounces tuna, cut into ⅛-inch-thick slices

1 tablespoon soy sauce

Pickled ginger (optional)

An unusual preparation, in which the tart is cooked in advance and the topping barely warmed. You can vary the garnish by substituting diced or julienned carrot and daikon tossed with a mixture of a tablespoon each of soy sauce and lemon juice for the cheese mixture.

Shiso is a wonderful Japanese herb that tastes a little like basil and mint combined; you may have had it in sushi bars, but it's only occasionally sold in supermarkets.

1 Preheat the oven to 400°F. Use a nonstick baking sheet or cover any baking sheet with a piece of parchment paper. Arrange the disks of pastry on the sheet, prick them with a fork, and bake until the pastry is nicely browned, 10 to 12 minutes. Transfer to a rack. (Leave the oven on.)

2 Meanwhile, mash together the ricotta, cream cheese, wasabi, mirin, salt and pepper to taste, and wine. Spread each of the disks with a thin layer of the cream cheese mixture, then sprinkle with 1 teaspoon of the sesame seeds. Return to the oven for 2 to 3 minutes, just until the slightest trace of browning begins. Spread each tart with another layer of cream, then the shiso, or basil and mint, and the tuna. Brush with the soy sauce, top with a few pieces of pickled ginger if you like, and serve.

MAKES 4 SERVINGS   TIME: 30 MINUTES, WITH PREMADE PASTRY

Leek and truffle **tart**

4 rounds puff pastry or other dough, each 5 to 6 inches across and about ¼ inch thick

6 tablespoons butter

1 pound leeks, trimmed, well washed, and chopped

Salt and freshly ground black pepper

4 ounces black truffle, thinly sliced, any trimmings reserved

4 ounces foie gras, trimmed and cut into ½-inch cubes

Coarse salt

This is not very difficult, nor that time-consuming. You can make it without the foie gras, but not without the truffles—so why not go all the way? It's a super recipe, and quite filling: A whole tart is an adequate main course, or it can be cut into two or even four for appetizers.

1 Preheat the oven to 400°F. Use a nonstick baking sheet or cover any baking sheet with a piece of parchment paper. Arrange the disks of pastry on the sheet, prick them with a fork, and bake until the pastry is nicely browned, 10 to 12 minutes. Transfer to a rack; leave the oven on.

2 Melt 2 tablespoons of the butter in a small saucepan and keep warm. Melt the remaining 4 tablespoons butter in a large skillet over medium-high heat; add the leeks, along with a big pinch of salt and pepper to taste, cover, and cook, stirring occasionally, until softened but not browned, 10 to 15 minutes. Mince any truffle trimmings and stir them in. Remove from the heat.

3 Cut four disks of parchment paper the same size as the disks of pastry; brush each with at least a teaspoon of the melted butter. Using one-quarter of the truffles for each one, make a ring of overlapping truffle slices on each of the paper disks—start with a single truffle slice in the center, then build out from there. Brush the truffles with a little more of the butter and refrigerate. The butter will act as a glue; when it hardens, the truffles will be stuck together.

4 Put a large skillet over medium-high heat for a minute or two, then add the foie gras and cook for just a minute, tossing. Stir the foie gras into the leeks and re-heat if necessary. Top the puff pastry circles with this mixture. When the truffle circles have hardened, turn one upside down on each tart, leaving the paper on top. Bake just for a minute to warm up the tarts. Remove the paper, brush with any remaining melted butter, sprinkle with coarse salt, and serve.

Simple to Spectacular

MAKES AT LEAST 4 SERVINGS   TIME: 1 HOUR, WITH PREMADE PASTRY

Pasta, noodles, and rice

SOME of these are traditional and some are our inventions, but they all have two things in common: They're made following the same basic steps, and they're all really good. Some are pretty too. Curried Pasta is a vibrant bright yellow, Herb-Printed Pasta is stunning, and the speckled Lobster-Roe Pasta is strikingly unusual, with its green and red coloring. The pastas made with mushroom and with garlic and thyme pack tremendous flavor.

KEYS TO SUCCESS

A manual pasta rolling machine is the best way to prepare these doughs, but they (and any other pasta doughs) can be rolled with a pin. Don't be afraid to use as much flour as you need to make it easy to work the dough, and roll it as thin as you can.

If the dough tears during rolling, fold it up and start rolling again. Usually the more you work it, the more pliable it becomes. Again, use as much flour as necessary.

You can dry the dough before cooking, and if you dry it thoroughly, it will keep for a few days. Or you can cook it immediately; cooking time will be no more than 3 minutes in that case, usually less.

Sauces for these doughs should be minimal—Beurre Noisette (page 192) is ideal for some of them, or a bit of garlic simmered in olive oil. We've included some other suggestions with the recipes.

Curried **pasta**

1 tablespoon curry powder (See note, page xii.)

2 cups flour, plus more for kneading and rolling

Salt

2 tablespoons extra-virgin olive oil

4 eggs

Use the Curry Powder on page 344 for best results, or any commercial curry powder (or other spice mix) that you like. A light marinara sauce, perhaps with some shrimp, would be great here, or a dressing of Jus Rôti (page 4).

1 Combine the curry powder and flour with a big pinch of salt in either a bowl or the container of a food processor. Add the oil and eggs and beat or process until the dough holds together; add a tablespoon or two of cold water if necessary.

2 By hand, knead the dough until smooth. Cut it into 3 pieces and roll them, one at a time, through a pasta machine: Start at the widest setting and gradually turn the dial so that the dough becomes thinner and longer with each subsequent trip through the rollers; sprinkle with flour as necessary to prevent sticking. On most pasta machines, you will want to roll to one short of the thinnest-possible thickness.

3 Put the pasta sheets through the cutters to make linguine or fettuccine, or cut the pasta by hand. Cook it right away, or spread it out to let dry on towels. (If you let it dry thoroughly, it will keep for a few days.)

4 To cook, plunge the pasta into boiling salted water. When fresh, it will cook in a minute; when dried, it will take a little bit longer. Sauce and serve.

MAKES 4 SERVINGS   TIME: 30 MINUTES

Mushroom **pasta**

¼ cup mushroom powder

2 cups flour, plus more for kneading and rolling

Salt

¼ cup extra-virgin olive oil

4 eggs

The best mushroom powder is made from porcini (cèpes); it is available from D'Artagnan (800–327–8246) or other suppliers of mushrooms. You can make your own powder by grinding any dried mushrooms as fine as possible in a spice mill or coffee grinder.

For sauce, try braised veal with its juices, or olive oil cooked with garlic, parsley, and mushrooms, or a mushroom-cream sauce.

1 Combine the mushroom powder and flour with a big pinch of salt in either a bowl or the container of a food processor. Add the oil and eggs and beat or process until the dough holds together; add a tablespoon or two of cold water if necessary (unlikely with this dough).

2 By hand, knead the dough until smooth. Cut it into 3 pieces and roll them, one at a time, through a pasta machine: Start at the widest setting and gradually turn the dial so that the dough becomes thinner and longer with each subsequent trip through the rollers; sprinkle with flour as necessary to prevent sticking. On most pasta machines, you will want to roll to one short of the thinnest-possible thickness.

3 Put the pasta sheets through the cutters to make linguine or fettuccine, or cut the pasta by hand. Cook it right away, or spread it out to let dry on towels. *(If you let it dry thoroughly it will keep for a few days.)*

4 To cook, plunge the pasta into boiling salted water. When fresh, it will cook in a minute; when dried, a little bit longer. Sauce and serve.

MAKES 4 SERVINGS   TIME: 30 MINUTES, PLUS OPTIONAL DRYING TIME

Simple to Spectacular

Garlic-thyme **pasta**

12 cloves garlic

3 tablespoons extra-virgin olive oil

2¼ cups flour

Salt

2 teaspoons freshly ground black pepper

2 teaspoons thyme leaves

2 eggs

A big-flavored pasta using roasted garlic. Any simple tomato sauce will set this off beautifully, although it is so flavorful that a simple dressing of warm olive oil would suffice.

1 Preheat the oven to 400°F. Wrap 10 of the garlic cloves, tossed with 1 tablespoon of the oil, in foil. Roast for about 30 minutes, or until the garlic is tender; cool and squeeze the garlic puree from the skins. Meanwhile, peel and mince the remaining garlic.

2 Combine the flour with a big pinch of salt in either a bowl or the container of a food processor; add the garlic puree and minced garlic, pepper, and thyme. Add the remaining 2 tablespoons oil and the eggs and beat or process until the dough holds together; add a tablespoon or two of cold water if necessary (unlikely with this dough).

3 By hand, knead the dough until smooth, adding more flour if necessary. Cut it into 3 pieces and roll them, one at a time, through a pasta machine: Start at the widest setting and gradually turn the dial so that the dough becomes thinner and longer with each subsequent trip through the rollers; sprinkle with flour as necessary to prevent sticking. On most pasta machines, you will want to roll to one short of the thinnest-possible thickness.

4 Put the pasta sheets through the cutters to make linguine or fettuccine, or cut the pasta by hand. Cook it right away, or spread it out to let dry on towels. (*If you let it dry thoroughly, it will keep for a few days.*)

5 To cook, plunge the pasta into boiling salted water. When fresh, it will cook in a minute; when dried, a little bit longer. Sauce and serve.

MAKES 4 SERVINGS   TIME: ABOUT 1 HOUR, PLUS OPTIONAL RESTING TIME

Pasta, Noodles, and Rice

Herb-printed **pasta**

2 cups flour

Salt

3 tablespoons extra-virgin olive oil

3 eggs

An assortment of fresh whole herb leaves, such as dill, tarragon, basil, chervil, and/or parsley

You can use any herbs you like to produce this stunning-looking dough. (This is a fun project to do with kids.) Sauce simply, with butter and Parmesan, Beurre Noisette (page 192), or garlic and oil. You might also use these to make "open" ravioli—just a couple of layers of pasta—with a filling of artichokes or asparagus and shrimp.

1 Combine the flour with a big pinch of salt in either a bowl or the container of a food processor. Add the oil and eggs and beat or process until the dough holds together; add a tablespoon or two of cold water if necessary.

2 By hand, knead the dough until smooth. Cut it into 3 pieces and roll them, one at a time, through a pasta machine: Start at the widest setting and gradually turn the dial so that the dough becomes thinner and longer with each subsequent trip through the rollers; sprinkle with flour as necessary to prevent sticking. Stop rolling about two settings before minimum thickness.

3 Put each of the pasta sheets on a board or table and place one third of the herbs on the bottom half of each sheet, side by side; don't layer the herbs, but put them fairly close together. Fold the top half of each sheet over the bottom. Put each sheet through the rollers again, starting at about the middle setting and working your way down to the third-thinnest setting or, if things are going well and the dough is not tearing, the second-thinnest. Again, use as much flour as you need to.

4 These are best cut by hand into wide strips or simply random shapes. Cook the pasta right away, or let it dry for a couple of hours on towels.

5 To cook, plunge the pasta into boiling salted water; it will be done in a minute. Sauce and serve.

MAKES 4 SERVINGS   TIME: 45 MINUTES, PLUS OPTIONAL DRYING TIME

Lobster-roe **pasta**

6 tablespoons uncooked lobster roe

2 cups flour

Salt

2 tablespoons extra-virgin olive oil

2 eggs

This is a delicate dough, so don't roll it too thin. It is also amazing-looking—the cooked roe is red, and the raw roe makes green polka dots.

You can get lobster roe out of female lobsters, or order it from Browne Trading (207-766-2402) or many other sources for fine seafood products. Sauce with Lobster Oil (page 366), garnished with lobster and herbs, or with a simple tomato sauce.

1 Poach half the roe in a small amount of boiling salted water. As soon as it turns red—this will take a matter of seconds—drain it in a fine sieve.

2 Combine the flour with a big pinch of salt in either a bowl or the container of a food processor. Add the oil and eggs and beat or process until the dough holds together; add a tablespoon or two of cold water if necessary, but do not make the dough too wet because the roe is moist.

3 By hand, knead the raw and cooked roe into the dough, adding more flour if necessary if the dough seems pasty. Cut the dough into 3 pieces and roll them, one at a time, through a pasta machine: Start at the widest setting and gradually turn the dial so that the dough becomes thinner and longer with each subsequent trip through the rollers; sprinkle with flour as necessary to prevent sticking. On most pasta machines you will want to roll a couple of steps thicker than the thinnest-possible thickness.

4 Put the pasta sheets through the cutters to make linguine or fettuccine, or cut the pasta by hand. Cook it right away, or spread it out and let dry for a couple of hours on towels.

5 To cook, plunge the pasta into boiling salted water; it will cook in a minute. Sauce and serve.

Simple to Spectacular

MAKES 4 SERVINGS   TIME: ABOUT 40 MINUTES, PLUS OPTIONAL DRYING TIME

TAKE fresh pasta dough, cut it into squares, fill them, and roll them up—these are cannelloni. You can take the same dough (and the same fillings) and make ravioli, tortellini, or any other shape of filled pasta you like, but cannelloni are the fastest and easiest; the process is really, really simple.

If our pasta dough is familiar, most of our fillings are a little unusual. One is the rather straightforward combination of ricotta and herbs, but others range from a spicy combination of potatoes and arugula to a rich, lusty filling of ground lamb with goat cheese and North African flavorings.

KEYS TO SUCCESS

You can make this dough in advance; well-wrapped and refrigerated, it will keep perfectly for a day or so before you roll it out.

Since you fill the cannelloni after the pasta dough has cooked and cooled, all of them are finished in the oven, where they cook a little more. Therefore, you should undercook the pasta slightly in the boiling water, just until tender enough to handle easily; then plunge into ice water to stop the cooking.

You can fill the pasta rather generously if you like; the proportion of wrapper to filling isn't critical here, because they are barely handled after rolling. (Ravioli are a different story; keep the amount of filling relatively small.)

The olive oil and broth added before baking help keep the cannelloni from sticking to the baking dish. They also create, with the juices that leak out of the filling, some nice pan sauces; drizzle them over the cannelloni before serving.

All of these can be run under the broiler for a little extra browning if you like; just be careful, because they will burn if left for too long.

Pasta dough

2 cups (about 10 ounces) flour

Salt

3 eggs

If, when you mix this dough, it seems dry and won't hold together, add another egg or a tablespoon or two of ice water.

1 Combine the flour and a pinch of salt in a food processor and pulse a couple of times. Add the eggs and turn the machine on until the dough begins to clump together.

2 Knead the dough on a lightly floured surface until smooth and firm. (If you have time, wrap it in plastic and refrigerate for an hour or more before rolling it out; it will be easier to handle.) Divide the dough in half and roll each piece, one at a time, through a pasta machine. Start at the widest setting and gradually turn the dial so that the dough becomes thinner and longer with each subsequent trip through the rollers; sprinkle with flour as necessary to prevent sticking. On most pasta machines, you will want to roll one short of the thinnest-possible thickness.

3 Bring a large pot of water to a boil and salt it. Cut the dough into rectangles about 4 × 6 inches. (You should be able to get at least 16 rectangles from one batch of pasta.) Cook them, a few at a time, for about 3 minutes each; they should just become tender. Remove carefully and place in a bowl of cold water, then remove and dry with paper towels.

4 With a short side facing you, make a line of filling on each rectangle of pasta. Roll up, then cook as directed in the individual recipe.

MAKES ABOUT 1 POUND, ENOUGH FOR THE FILLINGS IN THIS SECTION   TIME: 30 MINUTES

Simple to Spectacular

Cannelloni with potatoes and arugula

1 pound Yukon Gold or other good all-purpose potatoes, peeled and cut into big chunks

Salt

3 to 4 tablespoons extra-virgin olive oil

2 cloves garlic, peeled and chopped

½ teaspoon red pepper flakes, or to taste

1 pound arugula, tough stems trimmed, washed, and dried

1 cup freshly grated pecorino Romano

Pasta Dough (page 80), cut into rectangles for cannelloni and cooked as directed

½ cup any chicken stock

The strong flavors of arugula, red pepper, and pecorino may guarantee that this is not a pasta dish for kids, but they make it powerfully appealing to grown-ups.

1 Boil the potatoes in salted water until soft, 10 to 20 minutes depending on the size of your chunks; drain.

2 Meanwhile, put 1 tablespoon of the olive oil in a skillet and turn the heat to medium; add the garlic, some salt, and red pepper flakes and cook, stirring occasionally, for 3 to 5 minutes, or until the garlic is light gold. Add two-thirds of the arugula; cover and cook for 2 minutes, then turn off the heat and let steam for 5 minutes, still covered. Chop the remaining arugula; when the cooked arugula is done, chop that mixture too.

3 Preheat the oven to 450°F. Mash the potatoes with the raw and cooked arugula, another tablespoon of olive oil, and half the pecorino. Fill the pasta as directed on page 80.

4 Put the cannelloni in one layer in a baking dish. Drizzle with the stock, then sprinkle with 1 more tablespoon of olive oil and the remaining cheese. Bake until golden brown on top, about 10 minutes. Serve, drizzled with the pan juices, and another tablespoon of olive oil if you like.

MAKES 4 TO 6 SERVINGS   TIME: 40 MINUTES, WITH PREMADE PASTA

Pasta, Noodles, and Rice

Cannelloni with greens and herbs

5 tablespoons extra-virgin olive oil

2 pounds spinach, trimmed, washed, and dried

½ pound arugula, trimmed, washed, and dried

1 pound mesclun or other mixed tender greens, washed and dried

1 teaspoon minced garlic

10 sprigs chervil, minced

1 egg yolk

½ cup freshly grated Parmesan

¼ teaspoon grated nutmeg

Salt and freshly ground black pepper

Pasta Dough (page 80), cut into squares for cannelloni and cooked as directed

½ cup any chicken stock

To make this dish even better, garnish it with a few sliced artichoke hearts that have been sautéed in olive oil until tender.
Use about 20 basil leaves if you can't find chervil.

1 Preheat the oven to 450°F. Put 2 tablespoons of the olive oil in a large skillet and turn the heat to medium. Add the spinach, arugula, and mesclun, along with the garlic; cook, stirring occasionally, for about 5 minutes, or until the greens are tender (they will reduce in volume considerably). Let cool, then finely chop and transfer to a bowl.

2 Stir in the chervil, egg yolk, 1 tablespoon of the olive oil, half the Parmesan, and the nutmeg. Season with salt and pepper. Fill the pasta as directed on page 80.

3 Put the cannelloni in one layer in a baking dish. Drizzle with the stock, then sprinkle with another tablespoon of the olive oil and the remaining cheese. Bake until golden brown on top, about 10 minutes. Serve drizzled with the pan juices and the remaining 1 tablespoon olive oil.

MAKES 4 TO 6 SERVINGS   TIME: 30 MINUTES, WITH PREMADE PASTA

Pasta, Noodles, and Rice

Cannelloni with scallops and zucchini

2 tablespoons extra-virgin olive oil

2 zucchini (about 12 ounces total), washed, trimmed, and cut into 1/4-inch cubes

Salt

1 tablespoon thyme leaves

3/4 pound scallops, cut into 1/4-inch cubes

Pinch of cayenne pepper

Pasta Dough (page 80), cut into rectangles for cannelloni and cooked as directed

1/2 cup any chicken or fish stock

1/2 cup heavy cream

4 tablespoons butter

Freshly ground black pepper

1 tablespoon fresh lemon juice, or to taste

These are finished with a creamy thyme butter. You can use shrimp instead of scallops—or in addition to them. Just make sure to cut the pieces quite small, since they only cook during the brief oven time.

1 Preheat the oven to 450°F. Put the olive oil in a large skillet and turn the heat to medium-high. A minute later, add the zucchini, along with a big pinch of salt and 2 teaspoons of the thyme. Cook just until the zucchini begins to become tender, about 5 minutes.

2 Toss the zucchini with the scallops and cayenne. Fill the pasta as directed on page 80.

3 Put the cannelloni in one layer in a baking dish. Drizzle with the stock, then bake until golden brown on top, about 10 minutes.

4 Meanwhile, combine the cream, 1/2 cup water, and the remaining 1 teaspoon thyme in a small saucepan. Bring to a boil over medium-high heat, and reduce to about 1/4 cup. Lower the heat, then whisk in the butter, a little at a time; season with salt and pepper and the lemon juice.

5 Serve the cannelloni drizzled with the pan juices and the thyme butter.

MAKES 4 SERVINGS   TIME: 30 MINUTES, WITH PREMADE PASTA

Cannelloni with ricotta and herbs

1 pound ricotta

¼ cup minced parsley

2 tablespoons minced chives

2 tablespoons minced chervil

1 teaspoon minced thyme

¼ teaspoon grated nutmeg

Salt and freshly ground black pepper

1 egg yolk

½ cup freshly grated Parmesan

Pasta Dough (page 80), cut into squares for cannelloni and cooked as directed

½ cup any chicken stock

1 tablespoon extra-virgin olive oil

4 tablespoons butter

2 tablespoons minced sage

These are classic Italian flavors for pasta, especially the combination of butter, sage, and Parmesan. If you use commercial ricotta, place it in a strainer for about 10 minutes to drain the excess liquid.

1 Preheat the oven to 450°F. Mix together the ricotta, parsley, chives, chervil, thyme, nutmeg, salt and pepper to taste, egg yolk, and half the Parmesan. Fill the pasta as directed on page 80.

2 Put the cannelloni in one layer in a baking dish. Drizzle with the stock, then sprinkle with the olive oil and the remaining cheese. Bake until golden brown on top, about 10 minutes.

3 Meanwhile, put the butter in a small saucepan and turn the heat to medium. When the foam subsides and the butter begins to turn brown, add the sage and remove from the heat. Serve the pasta with the pan juices and the butter-sage mixture.

MAKES 4 TO 6 SERVINGS   TIME: 30 MINUTES, WITH PREMADE PASTA

Cannelloni with lamb and goat cheese

½ teaspoon cardamom seeds

2 teaspoons cumin seeds

1 teaspoon coriander seeds

1 cinnamon stick

12 ounces ground lamb

3 ounces soft fresh goat cheese

1 tablespoon minced cilantro

Salt and freshly ground black pepper

Pasta Dough (page 80), cut into rectangles for cannelloni and cooked as directed

½ cup any chicken stock

2 tablespoons extra-virgin olive oil

½ cup freshly grated Parmesan

½ cup peeled, seeded, and diced tomato

Much simpler than it sounds, because the lamb cooks once the pasta is filled and in the oven.

1 Preheat the oven to 450°F. Put the cardamom, cumin, coriander, and cinnamon in a small skillet and turn the heat to medium. Toast, shaking the skillet periodically, until the spices are fragrant, just a minute or two. Grind in a spice mill or coffee grinder or a mortar and pestle.

2 Combine 2 teaspoons of the spice mix with the lamb, cheese, cilantro, and salt and pepper to taste. Fill the pasta as directed on page 80.

3 Put the cannelloni in one layer in a baking dish. Drizzle with the stock, then sprinkle with half the olive oil and the cheese. Bake until golden brown on top, about 10 minutes. Drizzle with the pan juices and the remaining olive oil and serve, topped with the diced tomato.

MAKES 4 SERVINGS   TIME: 30 MINUTES, WITH PREMADE PASTA

Simple to Spectacular

LIKE our pasta doughs, some of these are traditional and some are not—but all are easy, and, with one exception, quite fast. To us, the most exciting of these recipes is the simplest, the Saffron Oil; it has the brilliant color you expect with a rich flavor you might not. The clam and oxtail ragu sauces are traditional, but we like our interpretations of these classics. And the red pepper—crème fraîche and lobster-chile are fresh and new.

KEYS TO SUCCESS

We created these for dried pasta—long, like linguine, and cut, like ziti. Perhaps it goes without saying, but the best dried pasta is imported from Italy. You can use fresh pasta if you like.

Pasta bowls should be hot, in order to keep the noodles and sauce warm through the serving process. Fill the bowls with hot water and drain them just before tossing the pasta and sauce together.

None of these sauces need cheese.

Pasta with saffron oil

¼ teaspoon saffron threads

Salt and freshly ground black pepper

⅓ cup extra-virgin olive oil

1 pound linguine or other pasta

Minced parsley for garnish

Though you can prepare this sauce in the time it takes to boil the water and cook the pasta, it is better if it sits for a little while. So if you have a little time, let it stand for an hour or more.

The best saffron is sold by the ounce, or at least the quarter-ounce. Steer clear of those tubes with just a few threads in them, and don't be suckered in by inexpensive saffron, which more than likely comes from marigolds rather than crocuses. An ounce of saffron will set you back at least forty dollars (and will last you several years, unless you use it fanatically).

1 Combine the saffron with 1 tablespoon hot water in a small saucepan and let sit for 5 minutes. Meanwhile, bring a large pot of water to a boil and salt it.

2 Add the olive oil to the saffron-water mixture and warm over very low heat; when the mixture begins to bubble, turn off the heat. (*At this point, you can let the mixture sit for 2 to 3 hours, or even overnight; rewarm before serving.*)

3 Cook the pasta until tender but not mushy. Drain, then toss with the saffron oil and salt and pepper to taste. Garnish with the parsley and serve.

MAKES 3 TO 4 SERVINGS   TIME: 20 MINUTES

Pasta with red pepper and crème fraîche

Salt

¼ cup extra-virgin olive oil

2 red bell peppers, peeled, cored, seeded, and minced

1 pound ziti or other pasta

1 cup crème fraîche or sour cream

Freshly ground black pepper

Minced fresh chervil or dill for garnish

A Jean-Georges special, more French than Italian, very contemporary, delicious, and easy. As in some traditional pasta dishes, the noodles finish cooking in the sauce. Use an ordinary vegetable peeler for the red peppers.

1 Bring a large pot of water to a boil and salt it. Meanwhile, put the olive oil in a large deep skillet and turn the heat to medium. Add the peppers and a large pinch of salt and cook, stirring occasionally, until the peppers are tender, about 10 minutes.

2 Cook the pasta until it is somewhat tender but still quite far from being done; drain it, reserving a little of the cooking water.

3 Stir the crème fraîche or sour cream and salt and pepper to taste into the red peppers, then add the pasta. Cook until tender, stirring, and adding some of the cooking liquid if necessary. Taste and adjust the seasoning, then serve, garnished with the herb.

MAKES 3 TO 4 SERVINGS   TIME: 25 MINUTES

Simple to Spectacular

Pasta with clams

Salt and freshly ground black pepper

¼ cup extra-virgin olive oil

3 pounds tiny hard-shell clams or cockles, washed

1 pound linguine or other pasta

1 tablespoon chopped garlic

3 tomatoes (about 1 pound), chopped

1 cup minced parsley

This is ultra-traditional, taught to us by a Roman friend. The best clams to use are tiny littlenecks or mahogany clams; cockles are a good substitute. Wash the shells well, even scrub them if necessary, to remove all traces of sand.

You can peel and seed the tomatoes for this dish if you like, but it's not necessary.

1 Bring a large pot of water to a boil and salt it. Meanwhile, put the olive oil in a large deep skillet and turn the heat to medium-high. Add the clams and cook, stirring occasionally, until the first few of them open. Turn off the heat and cover the skillet.

2 Cook the pasta until it still retains quite a bit of crunch; drain, reserving about 1 cup of the cooking liquid. Turn the heat under the clams to high and add the garlic and tomatoes. Stir, then add the pasta.

3 Cook, stirring, until the pasta is tender, adding a bit of the reserved cooking liquid if the mixture seems dry. Stir in the parsley, taste and add salt (if necessary) and pepper, and serve.

MAKES 4 SERVINGS   TIME: ABOUT 30 MINUTES

Pasta with lobster and chiles

2 lobsters (each about 1½ pounds)

8 bay leaves

8 cloves garlic, cut in half

4 small chiles, cut in half

Salt

¼ teaspoon red pepper flakes, or to taste

Juice of 3 to 4 lemons, or to taste

½ teaspoon minced garlic

½ cup extra-virgin olive oil

1 pound ziti or other pasta

½ cup minced parsley

An unusual dish, because many seafood sauces for pasta contain tomatoes. Here, we use bay leaves, lemon, garlic, and chiles for flavor. See pages 229–238 for more lobster recipes.

1 Put the lobsters in a pot with the bay leaves, halved garlic, and chiles; add water to cover. Bring to a boil, then turn off the heat and let sit. Bring another pot of water to a boil for the pasta; salt it.

2 Combine the red pepper flakes, three-quarters of the lemon juice, the minced garlic, and the olive oil in a big bowl. Crack the lobsters and remove their meat; cut it into chunks, but don't make them too small. Add the lobster to the bowl and let it sit there while you cook the pasta.

3 Cook the pasta until it is tender but not mushy. Drain it and toss with the sauce. Stir in the parsley and salt to taste; add more lemon juice and red pepper flakes if necessary, and serve.

MAKES 4 SERVINGS   TIME: 30 TO 40 MINUTES

Simple to Spectacular

Pasta with oxtail ragu

3 tablespoons extra-virgin olive oil

2 pounds oxtails, cut into approximately 2-inch sections

1 medium onion, peeled and chopped

1 carrot, peeled and chopped

1 stalk celery, chopped

2 cloves garlic, peeled and crushed

6 sprigs thyme

3 cups full-bodied red wine

Salt and freshly ground black pepper

1 tablespoon butter

1 pound ziti or other pasta

This slow-cooked sauce is plenty rich on its own, but if you'd like to make a wonderful garnish, sauté 3 cups of assorted sliced mushrooms along with 2 tablespoons minced shallots in 2 tablespoons butter until tender.
You can use veal shank or short ribs in place of the oxtail if you like.

1 Put the oil in a large skillet and turn the heat to medium-high. Brown the oxtail pieces, turning as necessary to brown on all sides—this will take a while, 20 minutes or so; don't rush it. As the oxtail pieces brown, transfer them to a casserole or large ovenproof saucepan.

2 Preheat the oven to 300°F. In the same skillet, brown the onion, carrot, celery, and garlic over high heat until really quite dark, at least 10 minutes. Combine with the oxtails, along with the thyme, wine, and salt and pepper to taste. Bring to a boil, then put in the oven and cook, uncovered, stirring only occasionally, until the meat is falling off the bone—probably a good 4 hours.

3 While the meat sauce is cooling, bring a large pot of water to a boil for the pasta; salt it. Take the meat off the bone and shred it. Strain the liquid and combine it with the meat. (If there is more than a cup of liquid, reduce it to a cup by boiling it over high heat before combining it with the meat; if there is less, dilute with a little water.) Season to taste and reheat gently; stir in the butter and adjust the seasoning.

4 Meanwhile, cook the pasta until it is tender but not mushy. Drain, toss with the sauce, and serve.

MAKES 4 SERVINGS   TIME: ABOUT 5 HOURS, LARGELY UNATTENDED

Spaetzle

WHAT is spaetzle? Noodles made easy. You make a very thick batter, close to a dough but as easy to produce as pancake batter—no kneading—and force it through a coarse colander, one with holes of about ¼ inch in diameter (or a spaetzle screen; you can buy these at most kitchen supply houses or specialty stores), into boiling water. The batter forms short, irregularly shaped noodles in just minutes. These can be dressed any way you like, with melted butter or a sauce.

Like pasta dough, the batter itself can be seasoned. So we go from plain spaetzle with butter to pepper spaetzle topped with crispy shallots to spaetzle made with chestnut flour, chickpea flour, or pureed squash, all served with different toppings. You'll soon get the idea, but remember that at their simplest, spaetzle are a great, fresh weeknight side dish.

KEYS TO SUCCESS

The best way to make spaetzle is by forcing the thick batter through a colander or strainer with ¼-inch holes, but you can drop it off a small spoon if you like; with a little practice, you'll be able to do this pretty quickly.

It's likely that you will have to cook the batter in batches; you really only want one layer of spaetzle in the boiling water at a time. But since they cook in just a couple of minutes, this is not a big deal.

When the spaetzle are done (they'll rise to the surface), remove them with a slotted spoon or strainer and plunge into ice water, then drain again. At this point, you can refrigerate them for 24 hours before reheating.

Spaetzle with butter

Salt and freshly ground black pepper

2 cups flour

½ cup milk

4 tablespoons butter or extra-virgin olive oil

Basic spaetzle. You can reheat the spaetzle in just a little oil and top them with any sauce you like. Or you can season the butter or oil with garlic or herbs, add a little ground meat to it, or top the spaetzle with grated cheese.

1 Bring a large pot of water to a boil and salt it. Combine the flour, milk, ¼ cup water, and a large pinch of salt in a bowl and beat well.

2 Strain the batter through a coarse colander or spaetzle maker into the boiling water and cook until the noodles rise to the top, just a couple of minutes. Drain and plunge into ice water to stop the cooking; drain again. *(You can prepare the noodles a day in advance up to this point; refrigerate, covered, until you're ready to cook.)*

3 Melt the butter or heat the oil in a large skillet over medium-high heat. Add the spaetzle and salt and pepper to taste and cook, stirring occasionally, until heated through, about 5 minutes. Serve hot.

MAKES 4 SERVINGS   TIME: 20 MINUTES

Spaetzle with pepper and crisp shallots

Salt and freshly ground black pepper

2 cups flour

½ cup milk

½ cup neutral oil, such as canola or grapeseed

1 cup peeled and sliced shallots

6 sage leaves, chopped, or 1 teaspoon crumbled dried sage

We use crisp-cooked shallots often (see page 124 for another example), mostly because they're easy and we love them; they're onion rings taken to another level. Here, the spaetzle is spiked with pepper—use more or less according to your taste.

1 Bring a large pot of water to a boil and salt it. Combine the flour, milk, ¼ cup water, a large pinch of salt, and a teaspoon of pepper in a bowl and beat well.

2 Strain the batter through a coarse colander or spaetzle maker into the boiling water and cook until the noodles rise to the top, just a couple of minutes. Drain and plunge into ice water to stop the cooking; drain again. *(You can prepare the noodles a day in advance up to this point; refrigerate, covered, until you're ready to cook.)*

3 Put the oil in a medium skillet and turn the heat to medium-high. Add the shallots and cook, stirring occasionally, until golden and crisp. Be careful—once they start to brown, they brown quickly, and may burn if you don't keep an eye on them. Remove the shallots with a slotted spoon and drain on paper towels; reserve the oil.

4 Heat about half the reserved oil in a large skillet over medium-high heat. Add the spaetzle and salt and pepper to taste and cook, stirring occasionally, until heated through, about 5 minutes. Stir in the sage and serve, topped with the crisp shallots.

MAKES 4 SERVINGS   TIME: 30 MINUTES

Simple to Spectacular

Chestnut spaetzle with mushrooms and chestnuts

Salt and freshly ground black pepper

8 chestnuts

1½ cups chestnut flour

½ cup flour

¼ cup milk

6 tablespoons butter or extra-virgin olive oil

8 ounces white mushrooms, trimmed and thinly sliced

Minced parsley for garnish

These are unbelievably good, and the hardest part may be finding chestnut flour—look in natural or specialty food stores.

1 Bring one small and one large pot of water to a boil; salt the water in the large pot. Use a paring knife to cut a ring around the equator of each chestnut. Plunge them into the small pot of boiling water for about 3 minutes, then turn off the heat, leaving the chestnuts in the water. Remove 2 or 3 chestnuts at a time and, using the knife and your fingers, peel off both shell and skin; use a towel to protect your hands from the heat if necessary. Slice the chestnuts into 3 or 4 pieces each and set aside.

2 Combine the flours, milk, and a large pinch of salt in a bowl and beat well. Strain the batter through a coarse colander or spaetzle maker into the boiling water and cook until the noodles rise to the top, just a couple of minutes. Drain and plunge into ice water to stop the cooking; drain again. (You can prepare the noodles a day in advance up to this point; refrigerate, covered, until you're ready to cook.)

3 Put 2 tablespoons of the butter or oil in a large skillet and turn the heat to medium. When the butter melts or the oil is hot, turn the heat to high and add the mushrooms; cook, stirring occasionally, until they are lightly browned, 5 to 10 minutes. Remove them from the pan and set aside. Wipe out the skillet, turn the heat to medium-high, and add the remaining 4 tablespoons butter or oil.

4 Add the chestnuts to the skillet and cook, stirring occasionally, for about a minute. Add the spaetzle and salt and pepper to taste and cook, stirring occasionally, until heated through, about 5 minutes. Stir in the mushrooms and cook for another minute, then garnish with parsley and serve.

Simple to Spectacular

MAKES 4 SERVINGS   TIME: 40 MINUTES

Chickpea spaetzle with eggplant

Salt

2 cups chickpea flour

¼ cup milk

5 tablespoons olive oil

Cayenne pepper

2 teaspoons cumin seeds

1 cup ½-inch cubes eggplant (peeled if skin is thick)

1 teaspoon minced garlic

¼ cup pitted black olives, chopped

Minced cilantro for garnish

Cumin seeds, unground, add a nice crunch here, and, of course, great flavor. Chickpea flour, like chestnut flour, can be found at many specialty and natural food stores. Note that this eggplant preparation would make a great pasta sauce or side dish on its own.

1 Bring a large pot of water to a boil and salt it. Combine the flour, milk, 1 tablespoon of the olive oil, a large pinch of salt, and a small pinch of cayenne in a bowl and beat well.

2 Strain the batter through a coarse colander or spaetzle maker into the boiling water and cook until the noodles rise to the top, just a couple of minutes. Drain and plunge into ice water to stop the cooking; drain again. (*You can prepare the noodles a day in advance up to this point; refrigerate, covered, until you're ready to cook.*)

3 Put the cumin seeds in a small skillet and turn the heat to medium. Toast, shaking the pan occasionally, until the cumin is fragrant, just a minute or two. Set aside. Put the remaining ¼ cup oil in a large skillet and turn the heat to medium. A minute later, add the eggplant and turn the heat to high. Cook, stirring occasionally, until the eggplant becomes tender and begins to brown, 10 to 15 minutes. Add the garlic and cook for another minute.

4 Add the spaetzle, cumin, olives, and salt and cayenne to taste and cook, stirring occasionally, until heated through, about 5 minutes. Garnish with cilantro and serve.

MAKES 4 SERVINGS   TIME: 40 MINUTES

Baked butternut spaetzle with cheese and walnuts

12 ounces peeled butternut squash, cut into 1-inch cubes
(buy a squash slightly larger than 1 pound)

4 cloves garlic, peeled

5 branches thyme

¼ cup extra-virgin olive oil

½ teaspoon red pepper flakes

Salt and freshly ground black pepper

½ cup walnuts, broken into pieces

2 eggs

1½ cups flour

Pinch of grated nutmeg

Pinch of cinnamon

3 tablespoons butter

½ cup ricotta

½ cup milk or cream, more or less

1 cup freshly grated Parmesan

Here, you make spaetzle laced with spiced and pureed butternut squash;
they're tender, sweet, and delicious. Then you bake them in a creamy
Parmesan sauce. The results are magnificent.

1   Preheat the oven to 450°F. Put the squash, garlic, thyme, olive oil, red pepper
    flakes, and a big pinch of salt in a roasting pan and roast, shaking and stirring
    occasionally, until the squash is tender, about 30 minutes.

2   Meanwhile, put the walnuts in a dry skillet and turn the heat to medium. Toast,
    shaking the pan occasionally, until the nuts are fragrant, just a minute or two.
    Set aside.

3   Bring a large pot of water to a boil and salt it. Combine the eggs, flour, nutmeg,
    cinnamon, squash and garlic, and salt and pepper to taste in a food processor
    and blend well.

4 Strain the batter through a coarse colander or spaetzle maker into the boiling water and cook until the noodles rise to the top, just a couple of minutes. Drain and plunge into ice water to stop the cooking; drain again. *(You can prepare the noodles a day in advance up to this point; refrigerate, covered, until you're ready to cook.)*

5 Preheat the broiler. Put the butter in a large skillet and turn the heat to medium. Add the spaetzle and cook, stirring occasionally, until heated through, about 5 minutes; add the ricotta and keep tossing, then thin with milk or cream so that the mixture is not dry.

6 Put the spaetzle in a gratin dish and top with the walnuts and Parmesan. Run under the broiler for about a minute, or until the cheese melts and begins to brown. Serve immediately.

MAKES 4 MAIN-COURSE OR 8 SIDE-DISH SERVINGS   TIME: ABOUT 1¼ HOURS

Sticky rice

STICKY or glutinous rice (also called sweet rice, although it isn't) is not your usual rice. It has real body, chewiness, and more flavor than the rice we're used to eating. When soaked and steamed—the best way to prepare it—it sticks together, making a tender mass that is easy to eat (it doesn't fall off the fork and can readily be picked up with chopsticks). It also takes to a wide variety of simple but unusual preparations, as you'll see here, from side dishes to dessert.

There are a couple of aspects of sticky rice that make it different: First of all, you buy it in Asian markets. It must be soaked before cooking, and it can hardly be overcooked; we recommend steaming it for 8 minutes, but that is the minimum. If it's more convenient to steam it and keep it hot for another few, that's fine; it will not change in texture or flavor.

KEYS TO SUCCESS

Soak the rice for as long as possible, up to 24 hours. You can get away with a single hour of soaking, but longer is better.

You need a steamer. You can use a bamboo or metal steamer, or improvise your own by propping a strainer above simmering water and covering it.

It's easiest to steam the rice by wrapping it loosely in a piece of cheesecloth, because removing it from the steamer just takes a second that way. But you can also use a strainer to hold the rice, or cook it directly in a steamer if the holes are fine enough.

You can cook the rice in advance. Keep it tightly wrapped and refrigerated, and steam again until hot just before serving.

Simple to Spectacular

Steamed **sticky rice**

1½ cups sticky (or glutinous) rice, soaked in water to cover
for at least 1 hour or, preferably, overnight

Salt and freshly ground black pepper

Sticky rice makes a fine side dish, even without sauce, because it has much
more flavor and body than most other rice. You can keep the rice hot over
the steaming water for up to an hour before serving.

1 Drain the soaked rice and wrap it loosely in a piece of cheesecloth; there's no
need to tie the cheesecloth closed.

2 Place the cheesecloth in the top of a steamer over boiling water, cover the
steamer, and steam for about 8 minutes, until all traces of chalkiness are gone
and the rice is fully tender. Keep the rice in the steamer until you're ready to
serve.

3 Mix the rice with salt and pepper and serve.

MAKES 4 SERVINGS   TIME: 15 MINUTES, PLUS 1 TO 24 HOURS SOAKING

Sticky rice salad with scallions

1½ cups sticky (or glutinous) rice, soaked in water to cover
for at least 1 hour or, preferably, overnight

2 tablespoons peanut or other oil

2 tablespoons soy sauce

½ cup chopped scallions

Juice of 1 lime, or more to taste

¼ cup minced cilantro

Salt and freshly ground black pepper

2 teaspoons sesame oil

Toss cooked sticky rice with some simple seasonings and you have a fast, warm, delicious salad. You can make this as grand as you like by adding a variety of vegetables. However you make it, it's great with fish or meat grilled with Asian seasonings.

1 Drain the soaked rice and wrap it loosely in a piece of cheesecloth; there's no need to tie the cheesecloth closed.

2 Place the cheesecloth in the top of a steamer over boiling water, cover the steamer, and steam for about 8 minutes, until all traces of chalkiness are gone and the rice is fully tender.

3 While the rice is still hot, toss it with the peanut oil, soy sauce, and scallions. Stir in the juice of 1 lime and about half the cilantro. Season with salt and pepper.

4 Just before serving (the rice should be warm or at room temperature), add the remaining cilantro, the sesame oil, and more lime juice if you like.

MAKES 4 SERVINGS   TIME: 20 MINUTES, PLUS 1 TO 24 HOURS SOAKING

Simple to Spectacular

Crunchy sticky rice pancakes

1½ cups sticky (or glutinous) rice, soaked in water to cover for at least 1 hour or, preferably, overnight

Salt and freshly ground black pepper

2 tablespoons butter

1 egg, lightly beaten

2 scallions, trimmed and minced

2 tablespoons minced cilantro

2 tablespoons peanut or other oil

1 tablespoon soy sauce

Juice of 1 lime

Like the salad on page 104, this is cooked sticky rice tossed with seasonings. But peanuts are added for crunch, butter for a velvety texture, and an egg for substance. You take the mixture and sauté it quickly to make crisp cakes that—with their quickly made sauce—make a great first course, snack, or Asian-style side dish.

1 Drain the soaked rice and wrap it loosely in a piece of cheesecloth; there's no need to tie the cheesecloth closed.

2 Place the cheesecloth in the top of a steamer over boiling water, cover the steamer, and steam for about 8 minutes, until all traces of chalkiness are gone and the rice is fully tender.

3 While the rice is still hot, toss it in a bowl with salt and pepper and half the butter. Stir in the egg, scallions, and cilantro. Gently shape the mixture into 4 large or 8 small cakes.

4 Heat a large skillet over medium-high heat for a minute or two, then add the oil. Cook the cakes in the hot oil until lightly browned on both sides, a total of 4 to 6 minutes.

5 Meanwhile, in a small saucepan, combine the remaining butter, the soy sauce, and lime juice. Turn the heat to low and melt the butter, then season with pepper. Serve the rice cakes hot, with a little of the sauce spooned over them.

MAKES 4 SERVINGS   TIME: 20 MINUTES, PLUS 1 TO 24 HOURS SOAKING

Twice-steamed sticky rice with chicken curry

2 cups sticky (or glutinous) rice, soaked in water to cover for at least 1 hour or, preferably, overnight

1 tablespoon plus 1 teaspoon nam pla (Thai fish sauce)

1 cup coconut milk

¼ teaspoon sugar

Banana leaves

1 recipe Curried Sautéed Chicken Chunks with Coconut Milk (page 261)

Here, we make sticky rice packages using banana leaves—you can buy them, frozen, at most Asian markets—and a spicy chicken curry; then we steam the packages. You can use many other moist fillings in a sticky rice package, including most braised or stir-fried meats. Prepare the chicken while the rice soaks or cooks.

1 Drain the soaked rice and wrap it loosely in a piece of cheesecloth; there's no need to tie the cheesecloth closed. Place the cheesecloth in the top of a steamer over boiling water, cover the steamer, and cook for about 8 minutes, until all traces of chalkiness are gone and the rice is fully tender.

2 Toss the rice with the nam pla, coconut milk, and sugar. Let sit for 15 minutes, or until the coconut milk is absorbed. Cut the banana leaves into four 8 × 12-inch rectangles, with the grain of the leaves running lengthwise. With one long side closest to your body, make a 4-inch square of rice on each rectangle, using half the rice. Top each with a portion of curry, leaving a 1-inch border around the rice, then cover completely with another layer of rice. Fold one long side of each banana leaf over, then the other, and finally the two shorter ends. Secure with a toothpick or string. (*You can refrigerate these packages for up to 2 days.*)

3 When you're ready to serve, steam the packages over boiling water until hot, about 15 minutes.

MAKES 4 SERVINGS   TIME: 1 HOUR, PLUS 1 TO 24 HOURS SOAKING

Sweet sticky rice with coconut milk and mango

1 cup sticky (or glutinous) rice, soaked in water to cover for at least 1 hour or, preferably, overnight

⅓ cup sugar

1 tablespoon sesame seeds

Salt

1 cup canned unsweetened coconut milk, more or less

1 ripe but not mushy mango, peeled, pitted, and sliced

Like many rices, sticky rice takes well to sugar and forms the basis of a fantastic dessert. This one is pure Thai, exotic but not at all difficult to prepare.

There is some judgment required, though: when you serve the rice, it should be moist and a little milky—like a perfect risotto—but not swimming in liquid. So first add the sugar syrup, a bit at a time, until the rice is sweet; then add just enough coconut milk to achieve the right texture. It's important to work the liquids into the rice while it is warm; but again, since the rice cannot be overcooked, you have plenty of flexibility here.

1 Drain the soaked rice and wrap it loosely in a piece of cheesecloth; there's no need to tie the cheesecloth closed.

2 Place the cheesecloth in the top of a steamer over boiling water, cover the steamer, and steam for about 8 minutes, until all traces of chalkiness are gone and the rice is fully tender. Unwrap and let cool for a minute.

3 While the rice is cooking, combine ¼ cup of the sugar with ¼ cup water in a small saucepan and bring to a boil; stir to dissolve the sugar. Remove from the heat. Toast the sesame seeds by placing them in a small skillet and cooking over medium heat, shaking the pan occasionally, until the seeds brown lightly and begin to pop; set aside.

4 Put the rice in a bowl and sprinkle with a little salt (the dish should have a slight saltiness when it's done), then combine it with the sugar syrup. Stir the remaining sugar into the coconut milk, then stir about ¼ cup of the coconut milk

into the rice. Continue to add coconut milk until the mixture is a little moister than a finished risotto, just slightly soupy; you will probably add just another ¼ cup or so. Let sit for about 5 minutes so the rice can absorb the excess moisture.

5 To serve, place a portion of the rice on each of four plates, then drizzle with a little of the remaining sweetened coconut milk. Top with the mango and sesame seeds, and finally a little more milk.

MAKES 4 SERVINGS   TIME: 20 MINUTES, PLUS 1 TO 24 HOURS SOAKING

Vegetables

Roast stuffed tomatoes

AN OLD-FASHIONED IDEA, but one that should never have fallen from favor. The basic technique is to hollow out a tomato, then fill it with its chopped pulp and a variety of other ingredients before roasting. The combination of the flavorful roast tomato, filling, and pan juices is really wonderful, and since you need not skin the tomato first (in fact, the skin holds the whole thing together), the preparation time is minimal.

And it's amazing how many flavors marry well with the tomato shell—we range from simple shrimp prepared in a Provençal manner to bitter greens smoothed with cheese to a combination of a couple of kinds of tomatoes. From there we go to a Middle Eastern– style stuffing of lamb (you can use other ground meat) and, finally, to an unusual dessert—tomato being, after all, a fruit.

KEYS TO SUCCESS

Stuff from the bottom (smooth) end of each tomato; you'll cut a thin slice from it that will serve as a "cap" during roasting, keeping the top of the stuffing moist.

With its stem end down, the tomato should sit flat in the roasting pan. If it does not, slice a thin piece off the stem end so it will stand up straight.

When removing the tomato pulp, scoop out enough to leave a wall of only about ¼ inch, but be careful not to pierce the sides or, especially, the bottom of the tomato. If you do, just patch the hole with a piece of pulp.

A medium-large tomato will take about ½ cup of dense stuffing and as much as 1 cup of loose stuffing, such as greens. Pack it in there, and pile it up over the top, as much as an inch if necessary. As it roasts, the stuffing will shrink and settle. If you're using mid-summer beefsteaks, big boys, brandywines, or another large variety, increase the amount of stuffing to as much as 1½ cups per tomato. Each of these babies will make a true main course or very large appetizer (even an appetizer for two if people don't mind sharing).

Roast tomatoes stuffed with shrimp

4 firm but ripe tomatoes (about 6 ounces each)

Salt and freshly ground black pepper

¾ pound fresh or frozen (thawed) shrimp, peeled (and deveined if you like)

1 teaspoon minced rosemary

1 tablespoon Mayonnaise (page 362), or use prepared mayonnaise

⅛ teaspoon cayenne pepper

2 tablespoons extra-virgin olive oil

Served hot or cold, as an impressive first course or a simple lunch dish, these are really quite magnificent. You need not use expensive large shrimp, because they will be chopped up. Substitute scallops, squid, or crabmeat for the shrimp if you like, and serve with bread and a green salad.

1   Preheat the oven to 450°F. Cut a ¼-inch slice from the smooth end of each tomato (reserve these slices) and use a spoon to scoop out all of the insides, leaving a wall about ¼ inch thick. Sprinkle the inside of the tomatoes with salt and pepper. Discard the woody core and seeds, and chop the tomato pulp with the shrimp. Toss this mixture with the rosemary, mayonnaise, cayenne, and salt and pepper to taste.

2   Stuff each tomato with one-quarter of the shrimp mixture and replace the top slices. Spread half the olive oil in a shallow roasting pan that will allow for a little room between the tomatoes, then place them in the pan and drizzle with the remaining olive oil. Sprinkle with salt and pepper and place the roasting pan in the oven.

3   Roast for 30 to 40 minutes, until the tomatoes are slightly shriveled and the stuffing is hot (pierce the stuffing to its center with a skewer and touch the skewer to your wrist or lip). Serve hot, warm, at room temperature, or chilled.

MAKES 4 SERVINGS   TIME: 1 HOUR

Roast tomatoes stuffed with bitter greens

4 firm but ripe tomatoes
(about 6 ounces each)

Salt and freshly ground black pepper

¼ cup extra-virgin olive oil

½ cup chopped scallions

2 tablespoons minced shallots

About 4 cups mixed bitter greens
(arugula, dandelion, radicchio, etc.),
washed, dried, and roughly chopped

⅓ cup soft fresh goat cheese

2 tablespoons balsamic or sherry
vinegar

To reduce the bitterness of the greens, we cook them quickly first; to keep them moist during roasting, we add a little goat cheese. The result is an assertive but creamy mixture that smacks of the farm. This variation is best hot or warm, rather than cold. Serve as a first course, as part of a buffet, or as a side dish.

1 Preheat the oven to 450°F. Cut a ¼-inch slice from the smooth end of each tomato (reserve these slices) and use a spoon to scoop out all of the insides, leaving a wall about ¼ inch thick. Sprinkle the inside of the tomatoes with salt and pepper. Discard the woody core and seeds; reserve the tomato pulp.

2 Place 2 tablespoons of the olive oil in a large skillet and turn the heat to medium-high. Add the scallions and shallots, with a large pinch of salt, and cook, stirring, for about 3 minutes, until they are wilted and translucent. Add the greens and cook, stirring, until they wilt, just a minute or two. Remove from the skillet and cool briefly.

3 Combine the greens with the tomato pulp and salt and pepper to taste. Fill the tomatoes about halfway, then spoon one-quarter of the goat cheese into each tomato. Finish stuffing the tomatoes with the remaining greens mixture and replace the top slices.

4 Spread 1 tablespoon of the olive oil in a shallow roasting pan that will allow for a little room between the tomatoes, then place them in the pan and drizzle with the remaining 1 tablespoon olive oil. Sprinkle with salt and pepper and place the roasting pan in the oven.

Simple to Spectacular

5　Roast for 30 to 40 minutes, until the tomatoes are shriveled and the stuffing is hot (pierce the stuffing to its center with a skewer and touch the skewer to your wrist or lip).

6　Transfer the tomatoes to a platter and place the roasting pan over high heat. Add the vinegar and cook, stirring, for just about 15 seconds. Drizzle the juices over the tomatoes and serve.

MAKES 4 SERVINGS   TIME: 1 HOUR

Sweet ginger roast **tomatoes**

4 firm but ripe tomatoes (about 6 ounces each)

2 tablespoons sugar

¼ cup dried currants, chopped

2 tablespoons minced orange zest

¼ cup unsalted pistachios, chopped

6 tablespoons brown sugar

6 tablespoons butter, softened

1 tablespoon candied ginger, minced

¼ cup almond powder, more or less (see page 407)

1 tablespoon peeled and minced ginger

2 tablespoons fresh lemon juice

Served hot, with vanilla ice cream, this is a most unusual, elegant, and instantly likable dessert. After all, the tomato is a fruit. The two kinds of ginger give it zing, but the combination of plenty of butter and brown sugar creates a butterscotch flavor that makes the dish familiar and homey.

1 Preheat the oven to 450°F. Cut a ¼-inch slice from the smooth end of each tomato (reserve these slices) and use a spoon to scoop out all of the insides, leaving a wall about ¼ inch thick. Sprinkle the tomatoes inside and out with the white sugar. Discard the woody core and seeds and reserve the tomato pulp.

2 Mix together the tomato pulp, currants, all but 1 teaspoon of the orange zest, the pistachios, 4 tablespoons of the brown sugar, 2 tablespoons of the butter, and the candied ginger. Add enough almond powder to make a mixture that you can handle easily.

3 Stuff each tomato with a little less than one-quarter of the mixture (you want about 2 tablespoons of the stuffing left over) and replace the top slices. Spread 2 tablespoons of the butter in a shallow roasting pan that will allow for a little room between the tomatoes, then place the tomatoes in the pan. Dot them with half of the remaining butter and sprinkle with the remaining stuffing.

4 Place the tomatoes in the oven and roast for 30 to 40 minutes, until they are shriveled and the stuffing is hot (pierce the stuffing to its center with a skewer and touch the skewer to your wrist or lip).

Simple to Spectacular

5 Transfer the tomatoes to a platter and pour the pan juices into a small saucepan; place the pan over a burner set to medium-high. Add the remaining 1 tablespoon butter, 1 teaspoon zest, and 2 tablespoons brown sugar, along with the minced ginger, and cook until the butter melts. Add the lemon juice and cook, stirring, until the sauce bubbles and turns light brown. Spoon this over the tomatoes and serve.

MAKES 4 SERVINGS   TIME: 1 HOUR

Roast tomatoes stuffed with lamb

4 firm but ripe tomatoes (about 6 ounces each)

Salt and freshly ground black pepper

¼ teaspoon red pepper flakes, or to taste

1 cinnamon stick, broken into pieces

10 coriander seeds

1 teaspoon fennel seeds

½ teaspoon cardamom seeds

¾ pound ground lamb (see headnote)

½ cup roughly chopped cilantro

3 tablespoons extra-virgin olive oil

1 large or 2 medium lemons, cut into wedges

¼ cup Jus Rôti (page 4) or good red wine

Lamb makes these stuffed tomatoes—which are best served right from the oven—far more hearty than the others here, so much so that it makes perfect sense to serve them as a main course, with a salad or an accompanying vegetable. With their quickly made, slightly sweet spice mix, they are deliciously intense, quite unusual, and a crowd pleaser.

If you grind your own lamb, you can use whatever cut you like. Leg or rack will be leanest and most tender; cook it to only about 135°F, which is about medium. Neck or shoulder will be fattier but more flavorful; cook it to about 145°F, which is nearly well done. If you buy preground lamb, assume that it is neck or shoulder, but if it looks very lean, cook it only to the lower temperature.

1 Preheat the oven to 450°F. Cut a ¼-inch slice from the smooth end of each tomato (reserve these slices) and use a spoon to scoop out all of the insides, leaving a wall about ¼ inch thick. Sprinkle the inside of the tomatoes with salt and pepper. Discard the woody core and seeds; reserve the tomato pulp.

2 Combine the red pepper flakes, cinnamon, coriander, fennel, and cardamom in a dry skillet. Toast over medium-high heat, shaking the pan occasionally, until the spices become ultra-fragrant, 2 to 3 minutes. Remove from the heat and grind to a coarse powder in a spice grinder or coffee mill or a mortar and pestle.

3 Mix the lamb with all but ½ teaspoon of the spice mixture, the tomato pulp, half the cilantro, salt and pepper to taste, and 1 tablespoon of the olive oil.

4 Stuff each tomato with one-quarter of the lamb mixture and replace the top slices. Spread 1 tablespoon of the olive oil in a shallow roasting pan that will allow for a little room between the tomatoes, then place them in the pan and drizzle with the remaining 1 tablespoon olive oil. Sprinkle with salt and pepper and the remaining spice mixture. Scatter the lemon wedges around the tomatoes and place the roasting pan in the oven.

5 Roast for 30 to 40 minutes, until the tomatoes are shriveled and the stuffing measures 135° to 145°F when tested with an instant-read thermometer (see headnote).

6 Transfer the tomatoes to a warm platter. If the lamb has thrown off a great deal of fat, drain the pan juices—trying to remove only the fat—so that only 2 tablespoons remain. Put the roasting pan on a burner over medium-high heat. Scoop the lemon flesh from the peel; add the flesh to the pan juices and discard the peel. Add the jus rôti or red wine and cook, stirring, for about 2 minutes, or until reduced by half. Drizzle the juices over the tomatoes, garnish with the remaining cilantro, and serve hot.

MAKES 4 SERVINGS   TIME: 1¼ HOURS

Roast tomatoes with tomato confit and basil oil

4 firm but ripe tomatoes (about 6 ounces each)

Salt and freshly ground black pepper

20 tomato halves, either from Tomato Confit (page 143; include their garlic) or marinated sun-dried tomatoes

1 clove garlic, peeled and minced (if using sun-dried tomatoes)

1½ cups loosely packed basil leaves

⅓ cup extra-virgin olive oil

If you have the time to make Tomato Confit for this recipe, you really should, because its soft, sweet garlic adds another dimension to the finished dish. But if you do not, sun-dried tomatoes marinated in olive oil make a fine substitute.

If using dried tomatoes (not oil-packed), soak them in very hot water to cover until tender (you may need to change the water once or twice, depending on their age). Drain well, then marinate in olive oil to cover for as little as an hour or as long as a day.

1 Preheat the oven to 450°F. Cut a ¼-inch slice from the smooth end of each tomato (reserve these slices) and use a spoon to scoop out all of the insides, leaving a wall about ¼ inch thick. Sprinkle the inside of the tomatoes with salt and pepper. Discard the woody core and seeds; reserve the tomato pulp.

2 Chop the tomato confit and its garlic or the sun-dried tomatoes. Select 8 nice basil leaves and set them aside. Roughly chop about ½ cup of the basil. Combine the chopped basil, tomato pulp, confit or sun-dried tomatoes, garlic, salt and pepper to taste, and 2 tablespoons of the olive oil.

3 Stuff each tomato with one-quarter of the mixture and replace the top slices. Spread half the remaining olive oil in a shallow roasting pan that will allow for a little room between the tomatoes, then place them in the pan. Sprinkle with salt and pepper and place the roasting pan in the oven.

Simple to Spectacular

4   Roast for 30 to 40 minutes, until the tomatoes are shriveled and the stuffing is hot (pierce the stuffing to its center with a skewer and touch the skewer to your wrist or lip).

5   While the tomatoes are roasting, drop the remaining basil leaves (reserving the 8 you selected before) into boiling water for 10 seconds, then remove and immediately rinse in cold water. Place them, still wet, in a blender, then turn on the blender and drizzle in the remaining olive oil.

6   Serve the tomatoes hot, warm, or at room temperature, drizzled with the basil oil, and the basil leaves scattered around.

MAKES 4 SERVINGS   TIME: 1 HOUR

POTATOES play an important role in both restaurant and home cooking in all of their forms—which are many, potatoes being among the most versatile of foods. Here we go from simple, more-or-less standard mashed potatoes to those laced with truffles. In between are mashed potatoes with cheese, with crisp shallots and sharp mustard, and, perhaps most surprising, with lightly cooked cucumber.

For these recipes (and any mashed potatoes recipes), you want starchy potatoes, often labeled Idaho or russet, or good all-purpose potatoes, sometimes called Eastern. The relatively new Yukon Gold potatoes are a starchy all-purpose type that produce beautiful mashed potatoes; we used those in testing and developing these recipes. What you do not want to use are so-called "new" potatoes, which are low-starch and waxy.

KEYS TO SUCCESS

For speed, peel the potatoes and cut them into chunks before cooking. But don't make the chunks too small—certainly not less than 1-inch cubes, and preferably larger—or the potatoes will become waterlogged as they cook.

One pound makes 4 adequate side-dish portions; but these recipes are easily doubled if you want more.

For super-smooth potatoes, use a ricer or a food mill. A potato masher or a fork will give you chunky mashed potatoes. Your choice.

Mashed potatoes can be made as long as half an hour in advance, then held over very low heat, or kept at room temperature and microwaved for brief intervals, stirring in between each, until hot. But what makes the most sense is to boil whole potatoes in advance, keep them in cold water, then reheat them and finish the recipe at the last minute.

Simple **mashed potatoes**

1 pound Yukon Gold or other all-purpose potatoes, peeled and cut into large chunks

Salt and freshly ground black pepper

½ cup milk

4 tablespoons butter

Yes, you can use less butter if you like, and certainly using skim milk won't make much of a difference, but these are rich and delicious this way.

1 Put the potatoes in salted water to cover and bring to a boil; adjust the heat so that the water bubbles, but not too rapidly, and cook until the potatoes are tender but not mushy, about 20 minutes. Meanwhile, warm the milk gently.

2 When the potatoes are done, drain them, mash them or put them through a ricer, and return them to the pot over the lowest possible heat. Add the milk and stir, then add the butter and stir until it melts. Season to taste and serve immediately.

MAKES 4 SERVINGS   TIME: 30 TO 40 MINUTES

Mashed potatoes aligoté

1 pound Yukon Gold or other all-purpose potatoes, peeled
and cut into large chunks

Salt and freshly ground black pepper

½ cup milk

4 tablespoons butter

4 ounces Tomme, Raclette, Gruyère, or similar cheese, cut
into ½-inch pieces

Minced chives for garnish

You could easily serve this as a main course for two; it not only is
substantial but has more flavor than almost anything you could serve with
it. As part of a meal for four, choose something simple, rustic, and flavorful
to accompany these—like a steak or some roast chicken with herbs.

1 Put the potatoes in salted water to cover and bring to a boil; adjust the heat so
that the water bubbles, but not too rapidly, and cook until the potatoes are tender but not mushy, about 20 minutes. Meanwhile, warm the milk gently.

2 When the potatoes are done, drain them, mash them or put them through a
ricer, and return them to the pot over the lowest possible heat. Add the milk and
stir, then add the butter and stir until it melts. Beat with a wooden spoon or rubber spatula.

3 Remove from the heat, add the cheese, and stir until it melts (if the cheese is
not especially ripe, you might have to do this over the lowest possible heat). Season to taste, then garnish with chives and serve.

MAKES 4 SERVINGS   TIME: 30 TO 40 MINUTES

Mashed potatoes with cucumber and sour cream

1 pound Yukon Gold or other all-purpose potatoes, peeled
and cut into large chunks

Salt and freshly ground black pepper

1 pound cucumbers (1 large English cucumber or 2 or
3 smaller cucumbers)

4 tablespoons butter

¾ cup sour cream

3 tablespoons chopped dill

This is a bigger dish, with more volume than the others; it could be stretched to serve six. Be generous with the salt—the cucumbers need it. These would make a wonderful bed for the Slow-Cooked Salmon with Parsley and Capers (page 177).

1 Put the potatoes in salted water to cover and bring to a boil; adjust the heat so that the water bubbles, but not too rapidly, and cook until the potatoes are tender but not mushy, about 20 minutes.

2 Meanwhile, peel the cucumbers, then cut them in half the long way; scoop the seeds out with a spoon and discard them. Chop the cucumbers into ½-inch cubes. Blanch them in boiling salted water for 3 to 4 minutes, until they begin to become tender but retain some crunch. Drain and plunge into ice water to stop the cooking.

3 When the potatoes are done, drain them, mash them or put them through a ricer, and return them to the pot over the lowest possible heat. Stir, then add the butter and stir until it melts. Stir in the sour cream and beat for a minute or so with a wooden spoon, then add the cucumbers and warm for just 15 seconds or so; you want to remove the chill, not really heat them up. Season to taste, garnish with the dill, and serve.

MAKES 4 SERVINGS   TIME: 30 TO 40 MINUTES

Mashed potatoes with mustard and crunchy shallots

4 ounces shallots, peeled

Neutral oil, such as canola or grapeseed, as needed

1 pound Yukon Gold or other all-purpose potatoes, peeled
and cut into large chunks

Salt and freshly ground black pepper

½ cup milk

4 tablespoons butter

¼ cup dry vermouth

2 tablespoons Dijon mustard

This is a real bistro-style dish, with crunch and sharp flavors offsetting the potatoes' smooth blandness. It would be great with grilled liver or other rich meats.

You can save time by boiling the potatoes while you cook the shallots.

1 Slice the shallots as thin as possible (a mandoline is ideal for this). Add about ⅛ inch of oil to a large skillet and turn the heat to medium-high. About 2 minutes later, add the shallots and cook, stirring frequently, until they brown, about 5 minutes. Be careful: Once they begin to brown, they will do so quickly, and might burn if you're not attentive. Remove with a slotted spoon and drain on paper towels; sprinkle them with salt. *(You can do this several hours in advance.)*

2 Meanwhile, put the potatoes in salted water to cover and bring to a boil; adjust the heat so that the water bubbles, but not too rapidly, and cook until the potatoes are tender but not mushy, about 20 minutes. While the potatoes cook, warm the milk gently.

3 When the potatoes are done, drain them, mash them or put them through a ricer, and return them to the pot over the lowest possible heat. Add the milk and stir, then add the butter, vermouth, and mustard and stir until the butter melts. Season to taste, top with the shallots, and serve immediately.

MAKES 4 SERVINGS   TIME: 40 MINUTES

Simple to Spectacular

Mashed potatoes with truffle sauce

1 pound Yukon Gold or other all-purpose potatoes, peeled and cut into large chunks

Salt and freshly ground black pepper

½ cup milk

5 tablespoons butter

1½ ounces black truffle, finely chopped

½ cup Jus Rôti (page 4)

This is no less than the ultimate expression of mashed potatoes with gravy. You have to try it to believe it. Expensive, yes, but barely more difficult than the first recipe in this series—once you have the truffles and Jus Rôti.

1 Put the potatoes in salted water to cover and bring to a boil; adjust the heat so that the water bubbles, but not too rapidly, and cook until the potatoes are tender but not mushy, about 20 minutes. Meanwhile, warm the milk gently.

2 While the potatoes are cooking, put 1 tablespoon of the butter in a small saucepan and turn the heat to medium. Add one-third of the truffle and cook until the butter bubbles for a minute. Add the jus rôti and cook, stirring occasionally, until reduced by about half. Keep warm while you finish the potatoes.

3 When the potatoes are done, drain them, mash them or put them through a ricer, and return them to the pot over the lowest possible heat. Add the milk and stir, then add the remaining 4 tablespoons butter and truffle and stir until the butter melts. Season to taste and serve, topped with the truffle sauce.

MAKES 4 SERVINGS   TIME: 30 TO 40 MINUTES

Oven-roasted vegetables

TOSSING a variety of vegetables and some olive oil in a pan and cranking up the heat is one good way to roast them, but here we explore the wonderful possibilities of roasting vegetables individually. Sometimes this means much less work, and a much simpler dish—as in Oven-roasted Zucchini, which takes about 5 minutes of preparation time and 15 minutes of roasting. At the other end of the spectrum is a big production, but one in which each vegetable retains its unique flavor. We also offer simply roasted beets with creamy goat cheese, an assemblage of roasted vegetables from the onion family, and probably the best roasted bell peppers you've ever tasted.

KEYS TO SUCCESS

Home ovens are almost never set hot enough for roasting. For many of these recipes, it's best to start at 450° or 500°F, then turn the temperature down to 400° or 450°F as the sizzle gets going. You want some browning to take place, and tame temperatures will not accomplish that.

Don't skimp on the olive oil, and use the best you can find.

Be attentive. Roasting is a slow process to get started, but once the vegetables' interior moisture has been cooked out, browning can take place rapidly.

Oven-roasted zucchini

1 pound zucchini

3 tablespoons extra-virgin olive oil

2 teaspoons minced garlic

1 teaspoon thyme leaves

Salt and freshly ground black pepper

Large chunks of zucchini turn buttery when roasted; these thin slices have some of that quality but also gain a measure of crispness. With the garlic, oil, and thyme, this is a sensational technique to use for a too-often bland vegetable. The zucchini is also great at room temperature.

1 Preheat the oven to 500°F. Wash and trim the zucchini and cut them the long way into slices ¼ inch thick (a mandoline is a good tool for this, but you can easily do it by hand).

2 Spread half the olive oil in the bottom of a baking pan. Spread the zucchini in the pan; they can overlap slightly if necessary, but keep it to one layer. Drizzle with the remaining oil and sprinkle with the garlic, thyme, and salt and pepper.

3 Roast for about 15 minutes, turning the oven heat to 450°F as soon as the oil starts sizzling. The zucchini is done when it is tender and just beginning to brown. Serve hot or at room temperature.

MAKES 4 SERVINGS   TIME: 30 MINUTES

Oven-roasted peppers with capers and anchovies

2 bell peppers, preferably 1 yellow and 1 red

¼ cup extra-virgin olive oil

8 cherry tomatoes (or, even better, 16 "grape" tomatoes)

4 anchovy fillets, cut in half both the long and short ways

1 large clove garlic, peeled and cut into thin slivers

12 fresh marjoram or oregano leaves, or 1 teaspoon dried marjoram, oregano, or thyme

24 capers

Salt and freshly ground black pepper

A staple at Jean-Georges' Mercer Kitchen restaurant in Soho, these are a notable step up from the usual roast peppers. We're tempted to say that this recipe actually serves two, rather than four, so you might consider doubling it.

1 Preheat the oven to 350°F. Cut the peppers in half the long way; remove the core and seeds. Spread half the olive oil in the bottom of a baking pan. Put the peppers cut side up in the pan.

2 Place one-quarter of the tomatoes, anchovies, garlic, herb, and capers into each pepper. Sprinkle with salt and pepper and drizzle with the remaining olive oil. Put ½ cup water in the bottom of the pan and cover with foil.

3 Bake for about 20 minutes, then uncover, lower the oven heat to 300°F, and cook for another 40 minutes, or until the peppers are tender (add a little more water if the bottom of the pan dries out). Serve hot or at room temperature, drizzled with a little of the pan juices.

MAKES 4 SERVINGS   TIME: ABOUT 1 HOUR, LARGELY UNATTENDED

Simple to Spectacular

Oven-roasted beets with goat cheese

1½ pounds beets

1 cup soft fresh goat cheese

Salt and freshly ground black pepper

¼ cup extra-virgin olive oil

2 tablespoons sherry vinegar

½ cup chopped beet greens

Baking beets is by far the best way to cook them—they don't become waterlogged, they're less messy to prepare, and their sweetness is intensified rather than leached out. Once you try it, you'll never go back to boiling. For the beet greens, you can substitute almost any herb, like parsley, chervil, or basil.

1 Preheat the oven to 350°F. Wash the beets. Leaving them wet, wrap them individually in foil. Place them in a roasting pan or on a baking sheet and bake for about 1½ hours, or until they're nice and tender (poke a thin-bladed knife right through the foil to test). Let cool in the foil.

2 Peel the beets and cut them into big chunks; arrange on a platter. Break up the goat cheese and scatter it on top of the beets. Sprinkle with salt and pepper, then drizzle with the olive oil and vinegar. Garnish with the beet greens and serve.

MAKES 4 SERVINGS   TIME: ABOUT 2½ HOURS, LARGELY UNATTENDED

Simple to Spectacular

Roasted alliums with chive oil

15 scallions, not too thin, trimmed

Extra-virgin olive oil as needed

Salt and freshly ground black pepper

2 large leeks, trimmed and well washed

12 spring or yellow onions, peeled and cut in half

8 large cloves garlic, cut in half (don't peel)

8 shallots, peeled

40 to 60 chives (a small handful)

2 tablespoons neutral oil, such as canola or grapeseed

Alliums being members of the onion family, the more the better. The best way to do this is to prepare and roast the various types separately, putting each in the oven as you ready it. Since they each have different, yet subtle, flavors, the effort is worth it. In fact, the results are amazing.

1 Preheat the oven to 450°F. Place the scallions on a baking sheet and drizzle with a little olive oil; sprinkle with salt and pepper and roast until tender, about 12 minutes.

2 Cut the leeks into 1-inch diagonal pieces; make sure you've removed all traces of sand and rinse again if necessary. Place them on a baking sheet and drizzle with a little olive oil; sprinkle with salt and pepper and roast until tender, about 15 minutes.

3 Place the onions, garlic, and shallots on a baking sheet, cut sides down, and drizzle with a little olive oil; sprinkle with salt and pepper and roast until tender, 15 to 18 minutes.

4 Meanwhile, tear the chives into pieces and put in the container of a blender with the canola oil and a little salt. Blend, stopping the machine to push the mixture down once or twice, until the oil has a cream-like consistency.

5 Serve the roasted vegetables hot or at room temperature, drizzled with the chive oil.

MAKES 4 SERVINGS   TIME: 1 HOUR

Roast vegetables with red pepper oil

4 small to medium beets

2 red bell peppers

Extra-virgin olive oil as needed

4 ounces shiitake mushrooms, stems removed and discarded

8 small carrots, peeled, or 2 medium carrots, peeled and cut into quarters the long way

1 ear corn, shucked and cut into quarters the long way

4 spring or small onions, peeled and cut in half

1 medium zucchini, washed, trimmed, and cut into thick diagonal slices

1 large tomato, peeled, cut into 16 wedges, and seeds and juice removed

Salt and freshly ground black pepper

8 ounces green beans, preferably haricots verts, trimmed

1 teaspoon sherry vinegar

Minced parsley or chervil for garnish

You can make the slightly hot red pepper oil with yellow or orange peppers as well; it will be a little bit milder and, obviously, have a different color. But don't try it with green peppers; the result will be bitter rather than sweet-hot.

1 Preheat the oven to 350°F. Wash the beets. Leaving them wet, wrap them individually in foil. Place them in a roasting pan or on a baking sheet and bake for about 1½ hours, or until they're nice and tender (poke a thin-bladed knife right through the foil to test). Let cool in the foil. Turn the oven to 450°F.

2 Core and seed the peppers and cut them into quarters. Drizzle a large roasting pan with oil and put 1 of the peppers in it, along with the shiitakes, carrots, corn, onions, zucchini, tomato, and beets (use two pans if you must; it's imperative that you roast these in one layer). Drizzle liberally with olive oil, sprinkle with salt and pepper, and put in the oven. Put the green beans in a small baking pan, drizzle with oil, sprinkle with salt and pepper, and add a few tablespoons of water. Put in the oven.

3 Meanwhile, put the remaining pepper through a juicer (or puree it in a blender, wrap the puree in a towel, and wring the juice out). Put the juice in a small

saucepan and boil over medium heat, stirring occasionally, until syrupy and reduced to about 2 tablespoons. Stir in 2 tablespoons olive oil and the sherry vinegar.

4 As the vegetables finish cooking, transfer them to a platter. They will probably finish in this order: mushrooms, beans, tomatoes, zucchini, beets, pepper, onions, corn (let it brown), and carrots. Arrange nicely and drizzle with the pepper oil. Garnish with the herb and serve hot or at room temperature.

MAKES 4 MAIN-COURSE OR 8 TO 12 SIDE-DISH SERVINGS
TIME: ABOUT 2 1/2 HOURS, LARGELY UNATTENDED

Sautéed vegetables in broth

THESE are among the most useful recipes in this book, because they can serve as side dishes, main courses (some are vegetarian, some not), or, with a little added liquid, as soups. Yet they are easy and fast, and contain no stock. Or, more accurately, they create their own stock, from the vegetables, from meat, or from seafood, beans, and herbs.

To a large extent, these are peasant, from-the-garden dishes, and more about shopping and chopping than about cooking. We begin with a variety of vegetables, simply cooked with olive oil and water, and go on to add meat, beans, herbs, and a seafood—the vegetables being the building block for everything else.

KEYS TO SUCCESS

Please, please feel free to substitute here. No single vegetable makes any of these dishes, and all of them are replaceable—leeks by onions, carrots by parsnips or turnips, beans by peas, turnips by carrots or parsnips, white potatoes by sweet potatoes, and so on. These ingredient lists should be seen as suggestions, not ironclad orders.

Since there is no stock in any of these recipes, it's even more important than usual that you use the best vegetables, oil, and even water possible. And try to use fresh herbs, because they will make a huge difference.

Cook by color and texture rather than by time. Vegetables cooked this way are done when they are bright and tender, and overcooking will muddy the flavor and color and degrade the texture.

Unless you want to make soup, keep the liquid here to the amounts we recommend. The vegetables should be brothy—and the juices are delicious—but not swimming in liquid.

Sautéed vegetables in their own broth

¼ cup extra-virgin olive oil, plus more for drizzling

2 leeks (white part only), well washed and roughly chopped

4 medium carrots, peeled and roughly chopped into ¼-inch dice

4 medium potatoes, peeled and roughly chopped into ¼-inch dice

1 branch thyme

Salt and freshly ground black pepper

8 ounces green beans, preferably haricots verts, trimmed and cut into 1-inch pieces

These are just as good topped with freshly grated Parmesan as with olive oil; and they're also great sprinkled with bread crumbs that have been briefly crisped in a skillet with a little butter or oil.

1 Put the olive oil in a large skillet and turn the heat to medium-high. A minute later, add all the vegetables except the beans, along with the thyme, and salt and pepper to taste. Turn the heat to high and cook, stirring occasionally, for about 3 minutes.

2 Add 2 cups water and stir. Bring to a boil and adjust the heat so that the mixture simmers, but not too rapidly. Cook, stirring occasionally, for about 10 minutes; add the green beans. Cook for another 5 minutes, or until the vegetables are tender but not mushy. Drizzle with olive oil and serve.

MAKES 4 SERVINGS   TIME: 30 MINUTES

Sautéed vegetables with ham

¼ cup extra-virgin olive oil

2 medium carrots, peeled and roughly chopped into ¼-inch dice

2 leeks (white part only), well washed and roughly chopped

2 medium potatoes, peeled and roughly chopped into ¼-inch dice

2 parsnips, peeled and roughly chopped into ¼-inch dice

2 turnips, peeled and roughly chopped into ¼-inch dice

4 ounces cremini or stemmed shiitake mushrooms, trimmed and sliced

2 small zucchini, washed, trimmed, and roughly chopped

1 branch thyme

Salt and freshly ground black pepper

6 ounces prosciutto or other dry-cured ham, with some of its fat, in 1 or 2 chunks

8 ounces green beans, preferably haricots verts, trimmed and cut into 1-inch pieces

¼ cup fresh peas (optional)

½ cup freshly grated Parmesan

An enhanced version of the previous recipe, in which we increase the number of vegetables. More important, we include a big piece of ham, which adds body and flavor. To turn this into a soup, increase the amount of water by 2 to 3 cups.

There is a lot of chopping here, so allow some time for it; the cooking takes just 20 minutes or so.

1 Put the olive oil in a large skillet and turn the heat to medium-high. A minute later, add all the vegetables except the beans and peas, along with the thyme, salt and pepper to taste, and the ham. Turn the heat to high and cook, stirring occasionally, for about 3 minutes.

2 Add 3 cups water and stir. Bring to a boil and adjust the heat so that the mixture simmers, but not too rapidly. Cook, stirring occasionally, for about 10 minutes. Add the beans, and peas if using, and cook for another 5 minutes, or until the vegetables are tender but not mushy; check and adjust seasoning.

3 Remove the ham and chop it up; return it to the broth. Sprinkle with the Parmesan and serve.

MAKES 4 SERVINGS   TIME: LESS THAN AN HOUR

Sautéed vegetables with beans and pistou

3 tablespoons pignoli nuts

2 large bunches basil, leaves only (about 2 firmly packed cups)

½ cup extra-virgin olive oil

2 cloves garlic, peeled

Salt and freshly ground black pepper

2 medium carrots, peeled and roughly chopped into ¼-inch dice

2 leeks (white part only), well washed and roughly chopped into ¼-inch dice

2 medium potatoes, peeled and roughly chopped into ¼-inch dice

2 parsnips, peeled and roughly chopped into ¼-inch dice

2 turnips, peeled and roughly chopped into ¼-inch dice

4 ounces cremini or stemmed shiitake mushrooms, trimmed and sliced

2 small zucchini, washed, trimmed, and roughly chopped into ¼-inch dice

6 ounces prosciutto or other dry-cured ham, with some of its fat, in 1 or 2 chunks

1 cup cooked white beans (rinse if canned)

½ cup freshly grated Parmesan

Pistou being the Provençal word for pesto, a traditional basil paste that works its magic when stirred into these cooked vegetables. The beans make this a substantial dish, one that should certainly be considered a main course.

1 Put the pignolis in a small skillet and turn the heat to medium. Toast, shaking the pan occasionally, until the nuts are fragrant and nearly brown, 2 to 3 minutes. Combine the nuts, basil, ¼ cup of the oil, the garlic, and salt and pepper to taste in a blender; whiz until blended, then taste and adjust the seasoning. Set aside.

2 Put the remaining ¼ cup olive oil in a large skillet and turn the heat to medium-high. A minute later, add all the vegetables except the beans, along with salt and pepper to taste and the ham. Turn the heat to high and cook, stirring occasionally, for about 3 minutes.

3 Add 3 cups water and stir. Bring to a boil and adjust the heat so that the mixture simmers, but not too rapidly. Cook, stirring occasionally, for about 10 minutes. Add the beans and cook for another 5 minutes, or until the vegetables are tender but not mushy. Remove the ham and chop it up; return it to the broth and stir in the basil pistou. Sprinkle with the Parmesan and serve.

MAKES 4 SERVINGS   TIME: 40 MINUTES

Sautéed vegetables with beans, clams, and herbs

¼ cup extra-virgin olive oil

2 medium carrots, peeled and roughly chopped into ¼-inch dice

2 leeks (white part only), well washed and roughly chopped into ¼-inch dice

2 medium potatoes, peeled and roughly chopped into ¼-inch dice

2 parsnips, peeled and roughly chopped into ¼-inch dice

2 turnips, peeled and roughly chopped into ¼-inch dice

4 ounces cremini or stemmed shiitake mushrooms, trimmed and sliced

2 small zucchini, washed, trimmed, and roughly chopped into ¼-inch dice

Salt and freshly ground black pepper

1 cup cooked white beans (rinse if canned)

About 2 pounds tiny clams (cockles are best), scrubbed

About 2 pounds mussels, the smaller the better, scrubbed and debearded

2 large tomatoes, peeled, seeded, and roughly chopped

1 teaspoon minced garlic

¼ cup chopped chervil

10 leaves tarragon

¼ cup chopped parsley

This is a feast. Shellfish give off their own special juices, so you need less water and wind up with more intense flavors. Make sure the clams and mussels are well washed; scrub their shells with a brush. Again, there is a lot of chopping here, so allow some time for it; but, again, the cooking itself is fast and easy.

1 Put the olive oil in a large skillet and turn the heat to medium-high. A minute later, add all the vegetables except the beans and tomatoes, along with salt and pepper to taste. Turn the heat to high and cook, stirring occasionally, for about 3 minutes.

2 Add 2 cups water and stir. Bring to a boil and adjust the heat so that the mixture simmers, but not too rapidly. Cook, stirring occasionally, for about 10 minutes. Add the beans, clams, mussels, and tomatoes and cover the pan. Cook for another 5 to 10 minutes, or until the clams and mussels are open.

3 Add the garlic and cook for another minute, then add the herbs and serve.

MAKES 4 SERVINGS   TIME: ABOUT 1 HOUR

Sautéed vegetables with orzo, monkfish, and red pepper relish

2 red bell peppers

1 to 2 small chiles, stemmed

½ cup extra-virgin olive oil

1 clove garlic, peeled

Salt and freshly ground black pepper

½ cup orzo or couscous

1 teaspoon turmeric

2 medium carrots, peeled and finely but roughly chopped into ¼-inch dice

2 leeks (white part only), well washed and roughly chopped

2 medium potatoes, peeled and finely but roughly chopped into ¼-inch dice

2 parsnips, peeled and finely but roughly chopped into ¼-inch dice

2 turnips, peeled and finely but roughly chopped into ¼-inch dice

4 ounces cremini or stemmed shiitake mushrooms, trimmed and sliced

2 small zucchini, washed, trimmed, and roughly chopped

1½ to 2 pounds monkfish, preferably bone-in (use the lesser amount if the monkfish has been filleted)

Thanks to the addition of toasted, cooked orzo, this is more of a stew—thick, rich, and very nice. For the monkfish, you can substitute swordfish or mako shark, cut into strips, or red snapper, catfish, or striped bass fillets.

1 Prepare a fire in a grill or preheat the broiler. Toss the bell peppers and chiles in a skillet or baking pan with 1 tablespoon of the olive oil. Roast them on the grill or under the broiler, turning frequently, until the skins char and begin to fall off, 10 to 15 minutes. Cover them with foil or paper until they cool.

2 Peel, stem, and seed all the peppers. Put them in a food processor with 3 more tablespoons of the oil, the garlic clove, and salt and pepper to taste; process until smooth. Taste and adjust the seasoning, and set aside.

3 Put the orzo or couscous in a dry saucepan and turn the heat to medium. Toast, shaking the pan occasionally, until the orzo begins to brown, about 5 minutes. Add the turmeric and 1 tablespoon of the olive oil; cook for about 30 seconds, then add 1 cup water. Turn the heat to low, cover, and cook until the water is absorbed, about 15 minutes. Remove from the heat.

4 Put the remaining 3 tablespoons olive oil in a large skillet and turn the heat to medium-high. A minute later, add all the vegetables, along with salt and pepper to taste. Turn the heat to high and cook, stirring occasionally, for about 3 minutes.

5 Add 4 cups water and stir. Bring to a boil and adjust the heat so that the mixture simmers, but not too rapidly. Cook, stirring occasionally, for about 5 minutes. Add the monkfish and cover the pan. Cook for another 10 minutes, or until the vegetables are tender and the monkfish cooked through.

6 Add the cooked orzo and stir for about a minute. Stir in a good tablespoon of the pepper puree and serve, passing the remaining pepper puree at the table.

MAKES 4 SERVINGS   TIME: ABOUT 1¼ HOURS

MAKE these and you'll never buy sun-dried tomatoes again. They are slow-cooked tomatoes, with garlic, thyme, and olive oil, and the long but simple process turns tomatoes into candy. At that point you can serve them by themselves, use them as a garnish for many dishes (especially those with white fish, for which they have both flavor and visual affinities), or include them in salads, as we do here.

We begin with straightforward tomato confit, then go to a quick and easy combination of confit with summer squashes and lots of lemon juice, then to a layered "napoleon" with crabmeat, an amazing shrimp cocktail, and, finally, a wonderful potato salad with scallops. In each, the confited tomatoes shine brightly.

KEYS TO SUCCESS

Needless to say, the riper and more flavorful the tomato, the better the confit. However, average-but-decent tomatoes become something wonderful given this treatment.

Peel the tomatoes and remove their seeds and pulp before confiting—all you want is the flesh. You can use plum tomatoes (which make 2 pieces per tomato) or larger round ones (which make 4 pieces per tomato).

Keep the oven heat low. You don't want to dry the tomatoes out entirely, and you certainly don't want them to brown. The lower the heat, the less you have to watch them.

Tomato confit

12 plum or 6 large tomatoes, ripe but not too soft

⅓ cup extra-virgin olive oil

6 cloves garlic, peeled and lightly crushed

6 sprigs thyme

1 teaspoon coarse salt

Sweet and garlicky. Double the recipe if your oven is big enough; there's no question you will find uses for these.

1 Preheat the oven to 275°F. Cut out the hard core of each of the tomatoes and make an X in the smooth flower end. Plunge into boiling water for about 15 seconds, or until the skins loosen, then plunge into ice water; drain. Peel; cut plum tomatoes in half, regular tomatoes into quarters, then remove all the seeds and pulp.

2 Cover a baking sheet with aluminum foil and brush with the olive oil. Place the tomatoes cut side down on the pan. Scatter the garlic and thyme around and sprinkle with the salt.

3 Bake for 2 hours or more, turning the tomatoes every 30 minutes or so to make sure that they are not browning (if they are, lower the heat) and turning the baking sheet so the tomatoes cook evenly. The tomatoes are done when they are very soft and shriveled. They will keep, refrigerated, for a few days.

MAKES 4 TO 6 SERVINGS   TIME: SEVERAL HOURS, LARGELY UNATTENDED

Tomato confit with arugula and zucchini

6 cups arugula, trimmed, washed, and dried

1 zucchini (4 to 6 ounces), washed and trimmed

1 summer squash (4 to 6 ounces), washed and trimmed

¼ cup extra-virgin olive oil

¼ cup fresh lemon juice

12 paper-thin slices Parmesan

12 pieces Tomato Confit (page 143)

Salt and freshly ground black pepper

A lovely midsummer salad, smacking of strong, fresh flavors.

1 Make a bed of arugula on each of four plates. Slice the squashes into long thin ribbons (a mandoline is ideal for this). Toss them with the olive oil and lemon juice, then lay the strips on the arugula; pour any remaining dressing over them.

2 Garnish with the Parmesan and tomato confit; drizzle with a little of the confit's oil if you have it. Sprinkle with salt and pepper and serve.

MAKES 4 SERVINGS   TIME: 20 MINUTES

Simple to Spectacular

Tomato confit and crab napoleon

1 pound crabmeat, picked over for shells and cartilage

1¼ cups sour cream

Juice of 2 lemons

¼ cup minced cilantro

Salt and cayenne pepper

24 pieces Tomato Confit (page 143)

½ cup minced chives

Tabasco sauce to taste

1 teaspoon good balsamic vinegar (optional)

Little cakes with alternating layers of tomato confit (that's the "crust") and crab salad. An impressive and tasty summer dish.

1 Mix together the crabmeat, ¼ cup of the sour cream, the lemon juice, cilantro, and salt and cayenne to taste. Taste and adjust the seasoning if necessary.

2 On a flat work surface such as a cutting board, make a layer of 2 pieces of tomato slightly overlapping; top with a spoonful of the crab mixture, then another layer of tomatoes, another of crab, and another of tomatoes. That's 1 napoleon; repeat to make 3 more.

3 Combine the remaining 1 cup sour cream with the chives, Tabasco, and salt to taste. Make a small pool of the sauce on each plate and top with a napoleon. Drizzle with a little balsamic vinegar if desired and serve.

MAKES 4 SERVINGS   TIME: 30 MINUTES

Shrimp cocktail with tomato confit and fresh tomatoes

8 pieces Tomato Confit (page 143), plus some of the confited garlic

1 medium ripe tomato, peeled and seeded

¼ cup olive oil (that from the confit is best, but extra-virgin olive oil is fine)

Grated fresh or prepared horseradish to taste

1 small chile, stemmed and minced

Salt and freshly ground black pepper

16 to 24 large shrimp, peeled and deveined

2 teaspoons thyme leaves

Most shrimp cocktail sauce is watery and insipid; this one is anything but.

1 Combine the tomato confit, ripe tomato, 2 tablespoons of the olive oil, the horseradish, chile, and salt and pepper to taste in the container of a blender and puree. Taste and adjust the seasoning; let rest while you prepare the shrimp.

2 Preheat a grill or broiler. Toss the shrimp with the thyme, the remaining 2 tablespoons olive oil, and salt and pepper to taste. Grill or broil for about 2 minutes per side, or until done. Serve hot, warm, at room temperature, or chilled, with the cocktail sauce.

MAKES 4 SERVINGS   TIME: 20 MINUTES

Simple to Spectacular

Potato salad with **tomato confit and scallops**

1½ pounds potatoes, preferably fingerlings or other small potatoes, scrubbed

1 stalk celery

4 sprigs thyme

Salt and freshly ground black pepper

3 tablespoons extra-virgin olive oil

16 bay scallops or 8 sea scallops (cut
sea scallops horizontally in half)

¼ cup minced scallions

2 teaspoons sherry vinegar

1 truffle, or 1 porcini mushroom, or
4 button or cremini mushrooms,
trimmed if necessary

12 to 16 pieces Tomato Confit
(page 143)

This can be as simple as a fine potato salad (if you omit the scallops and truffle) or about as elegant a dish as you can find, especially if you use bay scallops (in season only in the winter months) and the truffle. The middle ground is fine also.

1 Cook the potatoes, along with the celery and thyme, in boiling salted water to cover. When they're tender, drain, let cool a bit, and peel them; cut into thin slices.

2 Put 1 tablespoon of the olive oil in a large skillet and turn the heat to high. Sear the scallops on both sides, just a minute on each, seasoning with salt and pepper as they cook; remove the scallops. Add the remaining 2 tablespoons olive oil to the pan, add the scallions, season with salt and pepper, and cook until they are limp. Turn off the heat and stir in the sherry vinegar.

3 To make the salad, thinly slice the truffle or mushrooms. Make a layer of these on each of four plates. Top with a layer of the tomato confit, then a layer of the potatoes, and finally the scallops. Spoon the scallions and their liquid over all and serve.

MAKES 4 SERVINGS   TIME: 1 HOUR

THE LAST FEW YEARS have seen a surge in the availability of different kinds of mushrooms, both wild and farmed. White button mushrooms are still the most common, and they're actually pretty good, especially when mixed with other types. But almost everyone can get their hands on fresh creminis, oysters, porto-bellos, and the quite delicious shiitakes. Chanterelles and black trumpets are not that hard to find. Frozen porcini are increasingly available, and dried porcini (or cèpes, as they're often called)—which, when soaked in hot water for 10 minutes or so, can be treated the same as fresh—have come down in price to the point where no household should be without them.

The best treatment for mush-rooms is sautéing, and we explore that technique thoroughly here, starting with what the Italians call *funghi trifolati*, a nicely seasoned mix. Next we take the same base and turn it into a wonderful mushroom-cream sauce for as-paragus. A mushroom syrup—sautéed mushrooms used to create a thick vege-tarian stock—graces a mushroom bruschetta and a stack of mushroom crepes, and, finally, we put mushrooms to work in a spring roll.

KEYS TO SUCCESS

You can use any mushrooms in these recipes, and it need not be a mix. They'll all work just fine with plain old white mushrooms. (You can improve the flavor of white mushrooms by adding an equal or lesser amount of reconstituted dried mushrooms during cooking.)

Trim and wash mushrooms carefully before cooking, but do not soak them. The stems of most mush-rooms are edible, but those of shiitakes are too tough—save them for the stockpot.

Mushrooms throw off a lot of liquid during cooking: you can hasten this process by salting them as soon as you start cooking them. After the liquid evapo-rates, they will brown quickly, so be careful.

Sautéed mushrooms

1 tablespoon butter

1 tablespoon extra-virgin olive oil

1 pound mixed mushrooms, trimmed, washed, and chopped

2 shallots, peeled and minced

2 cloves garlic, peeled and minced

Salt and freshly ground black pepper

½ cup chopped parsley

A simple and basic mushroom preparation, a perfect side dish that, with a little more olive oil, becomes a pasta sauce.

1 Put the butter and oil in a skillet and turn the heat to medium-high. When the butter melts, add the mushrooms, shallots, garlic, and salt and pepper to taste and stir.

2 Cook, stirring occasionally, until the mushrooms have given up their liquid and begun to brown, about 10 minutes. Stir in the parsley and serve.

MAKES 4 SERVINGS   TIME: 20 MINUTES

Asparagus with mushroom-cream sauce

20 fat asparagus spears (1 to 1½ pounds)

1 tablespoon butter

1 tablespoon extra-virgin olive oil

1 pound mushrooms, trimmed, washed, and chopped

2 shallots, peeled and minced

Salt and freshly ground black pepper

1 cup heavy cream

2 tablespoons dry (fino) sherry

Chopped chives for garnish

This is a luxurious dish, but not a difficult one. Ideally, you'd use morels, but those are usually hard to come by—shiitakes will also work beautifully.

1 Bring a large pot of water to a boil. Meanwhile, break off the woody bottom sections of the asparagus and peel the spears up to the flower buds.

2 Put the butter and oil in a skillet and turn the heat to medium-high. When the butter melts, add the mushrooms, shallots, and salt and pepper to taste and stir. Cook, stirring occasionally, until the mushrooms have given up their liquid and it has begun to evaporate, about 5 minutes. Add the cream and boil, stirring occasionally, until mostly evaporated, about 10 minutes.

3 Meanwhile, salt the boiling water and blanch the asparagus for about 5 minutes, or until bright green and just about tender. Drain and keep warm.

4 When the mushroom mixture is creamy but not soupy, stir in the sherry. Cook for another minute, then spoon over the asparagus. Garnish with the chives and serve.

MAKES 4 SERVINGS   TIME: 30 MINUTES

Mushroom bruschetta with mushroom syrup

2 tablespoons butter

Extra-virgin olive oil as needed

8 ounces button mushrooms, washed and chopped

2 shallots, peeled and roughly chopped

2 cloves garlic, peeled and roughly chopped

Salt and freshly ground black pepper

4 thick slices sourdough bread or other good white bread

1 clove garlic, peeled and cut in half

1 pound mixed mushrooms, trimmed, washed, drained, and chopped

2 shallots, peeled and minced

2 cloves garlic, peeled and minced

½ cup chopped fresh herbs, such as parsley, dill, chervil, basil, and/or tarragon

Minced zest of 1 lemon

Lemon wedges for serving

The syrup is an easily made reduction of mushroom stock, and it can be used in the next recipe as well. Serve this with simply roasted or grilled meat.

1 Preheat the broiler or prepare a grill. Put half the butter and 1 tablespoon oil in a skillet and turn the heat to medium-high. When the butter melts, add the button mushrooms, shallots, chopped garlic, and salt and pepper to taste and stir. Cook, stirring occasionally, until the mushrooms give up their liquid and begin to brown, about 10 minutes. Add 2 cups water, stir, and cook for about 10 minutes, or until slightly reduced. Strain and return the liquid to the skillet; discard the mushrooms. Cook over high heat for 10 to 15 minutes more, or until quite thick and syrupy.

2 Meanwhile, brush the bread on both sides with oil and grill lightly, turning once. Rub with the cut garlic clove.

3 Put the remaining butter and another tablespoon of olive oil in a large skillet and turn the heat to medium-high. When the butter melts, add the mixed mushrooms, shallots, minced garlic, and salt and pepper to taste and stir. Cook, stirring occasionally, until the mushrooms have given up their liquid and begun to brown, about 10 minutes. Stir in the chopped herbs and lemon zest.

4 To serve, spoon the mushrooms onto the grilled bread and drizzle with the mushroom syrup. Serve with lemon wedges.

MAKES 4 SERVINGS   TIME: 40 MINUTES

Mushroom gâteau

8 tablespoons (1 stick) butter, more or less

1 cup flour

3 eggs

1 cup milk

Salt and freshly ground black pepper

3 tablespoons extra-virgin olive oil

3 pounds mixed mushrooms, trimmed, washed, and chopped

3 shallots, peeled and minced

3 cloves garlic, peeled and minced

½ cup parsley leaves

Mushroom Syrup (see preceding recipe) or any vinaigrette (see pages 355–360)

This mushroom-laden stack of crepes—for which it's worth shopping for an assortment of mushrooms—is a perfect appetizer or accompaniment to roast veal or other simple meat dishes; sauce it with the mushroom syrup from the preceding recipe or any vinaigrette. It's best to prepare the cake in advance, then refrigerate it, even overnight, before reheating; this will make it really easy to slice, and the reheating will crisp up the top nicely.

1 Melt 2 tablespoons of the butter in a small saucepan over medium heat. Stir, scraping down the sides with a rubber spatula, until the butter foam subsides and the butter turns nut-brown. Immerse the bottom of the pan in cold water to stop the cooking.

2 Put the butter in a blender, along with the flour, eggs, milk, and a large pinch of salt, then blend until smooth. Refrigerate while you prepare the mushrooms.

3 Combine the oil and 3 tablespoons of the butter in a large skillet and turn the heat to medium-high. When the butter melts, add the mushrooms, shallots, garlic, and salt and pepper to taste, and stir. Cook, stirring occasionally, until the mushrooms have given up their liquid and begun to brown, about 10 minutes. Add the parsley and remove from the heat. Finely chop the mixture (you can do this in a food processor, but be careful not to puree the mixture). Taste and adjust the seasoning.

4 Heat a 10-inch nonstick skillet over high heat for about 2 minutes. Add a small piece of the remaining butter and swirl it around. Pour in ¼ cup of the crepe batter and swirl it around so that it coats the bottom of the pan completely; pour the excess back into the remaining batter. Adjust the heat so that the batter dries on top before it burns on the bottom; it will be ready to turn in 1 to 2 minutes. (Bear in mind that the first crepe is almost always a throwaway.) Turn and cook the second side for about 30 seconds. Repeat to use up the batter, adding more butter to the pan if necessary (it may not be); you need 8 near-perfect crepes for this recipe. Let cool to room temperature.

5 To make the gâteau, put a crepe on a cake plate or other flat surface and spread a portion of the mushroom mixture on it. Repeat, using all the crepes and mushrooms; end with a crepe. Refrigerate until firm.

6 Slice the gâteau. Dot with butter and reheat in a 350°F oven for about 10 minutes, or carefully brown under the broiler. Drizzle with mushroom syrup or vinaigrette and serve.

MAKES 6 TO 8 SERVINGS   TIME: 1 HOUR, PLUS CHILLING TIME

Mushroom spring rolls

2 tablespoons neutral oil, such as grapeseed or canola, plus more for brushing the phyllo

2 pounds mixed mushrooms, trimmed, washed, and chopped

2 tablespoons peeled and minced ginger

2 teaspoons peeled and minced garlic

Salt and freshly ground black pepper

3 scallions, trimmed and minced

Twenty-four 6-inch squares of phyllo dough

½ cup salted peanuts, finely chopped

1 small chile, stemmed and minced, or cayenne pepper or Tabasco to taste

2 teaspoons sugar

1 cup canned unsweetened coconut milk

2 teaspoons soy sauce

1 teaspoon fresh lemon juice

A simple but convincing fusion dish, crispy spring rolls that are baked, not fried, and served with a spicy, nutty dipping sauce. White button mushrooms are perfectly fine here.

1   Put the 2 tablespoons oil in a large skillet and turn the heat to medium-high. Add the mushrooms and cook, stirring occasionally, until they give up their liquid. Add the ginger and garlic, along with salt and pepper to taste, and cook until the mixture is quite dry. Stir in the scallions and let cool.

2   Preheat the oven to 350°F. Brush 12 squares of phyllo lightly with oil and place the remaining phyllo on top of them. With a point of each square facing you, spoon a heaping tablespoon of the mushroom mixture across the center of each square, making a 4-inch-long log from left to right. Fold over the left and right of each square so that they overlap in the middle. Brush a bit of oil over the top half of the wrapper. Fold the bottom half up, then roll up tightly; the oil will seal the spring roll. As each of the rolls is done, place it on a lightly oiled baking pan. (*You can prepare the spring rolls in advance up to this point; refrigerate, well wrapped or in a covered container, for up to 2 hours before proceeding.*)

3   Bake the spring rolls for about 15 minutes, or until golden brown and hot.

4   While they are baking, make the dipping sauce: Combine the peanuts, chile, and sugar in a small skillet over medium-high heat and cook, tossing and stirring,

until the mixture is lightly browned, 2 to 3 minutes. Add the coconut milk and stir, then cook until reduced by about one-third and thick, about 5 minutes. Stir in the soy sauce and lemon juice and remove from the heat.

5 Serve the spring rolls hot, with the warm dipping sauce.

MAKES 4 SERVINGS   TIME: 1 HOUR

Lentils

THE FASTEST-COOKING dried legume is also among the most distinctive and flavorful. We offer three extremely simple recipes (and we include Foie Gras Poached in Lentils among these, because although it's expensive, it is child's play to prepare) and two that take a little more time and effort. Warm Lentil Salad and Lentil Soup are in fact quite similar, and the cooking of the lentils remains fairly consistent in all of these recipes, even the ones in which the lentils take on a different form, as in the pancakes and the terrine.

All of these—in fact, all lentil recipes—are best with the tiny dark green lentils known in France as lentilles du Puy, but sold under other names too. They're distinctively different in appearance from the larger, more common brownish-green lentils sold everywhere.

KEYS TO SUCCESS

You can certainly substitute brown lentils for lentilles du Puy—in fact, they will cook a little faster, so you might prefer them.

Do not use red lentils (they're actually orange in color) in these recipes, as they will fall apart.

Lentils, like most dried foods, are unpredictable in their cooking time—taste frequently, starting about 20 minutes after they come to a boil.

Always rinse lentils before cooking, and pick through them to find any stray pebbles that may have made it through the packing process.

Warm lentil salad

8 ounces small green lentils, rinsed and picked through

1 stalk celery, cut into ¼-inch dice

1 onion, peeled and cut into ¼-inch dice

1 small leek, trimmed, well washed, and cut into ¼-inch dice

1 carrot, peeled and cut into ¼-inch dice

1 teaspoon chopped garlic

3 sprigs thyme

2 bay leaves

2 tablespoons sherry vinegar

Salt and freshly ground black pepper to taste

½ cup chopped parsley

1 tablespoon Dijon mustard

2 tablespoons hazelnut oil

This makes a fine side dish, although it is much heartier than most salads, and it can also serve as a main course, especially if you add a little minced cooked meat to the mix.

1 Combine the lentils, celery, onion, leek, carrot, garlic, thyme, and bay leaves in a saucepan with water to cover. Bring to a boil over medium-high heat, then turn the heat to medium-low and cook, stirring occasionally, until the lentils are tender, 30 to 45 minutes. (Add more water if necessary, but no more than you need.)

2 Remove the thyme and bay leaves; drain the lentils if necessary. Toss with the remaining ingredients, let sit for 10 minutes, and serve warm.

MAKES 4 SERVINGS   TIME: ABOUT 1 HOUR, LARGELY UNATTENDED

Lentil soup

4 ounces prosciutto, roughly chopped

8 ounces small green lentils, rinsed and picked through

1 stalk celery, roughly chopped

1 onion, peeled and roughly chopped

1 small leek, trimmed well, washed, and roughly chopped

1 carrot, peeled and roughly chopped

1 teaspoon chopped garlic

3 sprigs thyme

2 bay leaves

1 tablespoon butter or extra-virgin olive oil

Salt and freshly ground black pepper

1 tablespoon sherry vinegar

Chopped chives for garnish

The addition of a piece of prosciutto to the preceding recipe is enough to produce a rich broth in the same amount of time it takes to cook the lentils. With bread, a great simple lunch. With bread and salad, a great simple dinner.

1 Combine the prosciutto, lentils, celery, onion, leek, carrot, garlic, thyme, and bay leaves in a saucepan with water to cover by about 2 inches. Bring to a boil over medium-high heat, then turn the heat to medium-low and cook, stirring occasionally, until the lentils are tender, 30 to 45 minutes.

2 Cool slightly, then remove 1 cup of the cooked lentils and set aside. Carefully puree the remaining lentil mixture (it's hot) in a blender, along with the butter or oil; add a little more water if necessary to achieve a thick but soupy puree. Season to taste, and add the vinegar. Return to the pan and reheat gently.

3 Put one-quarter of the reserved lentils in the bottom of each of four bowls, then top each with a portion of the soup. Garnish with chives and serve.

MAKES 4 SERVINGS   TIME: ABOUT 1 HOUR, LARGELY UNATTENDED

Foie gras poached **in lentils**

4 ounces bacon, cut into ½-inch dice

8 ounces small green lentils, rinsed and picked through

1 stalk celery, cut into ¼-inch dice

1 onion, peeled and cut into ¼-inch dice

1 small leek, trimmed well, washed, and cut into ¼-inch dice

1 carrot, peeled and cut into ¼-inch dice

1 teaspoon chopped garlic

3 sprigs thyme

2 bay leaves

1 pound foie gras, more or less, in one piece

Salt and freshly ground black pepper

1 tablespoon sherry vinegar

Fleur de sel or other coarse salt

All we can say is, open your wallet and buy the biggest piece of foie gras you can afford—this ridiculously easy preparation is sheer luxury, a four-star dish that anyone can make quickly and easily. There is some consolation in the cost of this dish: It serves 8.

1 Combine the bacon, lentils, celery, onion, leek, carrot, garlic, thyme, and bay leaves in a saucepan with water to cover. Bring to a boil over medium-high heat, then turn the heat to medium-low and cook, stirring occasionally, until the lentils are nearly tender, 20 to 30 minutes. (Add more water if necessary, but no more than you need.)

2 Put the foie gras in with the lentils, along with salt and pepper to taste. Simmer for about 20 minutes, undisturbed, until the internal temperature of the foie gras is 120°F (use an instant-read thermometer). Turn off the heat and let sit for 5 minutes more.

3 Remove the foie gras and stir the vinegar into the lentils; they should be a little brothy, so add some water if necessary, and adjust the seasoning. Slice the foie gras and serve it on top of the lentils, topping it with some coarse salt.

MAKES 8 SERVINGS   TIME: ABOUT 1 HOUR, LARGELY UNATTENDED

Simple to Spectacular

Lentil pancakes with smoked salmon and crème fraîche

8 ounces small green lentils, rinsed and picked through

1 stalk celery, roughly chopped

1 onion, peeled and roughly chopped

1 small leek, trimmed, well washed, and roughly chopped

1 carrot, peeled and roughly chopped

1 teaspoon chopped garlic

3 sprigs thyme

2 bay leaves

20 leaves tarragon

2 eggs

¼ cup flour

½ teaspoon baking powder

⅓ cup heavy cream

½ cup minced parsley

½ cup minced chervil

2 shallots, peeled and minced

About ¼ cup neutral oil, such as canola or grapeseed

1 cup crème fraîche

8 ounces smoked salmon, thinly sliced

These mysteriously flavored pancakes are a great foil for any cool mixture, from sour cream and caviar to chopped tomato salsa. They should be warm when you serve them, but need not be hot.

1 Combine the lentils, celery, onion, leek, carrot, garlic, thyme, and bay leaves in a saucepan with water to cover. Bring to a boil over medium-high heat, then turn the heat to medium-low and cook, stirring occasionally, until the lentils are tender, 30 to 45 minutes. (Add more water if necessary, but no more than you need.)

2 Remove the thyme and bay leaves; drain the lentils if necessary (they should be fairly dry). Combine in a food processor with the tarragon, eggs, flour, baking powder, and cream; puree, but not until completely smooth. Transfer to a bowl and stir in the parsley, chervil, and shallots.

3 Put 2 tablespoons of the oil in a large skillet and turn the heat to medium. A minute or two later, drop large tablespoonfuls of the batter into the skillet and cook as you would pancakes, 2 or 3 minutes per side. Repeat, adding more oil as necessary. Keep the pancakes warm in a low oven (200°F) as you finish them. When the pancakes are done, spread each one with a little crème fraîche, top with a bit of smoked salmon, and serve.

Simple to Spectacular

MAKES 8 TO 16 SERVINGS   TIME: ABOUT 1½ HOURS

Terrine of lentils and squab (or Cornish hen)

2 squab or 1 Cornish hen

2 tablespoons butter

2 tablespoons neutral oil, such as canola or grapeseed

2 stalks celery, 1 roughly chopped, the other cut into ¼-inch dice

2 onions, peeled, 1 roughly chopped, the other cut into ¼-inch dice

1 large leek, trimmed, well washed, ½ roughly chopped, and ½ cut into ¼-inch dice

2 carrots, peeled, 1 roughly chopped, the other cut into ¼-inch dice

3 cloves garlic, peeled

6 sprigs thyme

8 ounces small green lentils, rinsed and picked through

1 teaspoon chopped garlic

2 bay leaves

Salt and freshly ground black pepper

One 1¼-ounce packet or 1 leaf gelatin

1 cup minced chives

Vegetable Vinaigrette (page 359) or any other vinaigrette

With squab, this is rich and luxurious, but it's nearly as good with the far less expensive and easier-to-find Cornish hen. In either case, you can sauté the legs separately and serve them on a bed of greens with the same vinaigrette you use to top the terrine. Or save them for another use.

1   Cut straight down along each side of the breastbone of the bird(s) to remove the breast entirely; set aside. Cut off the legs and reserve for another use (see headnote). Chop the remaining carcass(es). Combine 1 tablespoon each of the butter and oil in a medium skillet and turn the heat to medium-high. When the butter melts, add the bones and turn the heat to high. Brown well on both sides, then add the roughly chopped celery, onion, leek, and carrot, the garlic cloves, and half the thyme. Cook until the vegetables begin to brown, around 10 minutes. Add 3 cups water and cook until only about ½ cup remains; strain, then transfer to a small saucepan and reduce over high heat to 3 tablespoons.

2   Meanwhile, combine the lentils with the remaining diced celery, onion, leek, carrot, and thyme, chopped garlic, and bay leaves in a saucepan with water to cover. Bring to a boil over medium-high heat, then turn the heat to medium-low and cook, stirring occasionally, until the lentils are tender, 30 to 45 minutes. (Add more water if necessary, but no more than you need.) Season with salt and pepper; set aside.

3 Season the breasts with salt and pepper. Put the remaining 1 tablespoon each butter and oil in a skillet and turn the heat to medium-high. When the butter foam subsides, sear the breasts on both sides. Squab is done when medium-rare, about 4 minutes per side; Cornish hen is done when cooked through, 4 to 6 minutes per side. Let cool slightly, then cut into 1-inch chunks.

4 Warm the stock gently in a small saucepan and add the gelatin; heat until it dissolves, just a minute or so.

5 Line a very small terrine, just large enough to hold the ingredients in a 3- or 4-inch-deep layer, with plastic wrap. Stir the stock-gelatin mixture into the lentils. Make a layer of one-third lentils in the terrine, then sprinkle it with salt and pepper, and chives. Place about half the meat on top. Make another layer of lentils, sprinkle with salt and pepper and chives, and then make another layer of the remaining meat. Finish with a layer of the remaining lentils. Cover and refrigerate overnight.

6 Use the ends of the plastic wrap to pull the terrine from the mold. Slice, then serve with the vinaigrette.

MAKES 8 SERVINGS   TIME: ABOUT 1 HOUR, PLUS CHILLING TIME

Simple to Spectacular

Fish and shellfish

THIS extremely basic technique makes quick work of any fish steak. Halibut, turbot, or any other fish steak with a bone is especially succulent, but swordfish is also delicious when prepared this way. The fish cooks mostly in the oven, so there is no spattering and very little fish odor. And because it is cooked in liquid, the fish remains supremely moist, and you have a great deal of latitude in cooking times, at least compared to fish that is grilled or sautéed.

The basic recipe is halibut braised with wine, from which you can easily progress to halibut with Provençal flavorings to one with a wonderful mustard-nut crust, one strongly flavored with fennel, and that redolent classic, fish braised in red wine. All can be completed in less than an hour, and most in far less time than that, which makes these suitable for weeknight cooking, yet elegant enough for dinner parties.

KEYS TO SUCCESS

Firm fish steaks, especially those with a bone, will retain their shape best with this technique, but you can also use firm fillets, such as those of red snapper or monkfish. Make sure the steaks are about 1 inch thick so they do not cook too quickly.

The wine you use, whether red or white, should be good and dry, because you need acidity. If you find yourself without any wine and must use water, add a tablespoon or so of lemon juice to the poaching liquid.

Many of these recipes are best with butter—it will give you the most delicate flavor—but you can substitute extra-virgin olive oil, or a neutral oil like canola.

Don't overcook the fish. Remove it from the oven before it is opaque all the way through (use a thin-bladed knife to peek into its interior); it will retain enough heat to finish cooking on the way to the table.

Halibut with white wine and shallots

1½ tablespoons butter

1 tablespoon minced shallots

Five 6- to 8-ounce bone-in halibut or other steaks, or
2 larger steaks, each at least 1 inch thick

Salt and cayenne pepper

1½ cups dry white wine

⅓ cup minced parsley

Barely seasoned, this subtly delicious dish features a light, delicate sauce made from the juices of the fish mingled with the delicate flavors of shallots, butter, and wine. Serve with bread or white rice, either of which makes a great vehicle for the sauce.

1 Preheat the oven to 500°F. Smear the butter in a shallow baking pan that will hold the fish without crowding. Sprinkle the shallots over the butter.

2 Season the fish on both sides with salt and cayenne; lay it in the pan. Pour the wine all around and bring to a boil on top of the stove.

3 Transfer to the oven and cook for 5 minutes. Turn the fish and cook until it is done, about 10 minutes total; the fish should be firm and just about opaque all the way through. Garnish with the parsley and serve.

MAKES 4 SERVINGS   TIME: 20 MINUTES

Provençal **halibut**

1½ tablespoons butter

1 tablespoon minced shallots

Four 6- to 8-ounce bone-in halibut or other steaks, or
2 larger steaks, each at least 1 inch thick

Salt and cayenne pepper

1 pound tomatoes (about 2 large), peeled, seeded, and diced

2 tablespoons capers

1½ cups dry white wine

⅓ cup minced parsley

The characteristic flavors of capers and tomatoes change the previous braised fish from a delicate northern-style French dish to a gutsy southern one. Serve this with a braised vegetable, such as asparagus or broccoli, dressed with olive oil and lemon, and perhaps some roasted peppers.

1 Preheat the oven to 500°F. Smear the butter in a shallow baking pan that will hold the fish without crowding. Sprinkle the shallots over the butter.

2 Season the fish on both sides with salt and cayenne; lay it in the pan. Scatter the tomatoes and capers around and over the fish, then pour the wine around all.

3 Bring to a boil on top of the stove, then transfer to the oven and cook for 5 minutes, basting once with the liquid. Turn the fish and cook until it is done, about 10 minutes total; the fish should be firm and just about opaque all the way through. Garnish with the parsley and serve.

MAKES 4 SERVINGS   TIME: 25 MINUTES

Simple to Spectacular

Halibut with mustard-nut crust

4½ tablespoons butter, softened

¼ cup grainy mustard, like moutarde de Meaux

½ cup shelled, skinned, and toasted finely ground or minced hazelnuts

Four 6- to 8-ounce bone-in halibut or other fish steaks, or 2 larger steaks, each at least 1 inch thick

Salt and cayenne pepper

6 sprigs thyme

1½ cups dry white wine

½ cup small black olives, such as Niçoise, with pits

With the addition of a rich, nutty crust and the step of finishing the fish under the broiler, braised fish becomes a simple luxury. The butter in the crust melts into the fish as it cooks, making it extra-moist. Refrigerate the fish once you've spread the crust mixture on top. Chilling will help the crust brown before it slides off. This dish is a star, so accompany it simply, perhaps with no more than bread and salad.

1 Cream 3 tablespoons of the butter with the mustard and hazelnuts in a small bowl. Season the fish with salt and cayenne pepper and spread the butter mixture all over one side of each steak. Refrigerate for 1 hour if time allows.

2 Preheat the oven to 500°F. Spread the remaining 1½ tablespoons butter in a shallow baking pan that will hold the fish without crowding. Place the fish in the pan, then top it with a couple of thyme sprigs. Pour the wine around the fish and scatter the olives around; strip the leaves from 4 sprigs of thyme and scatter them around as well.

3 Bring to a boil on top of the stove, then transfer to the oven and cook for 10 to 12 minutes, undisturbed, until the fish is just about done; it should be firm and just about opaque nearly all the way through.

4 Turn on the broiler and place the fish about 3 inches from the heat source. Broil for a minute or two, or until the crust is bubbly and light brown. Serve.

MAKES 4 SERVINGS   TIME: 30 TO 90 MINUTES, DEPENDING ON TIME AVAILABLE

Three-fennel **halibut**

2 pounds fennel

2 tablespoons fresh lemon juice

¼ cup extra-virgin olive oil

Four 6- to 8-ounce bone-in halibut or other steaks, or 2 larger steaks, each at least 1 inch thick

1 tablespoon fennel seeds, cracked in a mortar and pestle or minced with a knife

Salt and cayenne pepper

An all-fennel dish, in which fennel fronds and bulb, juice, and seeds combine for great depth of flavor and beautiful color. Olive oil replaces the butter here for a real sense of the Mediterranean. The dish is quite brothy and wonderful with crusty bread.

If you do not have a juicer, puree the fennel in a food processor and wring the pulp in a towel to extract the juice.

1 Preheat the oven to 500°F. Tear off some of the feathery fronds from the fennel and set aside. Juice half the fennel, which should produce about 2 cups of juice (see headnote); mix the lemon juice into it. Trim and core the remaining fennel and cut it into slices; cook in boiling salted water to cover until nearly tender, about 10 minutes. When it is done, drain it and plunge it into ice water to stop the cooking.

2 Spread 2 tablespoons of the olive oil in a shallow baking pan that will hold the fish without crowding. Add the fish and pour the fennel juice around it; season the fish. Scatter the cooked fennel into the pan around the fish, and top the fish with the fennel seeds and reserved fronds.

3 Bring to a boil on top of the stove, then transfer to the oven and cook, basting once with the liquid (do not turn), until the fish is just about done, about 10 minutes; it should be firm and just about opaque nearly all the way through.

4 Leaving the fish in the pan, pour the juices into a small saucepan; return the fish to the oven, turn the oven off, and prop the door ajar. Heat the liquid gently and whisk in the remaining 2 tablespoons olive oil and salt and cayenne to taste. Divide the fish and fennel among four bowls and spoon the sauce over them.

MAKES 4 SERVINGS   TIME: 40 MINUTES

Halibut braised in red wine

5½ tablespoons butter

1 pound meaty fish bones

1 leek, root end and most of the green part removed, well washed and roughly chopped

1 stalk celery, roughly chopped

1 small onion, peeled and cut in half

2 large cloves garlic, peeled

2 sprigs thyme

2 cups plus 1 tablespoon good red wine

16 pearl onions, peeled

Salt and freshly ground white pepper

2 ounces slab bacon, cut into ¼-inch cubes

Four 6- to 8-ounce bone-in halibut or other steaks, or 2 larger steaks, each at least 1 inch thick

16 medium button mushrooms, trimmed and cut into quarters

1 teaspoon sugar

Firm fish braised in a meat-like fish broth and hearty accompaniments produces one of the sturdiest fish dishes you've ever tasted. This is not a complicated recipe, but it does take some time because making a fish stock is necessary. The fish stock requires fish bones, which you can get when you buy the fish; halibut trimmings make excellent stock, but those from any white fish will do. This preparation demands bread, because the sauce is just too good to waste. Panfried potatoes would be good too.

1 Put 2 tablespoons of the butter in a large saucepan and turn the heat to medium-high. When the butter melts, add the fish bones and cook for about 2 minutes, stirring occasionally. Add the leek, celery, onion, garlic, and thyme and cook for about 5 minutes, stirring occasionally, until the vegetables begin to become soft. Add 1 cup of the wine and ½ cup water and cook at a steady simmer for about 15 minutes, or until about one-third of the liquid has evaporated. Meanwhile, cook the pearl onions in boiling salted water until tender, about 10 minutes; drain.

2 When the stock is done, let it cool a little, then strain. (*The recipe can be prepared a day or two in advance up to this point; cool the stock and onions, place in separate containers, and refrigerate.*)

Simple to Spectacular

3 Put 1 cup of the wine in a small saucepan over medium-high heat. You want to reduce it to a syrupy tablespoon or so; this will take 10 to 20 minutes. Meanwhile, place the bacon pieces in a saucepan with water to cover and bring to a boil; drain. When the wine is done, turn off the heat and use a rubber spatula to scrape the syrup into a wider saucepan. (You can begin cooking the fish while the wine is reducing.)

4 Preheat the oven to 500°F. Spread 1½ tablespoons of the butter in a shallow baking pan that will hold the fish without crowding. Season the fish with salt and pepper. Place the fish in the pan and scatter the mushrooms and onions around it. Top the fish with the bacon pieces. Pour the stock around all.

5 Bring to a boil on top of the stove and transfer to the oven. Cook the fish, basting once (do not turn), until it is just done, about 10 minutes; it should be firm and just about opaque nearly all the way through. Leaving the fish in the pan, pour the juices into the saucepan with the reduced wine; return the fish to the oven, turn the oven off, and prop the door ajar.

6 Reduce the wine-stock mixture over high heat until about ½ cup remains (in a wide saucepan, this will only take 5 minutes or so). Meanwhile, place the fish under the broiler, about 3 inches from the heat source; cook for just a minute or so, until the bacon begins to crisp up a bit.

7 When the sauce is reduced (and the fish is cooking), turn the heat to low and add the sugar; season with salt and pepper and stir in the remaining 2 tablespoons butter until it melts. Add the remaining 1 tablespoon wine, then taste and add a little more sugar if necessary. Cook for 10 seconds more, then turn off the heat, spoon over the fish, and serve.

MAKES 4 SERVINGS   TIME: 1 HOUR

Slow-cooked salmon

NOT so much slow-cooked, since we're talking about less than 15 minutes in the oven, but low-cooked—the oven temperature is 300°F. This results in salmon that is not browned, but superbly moist and evenly cooked, medium-rare throughout. It's delicious and, once you and your oven get the hang of it, virtually foolproof.

Our flavors begin with Mediterranean and then Thai influences. A horseradish puree accompanies one of the dishes, then a classic French mushroom "fondue," and finally a topping of coriander-scented mussels.

KEYS TO SUCCESS

The salmon must be cut to the right size: Buy a fillet that is about 11/4 inches thick at its center and cut it crosswise into strips weighing 6 or 12 ounces each.

Experiment with your oven. You don't want the salmon to brown at all, so the temperature has to be under 350°F. But whether it's 300° or 250°F. is hard to say—somewhere in that range will cook the salmon properly in about 12 to 15 minutes.

The salmon will appear to be undercooked when it is in fact done. You can tell because it will flake, the internal temperature will be 115°F or higher, and it will taste cooked.

Slow-cooked salmon with parsley and capers

1 teaspoon butter

Four 6-ounce center-cut salmon fillets (or two 12-ounce fillets), about 1¼ inches thick at the thickest point, preferably with skin on (but scaled)

Salt and freshly ground black pepper

2 tablespoons capers, chopped

2 tablespoons chopped parsley

1 tablespoon extra-virgin olive oil

1 tablespoon fresh lemon juice

Only the salmon requires cooking, making this combination of flavors a near-perfect weeknight dish.

1 Preheat the oven to 300°F. Smear the butter on a baking sheet and place the salmon on it, skin side up. Put the baking sheet in the oven.

2 Check the fillets after 12 minutes; the skin should peel off easily, the meat should flake, and an instant-read thermometer should display about 120°F. The salmon may look underdone, but if it meets these three criteria, it is done. (If it is not done, or you prefer it more well done, return it to the oven for about 3 minutes more.)

3 Remove the skin from each fillet and, if you like, scrape off the gray fatty matter on the skin side (or just turn the fish over). Sprinkle with salt and pepper, then top with the remaining ingredients and serve.

MAKES 4 SERVINGS   TIME: 20 MINUTES

Slow-cooked salmon with crunchy lemongrass

The inner core of 2 stalks lemongrass (page 287)

1 small chile, stemmed and seeded

1 large clove garlic, peeled

4 tablespoons butter

1 cup bread crumbs, preferably Japanese panko

1 tablespoon chopped cilantro

1 tablespoon chopped mint

1 tablespoon chopped basil, preferably Thai

Four 6-ounce center-cut salmon fillets (or two 12-ounce fillets), about 1¼ inches thick at the thickest point, preferably with skin on (but scaled)

Salt and freshly ground black pepper

Lime wedges (or the sauce described in headnote)

You can make a quick sauce for this dish if you like, and, if you plan to serve it with rice, it's a good idea: Combine ½ cup canned unsweetened coconut milk, 1 tablespoon nam pla (Thai fish sauce), and ¼ cup fresh lime juice in a small saucepan and warm gently. Spoon around the cooked salmon just before serving (omit the lime wedges).

1 Preheat the oven to 300°F. Mince together the lemongrass, chile, and garlic. Put the butter in a medium skillet and turn the heat to medium-high. When it melts, sauté the lemongrass mixture in it for about 2 minutes, stirring occasionally. Add the bread crumbs and cook, stirring, until they brown lightly, another minute or two. Turn off the heat and stir in the herbs.

2 Place the fillets on a baking sheet, skin side up, and sprinkle them with salt and pepper. Top the fish with the bread crumb mixture and put the baking sheet in the oven.

3 Check the salmon after 12 minutes; it should flake and an instant-read thermometer should display about 120°F. It may look underdone, but if it meets these two criteria, it is done. (If it is not done, or you prefer it more well done, return it to the oven for about 3 minutes more.) Serve immediately, with lime wedges (or the sauce).

Simple to Spectacular

MAKES 4 SERVINGS   TIME: 30 MINUTES

Slow-cooked salmon with horseradish

1 pound fresh horseradish, peeled and thinly sliced

Salt and freshly ground black pepper

2 tablespoons crème fraîche or sour cream

Four 6-ounce center-cut salmon fillets (or two 12-ounce fillets), about 1¼ inches thick at the thickest point, preferably with skin on (but scaled)

Chopped parsley for garnish

Serve this on a bed of lightly dressed mesclun salad (see page 39). You might also garnish it with salmon eggs.

1 Put the horseradish in a saucepan with water to cover, add salt, and bring to a boil. Simmer for about 1 hour, or until the horseradish is very tender, like a boiled potato. Drain, reserving some of the cooking liquid.

2 Puree the horseradish in a blender or food processor with the crème fraîche or sour cream and as much of the cooking liquid as you need to allow the machine to do its work. Season the puree to taste.

3 Preheat the oven to 300°F. Put the fillets on a baking sheet, skin side down, and sprinkle them with salt and pepper. Smear the fish with the horseradish puree and put the baking sheet in the oven.

4 Check the salmon after 12 minutes; it should flake and an instant-read thermometer should display about 120°F. It may look underdone, but if it meets these two criteria, it is done. (If it is not done, or you prefer it more well done, return it to the oven for about 3 minutes more.) Serve immediately, garnished with parsley.

MAKES 4 SERVINGS   TIME: 1 HOUR AND 20 MINUTES, LARGELY UNATTENDED

Slow-cooked salmon with herbs, mushrooms, and tomato fondue

1 pound tomatoes, peeled, seeded, and chopped

¼ cup extra-virgin olive oil

Pinch of sugar

Salt and freshly ground black pepper

6 tablespoons butter

½ cup trimmed and minced mushrooms

¼ cup peeled and minced shallots

Juice of 1 lemon

½ cup bread crumbs, preferably Japanese panko

½ cup roughly chopped chervil

1 egg

Four 6-ounce center-cut salmon fillets (or two 12-ounce fillets), about 1¼ inches thick at the thickest point, preferably with skin on (but scaled)

1 teaspoon slivered garlic

1 tablespoon slivered shallots

1 bay leaf

½ cup dry white wine

A food processor makes quick work of the mushroom-shallot mixture here.

1 Combine the tomatoes, oil, sugar, and salt and pepper to taste in a small saucepan and bring the mixture to a boil over medium-high heat. Turn the heat to low and simmer gently for about 20 minutes. (Keep warm if this is done before the salmon.)

2 Meanwhile, preheat the oven to 300°F. Put 1 tablespoon of the butter in a skillet and turn the heat to medium-high; when it melts, add the mushrooms, minced shallots, and a sprinkling of salt and pepper and cook, stirring occasionally, until the mushrooms give up their liquid and it evaporates, 5 to 10 minutes. Put the mushroom mixture in the container of a food processor, along with the lemon juice, bread crumbs, chervil, egg, and 4 tablespoons of the butter and process briefly to combine.

3 Put the fillets on a baking sheet, skin side down, and sprinkle them with salt and pepper. Smear the fish with the mushroom mixture, surround it with the slivered garlic and shallots, the bay leaf, bits of the remaining 1 tablespoon butter, and the white wine, and put the baking sheet in the oven.

4 Check the salmon after 12 minutes; it should flake and an instant-read thermometer should display about 120°F. It may look underdone, but if it meets these two criteria, it is done. (If it is not done, or you prefer it more well done, return it to the oven for about 3 minutes more.)

5 Turn on the broiler. Run the salmon over the broiler for less than a minute, just to brown the top a bit. Serve immediately, with the pan juices, garlic, and shallots spooned over it and the tomato fondue next to it.

MAKES 4 SERVINGS   TIME: 45 MINUTES

Slow-cooked salmon with mussels and coriander

1½ pounds mussels, scrubbed and debearded

⅓ cup peeled and chopped shallots

½ cup dry white wine

Several stems parsley

1 tablespoon coriander seeds

1 large slice good bread (about 2 ounces)

¼ cup minced shallots

3 tablespoons extra-virgin olive oil

Minced zest of 1 orange

1 hard-cooked egg, chopped

Salt and freshly ground black pepper

One 24-ounce center-cut salmon fillet (or two 12-ounce fillets), about 1¼ inches thick at the thickest point, preferably skin on (but scaled)

An elegant, lovely, and beautifully flavored dish, even better if served with lightly steamed or sautéed spinach.

1 Put the first 5 ingredients in a large covered saucepan and turn the heat to high. Steam, shaking the pan occasionally, until the mussels open, 5 to 10 minutes. Remove the mussels with a slotted spoon. Strain the liquid through cloth and reserve it. Put the bread in the liquid and let it stay there, turning once or twice, until it is completely saturated.

2 Remove the mussels from their shells; reserve 8 for garnish and chop the rest.

3 Preheat oven to 300°F. Combine the minced shallots and 1½ tablespoons of the olive oil in a small skillet and cook over medium heat, stirring occasionally, until the shallots are soft, 3 to 5 minutes. Combine the shallots, mussels, orange zest, and egg. Squeeze the excess liquid from the bread (continue to reserve the mussel cooking liquid), chop it, and add it to the mussel mixture, along with plenty of salt and pepper.

4 Put the salmon on a baking sheet, skin side down, and sprinkle it with salt and pepper. Make an aluminum foil collar around the salmon, then pile the mussel mixture onto the fish. Put the remaining 1½ tablespoons oil and the reserved mussel liquid on the bottom of the baking sheet and put it in the oven.

5 Check the salmon after 12 minutes; it should flake and an instant-read thermometer should display about 120°F. It may look underdone, but if it meets these two criteria, it is done. (If it is not done, or you prefer it more well done, return it to the oven for about 3 minutes more.) Remove the foil collar(s) and serve, garnished with the reserved mussels.

MAKES 4 SERVINGS   TIME: 45 MINUTES

THESE recipes all feature fish fillets of medium thickness—red snapper is the best example—gently cooked in butter or oil. They range from the exquisitely simple and delicate—fish with a supremely light coating of egg and flour—to crispy fish coated with Cream of Wheat or potatoes to those given flavorful coatings of spices or nuts.

KEYS TO SUCCESS

Start with fillets of sturdy white-fleshed fish, about ½ inch thick. Red snapper is the model, but you can also use sea bass, catfish, pollock, blackfish, ocean perch, rockfish, and many others.

Keep the heat high and the cooking time short—about 6 minutes is usually right. Don't overcook, or the fish will fall apart.

Classic **sautéed snapper**

2 eggs

Salt and freshly ground black pepper

¼ cup extra-virgin olive oil or butter

Four 6-ounce fillets red snapper, sea bass, or similar fish, skin removed

Flour for dredging

Lemon wedges

This is one of the best ways to cook fish on top of the stove because, as long as you don't overcook it, the fish will retain most of its moisture. It is delicate, however, rather than super-crunchy—if that's what you're looking for, try one of the next three recipes.

1 If you will be cooking in batches, preheat the oven to 200°F. Beat the eggs in a shallow bowl with salt and pepper to taste; put the bowl next to the stove.

2 Heat a 10- or 12-inch skillet, preferably nonstick, over medium-high heat for 2 to 3 minutes, then add the oil or butter. Immediately dredge one of the fillets very lightly in the flour, tapping the fillet lightly so excess flour falls off. Dip in the egg, then gently lay in the skillet. The egg should start to cook instantly but not immediately brown. Repeat with the remaining fillets. If you are only able to fit two fillets in the skillet at a time, that's fine—cook in batches.

3 Carefully turn each fillet as soon as it becomes light golden on the first side, about 2 minutes. Cook for about 2 minutes on the second side, then back on the first side for 30 seconds or so. Drain on paper towels for an instant. Keep warm in the oven while you cook the remaining fillets if necessary. Serve hot, with lemon wedges.

MAKES 4 SERVINGS   TIME: 20 MINUTES

Sautéed red snapper with potato crust

2 large baking potatoes (about 2 pounds)

Salt and freshly ground black pepper

Four 6-ounce fillets red snapper, sea bass, or similar fish, skin removed

2 tablespoons extra-virgin olive oil

2 tablespoons butter

1 cup dry white wine

2 tablespoons chopped shallots

3 tablespoons Dijon mustard

Chopped chives for garnish

We worked hard to get this one just right, because we originally thought it would be tricky. But it turns out to be a snap, as long as you use starchy (baking) potatoes—like Idahoes. Wrap them around the fish, and not only do they become crisp, they keep the fillet moist.

1   Peel and shred or grate the potatoes—ideally, you'll have long, thin strands, but any small shreds will do. Mix them with salt to taste and squeeze out some of their liquid. Sprinkle the fish on both sides with salt and pepper, then make a thick layer of potatoes on each side of each fillet, pressing with your hands to make it adhere.

2   Preheat the oven to 200°F. Heat a 10- or 12-inch skillet, preferably nonstick, over medium-high heat for 2 to 3 minutes, then add the oil and butter. When the butter foam subsides, add the fillets to the skillet (you might have to cook in batches, but that's okay). Cook the fillets, turning once, until the potato crust is nicely browned on both sides, about 10 minutes total. Keep the first batch warm in the oven while you cook the remaining fillets if necessary.

3   When the fish is done, remove it to the oven. Add the wine to the skillet and reduce by half over high heat, stirring with a wooden spoon. Add the shallots and cook for a minute. Add the mustard and salt and pepper, then taste and adjust the seasoning as necessary.

4   To serve, make a small pool of the mustard sauce on each of four plates, then top with one of the fillets. Garnish with chives.

MAKES 4 SERVINGS   TIME: 40 MINUTES

Simple to Spectacular

Crunchy red snapper with spice mix

6 hazelnuts, shelled and peeled

6 almonds, shelled and peeled

1 tablespoon coriander seeds

1 tablespoon sesame seeds

½ teaspoon freshly ground black pepper

½ cup heavy cream

3 tablespoons butter

1 tablespoon neutral oil, such as canola or grapeseed

Four 6-ounce fillets red snapper, sea bass, or similar fish, skin removed

Salt and cayenne pepper

Spices and nuts give this fish great crunch and flavor at once. Here, it's best to cook the fish over not-too-high heat, because nuts burn easily. Still, the cooking time should be less than 10 minutes.

1 Combine the first 5 ingredients in a small skillet and toast over medium heat, shaking the pan occasionally, until fragrant, about 3 minutes. Grind to a coarse powder in a coffee or spice grinder.

2 If cooking in batches, preheat the oven to 200°F. Put the heavy cream in a bowl and put the spice mixture on a plate.

3 Heat a 10- or 12-inch skillet, preferably nonstick, over medium heat for 2 to 3 minutes, then add the butter and oil. Season the fish with salt and cayenne, then dip one side of each fillet in the cream; press the wet side into the spice mixture and then reserve remaining spice mix for garnish. When the butter foam subsides, add the fillets to the skillet (you might have to cook in batches, in which case you'll need a little more butter and oil), coated side down. Cook the fillets until just browned, on the first side, 2 to 3 minutes, then turn carefully and cook on the other side for 4 to 6 minutes, or until done. (Keep the first batch warm in the oven while you cook the remaining fillets if necessary.)

4 Serve the fillets dusted with a tiny bit of the remaining spice mix, or garnished with chopped toasted nuts.

MAKES 4 SERVINGS   TIME: 1 HOUR

Red snapper with Cream of Wheat-and-buttermilk sauce

Four 6-ounce fillets red snapper, sea bass, or similar fish, skin removed

2 cups buttermilk, more or less

2 tablespoons minced dill, plus more for garnish

Salt and freshly ground black pepper

2 cups Cream of Wheat, preferably not instant

¼ cup extra-virgin olive oil or butter

2 tablespoons butter

2 tablespoons fresh lemon juice

A lovely dish, crisp-coated fish in a creamy, slightly sour broth. The combination of ingredients may sound odd, but, trust us, the results are unique. Dill is our herb of choice, but chervil, parsley, or fennel fronds will work just as well. Try to avoid skim buttermilk—that with 2 percent fat is better here. And eat this with a spoon.

1 Put the fillets in a shallow dish and add enough buttermilk to cover. Sprinkle with the dill and salt and pepper, and let sit for about 10 minutes, turning frequently.

2 Preheat the oven to 200°F. Place the Cream of Wheat in a bowl. Heat a 10- or 12-inch skillet, preferably nonstick, over medium-high heat for 2 to 3 minutes, then add the oil or butter. A minute later, dredge each fillet in turn in the Cream of Wheat, turning it gently a few times so lots of the cereal adheres to the fillet; as the fillets are coated, add them to the skillet. It's likely that you'll only be able to fit two fillets in the skillet at a time, but that's fine—just cook in batches.

3 Carefully turn each fillet as soon as it becomes light golden on the first side, about 2 minutes. Cook for about 2 minutes on the second side, then back on the first side for 30 seconds or so. Drain on paper towels for an instant, then keep warm in the oven while you make the sauce.

4 Place 1 cup of the buttermilk you used for soaking in a small saucepan with salt and pepper to taste and the butter. Bring to a boil and stir until the butter melts. Add the lemon juice and whisk or zap with an immersion blender. Serve the fillets in bowls, with a little of the buttermilk sauce around each of them, and garnish with dill.

Simple to Spectacular

MAKES 4 SERVINGS   TIME: 30 MINUTES

Pistachio-crusted red snapper with pistachio oil and spinach

4 tablespoons butter

½ cup roughly chopped carrots

1 small leek, trimmed, well washed, and chopped

1 clove garlic (don't bother to peel it)

5 stems parsley

1 sprig thyme

1 bay leaf

5 peppercorns

1 pound fish bones, preferably from red snapper or other white-fleshed fish

½ cup dry white wine

1 cup shelled pistachios

Four 6-ounce fillets red snapper, sea bass, or similar fish, skin removed

Salt and cayenne pepper

¼ cup extra-virgin olive oil

1 clove garlic, peeled and crushed

1 pound spinach, trimmed, washed, and dried

Freshly ground black pepper

2 tablespoons fresh lemon juice

2 tablespoons pistachio or other nut oil

Pistachio oil is a wonderful ingredient. It's available at many specialty food stores, but if you can't find it, substitute hazelnut or walnut oil (you can use those nuts if you prefer too).

1 Place 2 tablespoons of the butter in a medium saucepan and turn the heat to medium-high. When the butter melts, add the carrots, leek, garlic, parsley, thyme, bay leaf, and peppercorns. Stir and cover, then reduce the heat to medium. Cook, stirring once or twice, for 10 minutes, or until the vegetables are tender. Add the fish bones and cook, covered, for about 5 minutes, stirring once or twice. Add the wine and 1 cup water, cover, and bring to a boil, then uncover and simmer, skimming any foam that forms, for about 20 minutes. Turn off the heat and let cool for 10 minutes, then strain and measure; you want about ⅔ cup of liquid. If there is much less, add water; if there is more, reduce over high heat until there is about ⅔ cup. *(This can be done a day or two in advance if you like.)*

2 Chop the pistachios fine, either by hand or with a food processor, but do not grind them to a powder. Season the fish with salt and cayenne, then press the rough (non-skin) side of each fillet into the nuts; there will be nuts left over, but that's fine. Set the fish and the remaining nuts aside for the moment.

3 Place 2 tablespoons of the olive oil in a 10- or 12-inch skillet and turn the heat to medium-high. Add the garlic clove and, when it browns, the spinach, along with salt and black pepper to taste. Cook, stirring almost constantly, until the spinach wilts. Remove the garlic clove and keep the spinach warm.

4 If cooking in batches, preheat the oven to 200°F. Bring the fish stock to a boil, then reduce to a simmer and add the remaining pistachios, along with the lemon juice, salt and cayenne to taste, and the nut oil. Whisk until smooth or zap with an immersion blender, then taste and adjust the seasoning. Keep warm.

5 Heat a 10- or 12-inch skillet, preferably nonstick, over medium heat for 2 to 3 minutes, then add the remaining 2 tablespoons each olive oil and butter. When the butter foam subsides, add the fillets to the skillet (you might have to cook in batches, but that's okay), crust side down. Cook the fillets until just browned, 2 to 3 minutes, then turn carefully and cook on the other side for 4 to 6 minutes, or until done. Keep the first batch warm in the oven while you cook the remaining fillets if necessary.

6 Serve in bowls, with the spinach as a base, the fish on top, and the sauce all around.

MAKES 4 SERVINGS   TIME: 1 HOUR

Fish with beurre noisette

BEURRE noisette, brown or nut-colored butter, is a classic French sauce with one ingredient: butter. Left as is or spiked with other flavors, it makes a great topping for fish of all kinds. We keep the fish preparations simple and play with the sauce, which can make for some lightning-quick dishes.

Trout with Beurre Noisette, for example, takes 10 minutes, and the skate, shrimp, and scallop dishes don't take much longer. Sea Bass Fillets with Mushroom Beurre Noisette is a more complicated preparation, one with a deep, rich stock and potent spice mix, and consequently takes longer; we think it's worth it.

KEYS TO SUCCESS

There's a moment at which beurre noisette is perfect, a deep golden brown. The best way to stop the cooking at this moment is to plunge the bottom of the saucepan into a bowl of cold water. (You can simply turn off the heat, but you run the marginal risk of overcooking the butter.)

Substitute freely here; the sauces can be used with almost any fish cooked in almost any way.

Fish fillets with beurre noisette

5 tablespoons butter

Four 6-ounce fillets trout, red snapper, or other fish

Salt

Pinch of cayenne pepper

Juice of ½ lemon

A truly minimalist dish, in which the simplicity of preparation and paucity of ingredients completely belie the wonderful results. Astonishing, really.

1 Put 3 tablespoons of the butter in a small saucepan over medium heat. Stir, scraping down the sides with a rubber spatula, until the butter foam subsides and the butter turns nut-brown. Immerse the bottom of the pan in cold water to stop the cooking, then keep warm over the lowest possible heat.

2 Put the remaining 2 tablespoons butter in a skillet large enough to hold the fish in one layer (work in batches if you have to; you'll need a little more butter). Turn the heat to medium-high; when the butter melts, add the fish and turn the heat to high. Cook for 3 to 4 minutes per side, sprinkling the fish with salt and the cayenne and turning once, until the fish is cooked through.

3 Drizzle the fish with lemon juice, spoon the beurre noisette over it, and serve.

MAKES 4 SERVINGS   TIME: 10 MINUTES

Simple to Spectacular

Skate with sesame beurre noisette

5 tablespoons butter

1 tablespoon roasted sesame oil

2 tablespoons balsamic vinegar

1 tablespoon sesame seeds

2 skate wings (about 1½ to 2 pounds)

Salt

Pinch of cayenne pepper

1 tablespoon minced tarragon

We add a little vinegar and sesame oil to the beurre noisette here, and we finish the dish with a couple of seasonings; the combination of sesame and tarragon is transcendent. Buy skate skinned, but with the center cartilage intact, and cook it that way. To eat, lift the "fillets" of meat off the center cartilage, which is itself edible, if you like crunchy things.

1 Put 3 tablespoons of the butter in a small saucepan over medium heat. Stir, scraping down the sides with a rubber spatula, until the butter foam subsides and the butter turns nut-brown; then cook for about 30 seconds longer. Immerse the bottom of the pan in cold water to stop the cooking, then add the sesame oil and vinegar, stir, and keep warm over the lowest possible heat.

2 Put the sesame seeds in a small dry skillet and turn the heat to medium. Toast, shaking the pan occasionally, until the seeds begin to pop, 2 to 3 minutes.

3 Put the remaining 2 tablespoons butter in a skillet large enough to hold the skate in one layer (work in batches if you have to; you'll need a little more butter). Turn the heat to medium-high. When the butter melts, add the fish and turn the heat to high. Cook for about 5 minutes per side, sprinkling the skate with salt and the cayenne and turning once, until it is cooked through.

4 Serve the fish topped with the beurre noisette and garnished with the sesame seeds and tarragon.

MAKES 4 SERVINGS   TIME: 20 MINUTES

Shrimp with spicy beurre noisette, mango, and tomato

5 limes

5 tablespoons butter

1 small chile, stemmed, seeded, and minced

½ cup diced mango

½ cup peeled, seeded, and diced tomato

24 to 36 large shrimp

Salt and cayenne pepper

Minced cilantro for garnish

This is a fruity, colorful, and spicy combination, perfect for summer and for those who like Caribbean flavors.

1 Juice 3 of the limes; set the juice aside. Cut the remaining 2 limes in half along their equators. Segment them as you would a grapefruit, remove any seeds, and set the segments aside.

2 Put 3 tablespoons of the butter in a small saucepan over medium heat. Stir, scraping down the sides with a rubber spatula, until the butter foam subsides and the butter turns nut-brown. Add the chile, mango, and tomato and cook for another 10 seconds, then immerse the bottom of the pan in cold water to stop the cooking. Keep warm over the lowest possible heat.

3 Put the remaining 2 tablespoons butter in a skillet large enough to hold the shrimp in one layer. Turn the heat to medium-high; when the butter melts, add the shrimp and turn the heat to high. Cook for 2 to 3 minutes per side, sprinkling the shrimp with salt and a pinch of cayenne and turning once, until they are cooked through.

4 Stir the lime juice and segments into the beurre noisette, along with salt and cayenne; taste and adjust the seasoning. Serve the shrimp with the beurre noisette spooned over it; garnish with cilantro.

MAKES 4 SERVINGS   TIME: 30 MINUTES

Simple to Spectacular

Scallops with ginger-lemongrass beurre noisette

16 large sea scallops (about 1½ pounds)

2 tablespoons peeled and minced ginger

Salt

5 tablespoons butter

2 tablespoons trimmed and minced lemongrass

½ cup chopped scallions

1 tablespoon nam pla (Thai fish sauce)

¼ cup chopped mint

Pinch of cayenne pepper

30 snow peas, trimmed and cut into long thin strips

2 tablespoons fresh lime juice

Beurre noisette takes well to Asian flavors (the combination of butter and nam pla is one of our favorites). For the snow peas, you can substitute any crunchy vegetable, cut into tiny pieces—carrots, for example.

1 Cut the scallops nearly in half along their equator. Mix half the ginger with a large pinch of salt and smear this mixture on the inside of the scallops.

2 Put 3 tablespoons of the butter in a small saucepan over medium heat. Stir, scraping down the sides with a rubber spatula, until the butter foam subsides and the butter turns nut-brown. Immerse the bottom of the pan in cold water to stop the cooking, then add the remaining ginger, the lemongrass, scallions, nam pla, and half the mint. Keep warm over the lowest possible heat.

3 Put the remaining 2 tablespoons butter in a skillet large enough to hold the scallops in one layer. Turn the heat to medium-high; when the butter melts, add the scallops and turn the heat to high. Cook for 2 to 3 minutes per side, sprinkling the scallops with salt and the cayenne. Just before you turn the scallops, add the snow peas to the skillet. The scallops are done when not quite cooked through (the snow peas are done almost instantly).

4 Stir the lime juice into the beurre noisette. Serve the scallops with the beurre noisette spooned over them; garnish with the remaining mint.

MAKES 4 SERVINGS   TIME: 25 MINUTES

Sea bass fillets with mushroom beurre noisette

8 ounces white mushrooms, trimmed and sliced

7 tablespoons butter, preferably salted

1½ tablespoons honey

1 tablespoon fresh lime juice

1 tablespoon sherry vinegar

1 tablespoon soy sauce

2 hazelnuts, shelled and skinned

2 blanched almonds

1 tablespoon coriander seeds

1 tablespoon sesame seeds

1½ teaspoons freshly ground black pepper

10 pearl onions, peeled and cut in half

20 lima beans or peeled fava beans

1 cup heavy cream

Flour for dredging

Four 6-ounce fillets sea bass, red snapper, or other fish

Salt

Pinch of cayenne pepper

20 cherry tomatoes, cut in half

2 tablespoons minced marjoram or oregano

All the work goes into the sauce here; the fish takes just a few minutes to cook. And the vegetarian mushroom sauce is a lesson in combining a few simple flavors to produce something rich and almost luxurious. Between it and the spice mix, the dish packs a real wallop.

1 Combine the mushrooms and 2 tablespoons of the butter in a skillet and turn the heat to high. Cook for about 2 minutes, stirring occasionally, then drizzle with the honey. When the mushrooms brown—this will happen quickly, thanks to the honey—add the lime juice, vinegar, and soy sauce, and pour into a small saucepan. Add 1 cup water to the skillet and cook over high heat, stirring occasionally, for about a minute. Add the water to the saucepan and simmer this mixture over medium-low heat for about 30 minutes. Strain; reserve the liquid and discard the solids.

2 Meanwhile, combine the nuts, coriander, sesame seeds, and pepper in a small dry skillet; turn the heat to medium. Toast, shaking the pan occasionally, until the spices are fragrant, just a minute or two. Grind to a powder in a spice or coffee mill or a mortar and pestle.

3   Bring a medium pot of water to a boil and salt it. Add the pearl onions and cook for about 5 minutes, or just until tender. Remove with a slotted spoon. Add the beans to the pot and cook for about 2 minutes, or just until tender. Drain and set aside.

4   Put 3 tablespoons of the butter in a small saucepan over medium heat. Stir, scraping down the sides with a rubber spatula, until the butter foam subsides and the butter turns nut-brown. Immerse the bottom of the pan in cold water to stop the cooking, then keep warm over the lowest possible heat.

5   Dip the fillets in the cream, then press the skin side into the spice mix, and finally the flour.

6   Put the remaining 2 tablespoons butter in a skillet large enough to hold the fish in one layer (work in batches if you have to; you'll need a little more butter). Turn the heat to medium-high; when the butter melts, add the fish and turn the heat to high. Cook for 3 to 4 minutes per side, sprinkling the fish with salt and the cayenne and turning once, until cooked through.

7   Combine the mushroom stock and beurre noisette and heat through; season to taste, then stir in the onions, beans, and tomatoes. Put each fish fillet in a bowl and surround with the broth and vegetables. Garnish with the marjoram or oregano and serve.

MAKES 4 SERVINGS   TIME: ABOUT 1 HOUR

SEVICHE is fish barely cooked by chemistry rather than heat; acidity does the trick. (In fact, you can fully cook fish with acidity, but it defeats the purpose.) The result is delicate, lightly flavored, and wonderful.

We rely almost exclusively on citrus juices for the "cooking," since we love their flavor with fish. With these, we use European or Asian herbs, green peppercorns, even miso as seasonings. All of these make quick, easy, and impressive appetizers.

KEYS TO SUCCESS

The fish and shellfish used in these recipes must be spanking fresh; be absolutely sure of its quality. It's best to tell your fishmonger how you will be using the fish.

To cut fish thin, start with a fillet and use a sharp knife to cut slices parallel to the cutting board. Aim for slices less than ¼ inch thick. The process is a little easier if the fish is very, very cold; putting it in the freezer for 15 minutes before slicing will help. (The easiest thing to do, of course, is to find a cooperative fishmonger to slice it for you.)

All the fish can be sliced ahead of time, then marinated as you need it; keep it very cold in the meantime.

Substitute freely; you can use almost any fish you want in most of these recipes.

Sea bass **seviche**

8 to 10 ounces sea bass fillet, sliced as thin as possible (see Keys to Success, page 198)

Salt and freshly ground black pepper

¼ cup extra-virgin olive oil

¼ cup fresh lime juice

2 tablespoons roughly chopped mint

2 tablespoons roughly chopped cilantro

1 teaspoon coriander seeds, lightly crushed

Serve this simple appetizer with toasted sourdough or other bread, along with butter and salt.

1 Put each slice of fish in turn between two sheets of plastic wrap and pound lightly with the bottom of a pot or the flat side of a cleaver. You want to make them as thin as possible without tearing them. Arrange a portion of the fillets on each of four plates.

2 Sprinkle evenly with salt and pepper, then drizzle with the olive oil and lime juice. Sprinkle with the herbs and coriander seeds and serve immediately.

MAKES 4 SERVINGS   TIME: 15 MINUTES

Scallop seviche with citrus

1 tablespoon fresh orange juice

1 tablespoon fresh grapefruit juice

2 tablespoons fresh lemon juice

¼ cup neutral oil, such as canola or grapeseed

2 tablespoons almond or hazelnut oil

Salt and freshly ground black pepper

12 ounces scallops, preferably bay scallops; if sea scallops,
cut into quarters

1 red bell pepper

Minced dill or fennel fronds for garnish

A mild, unaggressive seviche, one that does not overwhelm the delicate nature of the scallops. Smell the nut oil to make sure it is fresh; if there are any off-odors, open a new bottle.

1 Whisk together the citrus juices, oils, and salt and pepper to taste. Toss with the scallops and refrigerate, covered, for 1 hour.

2 Meanwhile, preheat the oven to 450°F. Roast the pepper in a small foil-lined pan or ovenproof skillet, turning occasionally, until blackened all over. (Alternatively, you can grill or broil the pepper; just blacken the outside and it will collapse.) Fold the foil over the pepper and let it cool for a few minutes; then peel, core, seed, and mince.

3 Serve the scallops garnished with the pepper and dill or fennel.

MAKES 4 SERVINGS   TIME: ABOUT 1 HOUR, LARGELY UNATTENDED

Simple to Spectacular

Mackerel seviche with soy

10 to 12 ounces mackerel fillet (preferably skin on), cut on a diagonal into ½-inch-thick slices

3 tablespoons fresh orange juice

3 tablespoons fresh lemon juice

1 tablespoon soy sauce

1 tablespoon sherry vinegar

1 Thai or other small chile, stemmed and minced (about 1 teaspoon)

1 tablespoon peeled and minced ginger

Minced chives or mint for garnish

Coarse salt

Mackerel is a rich-flavored dark fish that can take a lot of seasoning, and here we pile it on.

1 Place the mackerel slices in a wide shallow bowl or deep plate in one layer, skin side up. Combine the orange and lemon juices with the soy, vinegar, and chile; pour this over the fish. Spread the ginger on top, then cover and refrigerate for 1 hour.

2 Just before serving, garnish with the herb and sprinkle with the salt.

MAKES 4 SERVINGS   TIME: ABOUT 1 HOUR, LARGELY UNATTENDED

Salmon seviche with green peppercorns

8 to 10 ounces fresh salmon fillets, sliced as thin as possible

Salt

3 tablespoons canned green peppercorns, drained

¼ cup extra-virgin olive oil

2 tablespoons fresh lime juice, or to taste

¼ cup chopped chives, for garnish

Serve this with thin slices of toast and champagne.

1 Arrange the salmon slices in one layer on four plates. Sprinkle lightly with salt.

2 Mince the peppercorns so fine they are almost pureed. Combine with the olive oil and lime juice. Brush this onto the salmon slices, then garnish with the chives and serve immediately.

MAKES 4 SERVINGS   TIME: 15 MINUTES

Fish and Shellfish

Nearly raw lobster with miso, mustard, and caviar

Two 1-pound lobsters

Salt

1 tablespoon dry mustard

2 teaspoons miso (preferably white)

2 teaspoons rice wine vinegar

1 tablespoon fresh lime juice

2 teaspoons soy sauce

1 teaspoon sugar

2 tablespoons caviar (optional)

¼ cup minced shiso or basil

¼ cup toasted and crumbled nori (optional)

You can make this dish—which is not a true seviche, but close—with shrimp as well, using about 4 per person; it will be less expensive and easier, though not as impressive. When cooking the lobsters, use plenty of water so it doesn't stop boiling when you add the lobsters to the pot.

1 Bring a very large pot of water to a boil and salt it. Add the lobsters and cook for 2 minutes. Drain and immediately plunge them into ice water, or run under cold water until chilled. Shell the lobsters. Cut the tail into thin slices, about ¼ inch thick. Cut the claws into thicker chunks.

2 Divide the lobster pieces evenly among four plates and sprinkle with salt. Combine the mustard, miso, vinegar, lime juice, soy, and sugar and drizzle over the lobster. Let sit at room temperature for 5 minutes.

3 Dot with the caviar, if using, then sprinkle with the shiso or basil and optional nori and serve.

MAKES 4 SERVINGS   TIME: 30 MINUTES

Simple to Spectacular

Raw tuna

TUNA has replaced beef as the most common animal food eaten raw, at least in our experience. Jean-Georges has long featured raw tuna in various forms on his menus; these are the most popular of those recipes.

They begin with the wonderful and simple tuna tartare. Next up are three dishes with Asian flavors—tuna and vegetables in a Vietnamese-style summer roll, a roll in which the wrapper is daikon radish, and a deep-fried spring roll in which the tuna stays nearly raw. Finally, there is the elegant tuna and fennel tart, baked just long enough to take the chill off the tuna.

KEYS TO SUCCESS

Start with spanking-fresh tuna, of course. This is easy to find in good fish markets, but do tell the fishmonger you want sushi-quality tuna.

To cut thin slices, semi-freeze the tuna to firm it up. Fifteen to 30 minutes in the freezer will do the trick (wrap it well in plastic first).

These are appetizers. Although people love raw tuna, no one wants to eat a half-pound of it.

Tuna tartare

1 pound tuna, any dark meat removed, cut into ¼-inch cubes

½ teaspoon Tabasco sauce, or more to taste

Salt to taste

2 tablespoons extra-virgin olive oil

Minced chives for garnish

Don't go too easy on the Tabasco sauce; the flavors here should be quite intense. Serve with crackers, toasted bread, or potato chips.

1 Combine the tuna, Tabasco, salt, and olive oil; taste and adjust the seasoning.

2 Serve immediately, or refrigerate for up to 2 hours. Garnish with chives just before serving.

MAKES 4 SERVINGS   TIME: 15 MINUTES

Simple to Spectacular

Tuna and vegetables in rice paper

1 tablespoon sugar

1 Thai chile, stemmed and minced

2 teaspoons peeled and minced ginger

2 tablespoons fresh lime juice

2 tablespoons nam pla (Thai fish sauce)

4 sheets rice paper, 8 to 10 inches in diameter

1 cup peeled and grated, shredded, or julienned carrots

2 scallions (white part with a little of the green), cut into slivers the long way

1 small (pickling) cucumber, peeled and cut into thin strips or shredded

4 avocado wedges

12 ounces tuna, cut into 8 strips about 4 inches long

About 1 cup rice vermicelli

20 or more mint leaves

About 8 sprigs cilantro

This is a bit of a procedure, but nothing about it is complicated. You can use almost any fish in these Vietnamese-style "summer" rolls—the Thai-Style Grilled Shrimp on Lemongrass Skewers (page 219) is especially wonderful.

Be careful with the rice paper; it should soak for only a few seconds in the water, and it must be rolled immediately thereafter.

1 Combine the first 5 ingredients in a small serving bowl and set aside. Soak the rice noodles in fairly hot water (about 120°F, just too hot to touch) for 10 to 20 minutes, or until soft; drain thoroughly.

2 Meanwhile, get a bowl of hot water (110° to 120°F) and a clean kitchen towel.

3 Put a sheet of rice paper into the water for about 10 seconds, just until soft (don't let it become too soft; it will continue to soften as you work). Lay it on the towel. Lay a quarter each of the carrots, scallions, cucumber, and avocado on the rice paper; finish with the tuna and noodles in the middle. Do not overfill. Top with mint and cilantro; don't skimp on the herbs.

4 Working quickly, roll up the rice paper, keeping it fairly tight. Now roll the rice paper roll up in a sheet of plastic wrap, again making it tight. Fold the last bit of plastic wrap back over itself, forming a tab that will make it easy to unwrap. Twist the ends and repeat to make 3 more rolls. *(The rolls can be refrigerated for up to a day.)*

5 To serve, use a sharp knife to trim the ends of each roll, then cut into 1-inch sections, right through the plastic wrap. Unwrap each section and place, cut side up, on a plate. Serve with the dipping sauce.

MAKES 4 SERVINGS   TIME: 45 MINUTES

Tuna wrapped in daikon

1 daikon radish (about 1 pound)

12 ounces tuna, cut into 16 matchstick pieces, each about
$\frac{1}{2} \times \frac{1}{2} \times 2$ inches

$\frac{1}{2}$ cup radish sprouts or other sprouts of your choosing

$\frac{1}{4}$ cup pickled ginger

2 tablespoons rosemary leaves

$\frac{1}{4}$ cup peeled and roughly chopped ginger

2 small chiles, stemmed and seeded, or 1 dried chile

3 tablespoons soy sauce

2 tablespoons honey

2 tablespoons sherry vinegar

2 tablespoons neutral oil, such as canola or grapeseed

Lovely, and rich in flavors. To get the best slices, you need a big daikon, a large, sweet Asian radish, although you won't use most of it. Substitute cooked lobster, crab, or shrimp for the tuna if you like.

1 Peel the daikon and cut a rectangle $2 \times 2 \times 4$ inches long from it. Cut it the long way into wafer-thin slices, each measuring 2×4 inches; you need 16 of these slices. In turn, lay each one down with a long side facing you; top with a piece of tuna, a few sprouts, and a piece of pickled ginger. Roll up tightly and set aside.

2 To make the dipping sauce, combine the rosemary, chopped ginger, chile, soy, honey, vinegar, and oil in the container of a blender. Blend until smooth, scraping down the sides if necessary.

3 Serve 4 of the rolls to each person, with a little dipping sauce on the side.

MAKES 4 SERVINGS   TIME: 30 MINUTES

Tuna spring rolls with soybean coulis

1 pound edamame (soybeans), fresh or thawed frozen

1 large bunch of cilantro, thick stems removed, washed and left wet

1 tablespoon nam pla (Thai fish sauce)

1 clove garlic, peeled and chopped

2 Thai chiles, stemmed, seeded and chopped

1 tablespoon fresh lime juice

4 large leaves Savoy cabbage

12 ounces tuna, cut into 4 equal rectangles, each about 1 × 3 inches

2 tablespoons pickled ginger

Cracked black pepper

4 spring roll wrappers, each 8 inches square

2 egg yolks, beaten in a bowl

Oil for deep-frying

Salt

Soy sauce

Although these spring rolls are cooked, the tuna remains raw, or essentially so. With the soy and cilantro "pesto" and the double-wrapping, this is a really beautiful presentation, one that has been served at Jean-Georges' Vong restaurants for years.

This makes 4 spring rolls, enough for 4 good appetizers. It is not a difficult recipe to double.

1 Shell the soybeans. Cook them in boiling salted water to cover for about 2 minutes, or until tender; drain. Set aside about ¼ cup for garnish and put the rest in the container of a blender, with the cilantro, nam pla, garlic, chiles, and lime juice. Puree, adding water as necessary (about ¼ cup is usually right) to allow the machine to do its work; taste and add more nam pla or lime juice as necessary. Set aside.

2 Blanch the cabbage leaves in boiling salted water to cover until tender but still a little crunchy, about 3 minutes. Drain and dry on towels; cut out the tough center veins.

3 Lay a rectangle of tuna on each leaf, along with some of the pickled ginger; sprinkle with pepper. Roll up each leaf and dry again. Arrange one of the spring roll wrappers with a point facing you. Put the cabbage-wrapped tuna in the center of the wrapper and fold over the left and right corners so that they overlap in the middle. Brush a bit of the egg yolk over the top half of the wrapper. Fold the bottom half up, then roll up tightly; the yolk will seal the spring roll. *(You can prepare the spring rolls in advance up to this point; refrigerate, well wrapped or in a covered container, for up to 2 hours.)*

4 Heat the oil to 375°F. Deep-fry the spring rolls for a minute or two, just until they are pale gold; the outside will become crisp but the tuna will remain raw. Use a serrated knife to cut each roll into three pieces, and sprinkle the cut side of each piece with a tiny bit of salt and soy sauce (it also looks nice if you drizzle a little soy sauce on each plate). Serve with the soybean coulis, garnished with the reserved soybeans.

MAKES 4 SERVINGS   TIME: 1 HOUR

Tuna and fennel tart

4 rounds puff pastry or other dough, each 5 to 6 inches across

3 tablespoons butter

1 pound fennel, trimmed, some of the feathery fronds reserved, and thinly sliced

Salt and freshly ground black pepper

1 tablespoon fennel seeds

½ cup any stock

10 ounces tuna, very thinly sliced

Coarse salt

Vegetable Vinaigrette (page 359) or other vinaigrette

Like all of the savory tarts on pages 68–70, this can be made with puff pastry, phyllo, or pizza or pie crust dough. All should be prebaked at 400°F for about 10 minutes, or until golden-brown.

You can make this with salmon instead of tuna if you prefer.

1 Preheat the oven to 400°F. Use a nonstick baking sheet or cover any baking sheet with a piece of parchment paper. Arrange the disks of pastry on the sheet, prick them with a fork, and bake until the pastry is nicely browned, 10 to 12 minutes. Transfer to a rack and increase oven temperature to 450°.

2 Meanwhile, put the butter in a skillet and turn the heat to medium-high. When it melts, add the sliced fennel, a big pinch of salt, and several grindings of pepper, along with the fennel seeds. Cook, stirring occasionally, until the fennel begins to soften, about 5 minutes. Add the stock, stir, cover, and cook for about 15 minutes, until the fennel is very soft. Puree in a blender, with the liquid.

3 Put the pastry disks on a parchment-lined or nonstick cookie sheet. Top each with a portion of the fennel puree, then with a few slices of tuna. Bake just long enough to take the chill off the tuna; it should not change color, or even become warm.

4 Sprinkle the tarts with a little coarse salt and top each with a few of the reserved fennel fronds. Serve with the vinaigrette.

MAKES 4 SERVINGS   TIME: 30 MINUTES, WITH PREMADE PASTRY

SHRIMP are the ultimate convenience food. They cook in minutes, contain very little fat, and are loved by almost everyone. And they're at their best when grilled.

There are hundreds of ways to grill shrimp, and our recipes run the gamut. We begin with a simple, fast marinade of thyme and lemon, then go to shrimp grilled on rosemary skewers, served with zucchini. These are followed by shrimp served with apple "ketchup," and then Thai-style shrimp. Finally, we demonstrate the versatility of shrimp and grind them in order to grill them as small meatballs—unusual, foolproof, and delicious.

KEYS TO SUCCESS

Look for Pacific or Gulf white shrimp, which are generally the best. If you buy shrimp that range in the 15 to 20 per pound range, you'll have fewer to peel than if you buy smaller ones.

Buy still-frozen shrimp (most shrimp are frozen before sale) if possible, and thaw in cold water on the day you plan to cook.

The shrimp must be peeled for these recipes, and should be deveined as well.

Use a hot fire for shrimp; there is very little danger of them burning, and they'll brown and cook quickly.

Grilled shrimp with thyme and lemon

1½ pounds medium-to-large shrimp

Salt and freshly ground black pepper

¼ cup extra-virgin olive oil

1 teaspoon fresh thyme leaves

1 lemon, quartered

Basic grilled shrimp—use any herb you like. If you're short on time, skip the marinating, and just dip the shrimp into the olive oil mix and grill.

1 If you want to skewer the shrimp, soak wooden skewers in water for at least 30 minutes before beginning (or use metal skewers). Start a charcoal or gas grill or preheat the broiler; the fire should be hot and the rack 2 to 4 inches from the heat source.

2 Meanwhile, peel the shrimp and devein them. Sprinkle them with salt and pepper and toss them on a plate with the olive oil and thyme. Let sit while the grill heats.

3 Skewer if desired, then grill or broil the shrimp for about 2 minutes per side. Serve with the lemon wedges, spooning the olive oil and thyme that remained behind over them.

MAKES 4 SERVINGS   TIME: 30 MINUTES

Simple to Spectacular

Grilled shrimp and zucchini on rosemary skewers

4 branches rosemary, each about 1 foot long

½ cup extra-virgin olive oil

1 teaspoon minced garlic

1½ pounds medium-to-large shrimp

Salt and freshly ground black pepper

1 lemon

4 small zucchini (about 1 pound total)

Chopped parsley for garnish

Here the fire cannot be quite as hot as in the preceding recipe, or the zucchini will burn. If you cannot find fresh rosemary, use ordinary skewers (soak wooden ones in water for at least 30 minutes before using) and dried rosemary for the marinade.

1 Strip the leaves from all but the top 3 inches of each of the rosemary branches. Reserve about 1 tablespoon of the leaves and mince them.

2 Combine the minced rosemary, olive oil, and garlic on a large platter. Peel the shrimp and devein them. Sprinkle them with salt and pepper and toss them on the platter with the olive oil mixture. Cut the lemon in half through its equator and remove the sections as you would with a grapefruit, discarding any seeds. Tuck this pulp in among the shrimp. Wash and trim the zucchini and cut them into long ¼-inch-thick ribbons. Marinate along with the shrimp.

3 Start a charcoal or gas grill or preheat the broiler; the fire should be moderately hot and the rack about 4 inches from the heat source.

4 When you're ready to grill, skewer the shrimp on the rosemary branches. The zucchini will be grilled separately, flat; if your grill is not large enough to do both zucchini and shrimp at the same time, start with the zucchini, grilling the slices for about 3 minutes per side, or until nicely browned and tender. Grill (or broil) the shrimp for about 2 minutes per side until lightly browned.

5 Serve the shrimp and zucchini with a little of the marinade spooned over them, garnished with a sprinkling of parsley.

MAKES 4 SERVINGS   TIME: 30 MINUTES

Grilled shrimp with apple ketchup

1½ pounds medium-to-large shrimp

Salt and freshly ground black pepper

¼ cup extra-virgin olive oil

2 tablespoons butter

2 tablespoons ketchup

2 tablespoons sherry vinegar

1 large tomato, peeled, seeded, and diced

1 Golden Delicious or Granny Smith apple, peeled, cored, and diced

½ lemon, segmented as you would a grapefruit, seeded, and chopped

2 tablespoons chopped parsley

Tabasco sauce to taste (optional)

The added flavor here comes from the sauce, a Jean-Georges classic that can be made in the time it takes the grill to preheat. It's crunchy and unusual, and, with the addition of Tabasco, can be made quite hot.

1 If you want to skewer the shrimp, soak 8 wooden skewers in water for at least 30 minutes before beginning (or use metal skewers). Start a charcoal or gas grill or preheat the broiler; the fire should be hot and the rack 2 to 4 inches from the heat source.

2 Peel the shrimp and devein them. Sprinkle them with salt and pepper and toss them on a plate with the olive oil. Let sit while the grill preheats and you make the sauce.

3 Place the butter in a small heavy saucepan and turn the heat to medium-high. Cook, swirling and stirring frequently, until the butter is nut-brown. Add the ketchup and cook for 30 seconds. Add the vinegar and cook for 15 seconds. Turn the heat to low and cook for about 2 minutes. Add the tomato and apple and stir; turn the heat as low as possible.

4 Grill or broil the shrimp for about 2 minutes per side until lightly browned. When the shrimp are done, add the lemon, parsley, and Tabasco, if using, to the sauce. Drizzle the sauce over the shrimp and serve.

MAKES 4 SERVINGS   TIME: 30 MINUTES

Thai-style grilled shrimp on lemongrass skewers

24 medium-to-large shrimp

5 stalks lemongrass

2 teaspoons minced chiles

1 teaspoon minced garlic

2 tablespoons plus 2 teaspoons nam pla (Thai fish sauce)

Salt and freshly ground black pepper

2 teaspoons grapeseed oil

2 tablespoons fresh lime juice

2 teaspoons sugar

Chopped mint and/or cilantro leaves for garnish

Grilled on lemongrass stalks, these shrimp have a wonderful flavor that you may consider a revelation if you've ever wondered, "What is that flavor?" when eating Thai food. If you like, you can grill shrimp this way, then use them in place of the tuna in Tuna and Vegetables in Rice Paper (page 207).

1 Peel the shrimp and devein them. Trim and mince 1 of the lemongrass stalks, then toss it and the shrimp in a bowl with 1 teaspoon of the minced chiles, the garlic, 2 teaspoons of the nam pla, a little salt and pepper, and the grapeseed oil.

2 Remove the outer sheath from the remaining lemongrass stalks and trim them so they are about 10 inches long and less than ¼ inch thick at the thin end. Bang each of the stalks several times with the back of a knife. Skewer the shrimp onto them and marinate in the minced lemongrass mixture.

3 Start a charcoal or gas grill or preheat the broiler; the fire should be hot and the rack 2 to 4 inches from the heat source. Combine the remaining 1 teaspoon chiles, 2 tablespoons nam pla, the lime juice, and sugar to make a dipping sauce and set aside.

4 Grill or broil the shrimp for about 2 minutes per side, until lightly browned. Serve immediately, with the dipping sauce.

MAKES 4 SERVINGS   TIME: 30 MINUTES

Grilled shrimp balls with cucumber and yogurt

1¼ pounds shrimp

Salt and cayenne pepper

2 teaspoons paprika

3 tablespoons minced dill

1 English cucumber (about 1 pound)

Extra-virgin olive oil

1 cup plain yogurt

Fresh lemon juice to taste

1 shallot, peeled and minced

2 tablespoons salmon eggs (optional)

The combination of hot—from the spices—and cold—from the yogurt—and the chewy texture of the shrimp balls is surprisingly pleasant. The grill heat should be a little lower here to avoid burning, since the grilling time will be slightly longer.

For true luxury add a tablespoon or two of caviar to the mix, and decorate the plate with salmon eggs—but this isn't necessary.

1   If you want to skewer the shrimp balls, soak 4 wooden skewers in water for at least 30 minutes before beginning (or use metal skewers).

2   Peel the shrimp and devein them. Finely chop the shrimp by hand or in a food processor; be careful not to puree them. Mix with salt and cayenne to taste, 1 teaspoon of the paprika, and 1 tablespoon of the dill. Wet your hands and knead the mixture together, then roll it gently into 1-inch balls. Dust lightly with the remaining 1 teaspoon paprika and refrigerate for at least an hour. (You can make the shrimp balls up to a day in advance.)

3   Start a charcoal or gas grill or preheat the broiler; the fire should not be very hot, and the rack should be at least 4 inches from the heat source. Peel the cucumber, cut it in half the long way, and scoop out the seeds. Thinly slice it into crescents (a mandoline is best for this) and put it in a bowl with salt to taste and a little cayenne.

4   Skewer the shrimp balls, brush them lightly with olive oil, and grill them slowly, about 3 minutes per side, until just cooked through. Drain the cucumbers of any accumulated liquid and stir in the yogurt, lemon juice, shallot, and the remaining 2 tablespoons dill. Put a portion of the salad and the shrimp on each plate. Garnish, if you like, with salmon eggs.

Simple to Spectacular

MAKES 4 SERVINGS   TIME: ABOUT 1¼ HOURS, LARGELY UNATTENDED

Shrimp tempura

THESE are great appetizers, especially if your friends like to watch you cook, because they're best right out of the pan. And with salad greens and a variety of accompanying sauces, they become main courses. They're very, very fast, the actual cooking time being only a minute or two. The differences here are in the sauces, and, to some extent, in the spices added to the shrimp themselves or the batter—but those are minimal.

Tempura batter and technique can be used with almost any seafood—scallops, lobster, fish fillets, or clams, for example—and with many vegetables. Just make sure everything is cut into pieces that will cook through in the extremely short cooking time.

KEYS TO SUCCESS

For best results, use large shrimp here, fewer than 15 or so per pound. They must be peeled, but need not be deveined.

Use ice water—not just cold water—for the batter. It really does make a difference. And don't overmix the batter.

The coating is very light; don't try to gob it on. It is thin, but will become quite crisp when fried.

Shrimp tempura

Neutral oil, such as canola or grapeseed, for deep-frying

½ cup flour, plus more for dredging

2 egg yolks

12 large shrimp, peeled (and deveined if you like)

Salt and freshly ground black pepper

1 lemon, cut into quarters

This is really great served with Ginger Salt (page 339)—or you can use a simple mixture of soy and ginger for a dipping sauce. The lemon, of course, works fine too.

1 Heat the oil in a deep-fryer or deep saucepan; use a thermometer to make sure the temperature stays between 350° and 375°F. Do not prepare the shrimp until the oil is ready.

2 Combine 1 cup water and 1 cup ice; let sit for a minute, then measure 1 cup water from this. Use chopsticks to lightly stir in the flour and egg yolks—the batter should remain *very* lumpy.

3 Dredge the shrimp very lightly in flour, tapping to remove the excess, then dip in the batter and immediately put in the oil—you can cook 4 to 6 shrimp at a time, depending on the size of your fryer. Cook for 1 minute, no more.

4 Sprinkle with salt and pepper and serve immediately, with the lemon wedges.

MAKES 4 SERVINGS   TIME: 20 MINUTES

Shrimp tempura with fast mustard sauce

    1 tablespoon dry mustard, preferably Coleman's

    1 tablespoon sugar

    Neutral oil, such as canola or grapeseed, for deep-frying

    ½ cup flour, plus more for dredging

    2 egg yolks

    12 large shrimp, peeled (and deveined if you like)

    Salt and freshly ground black pepper

This is a great all-purpose mustard sauce; it can be drizzled on any fried or grilled food for instant flavor.

1 Combine the mustard, sugar, and 1 tablespoon water in a small bowl; whisk to blend thoroughly. Let sit while you proceed with the recipe.

2 Heat the oil in a deep-fryer or deep saucepan; use a thermometer to make sure the temperature stays between 350° and 375°F. Do not prepare the shrimp until the oil is ready.

3 Combine 1 cup water and 1 cup ice; let sit for a minute, then measure 1 cup water from this. Use chopsticks to lightly stir in the flour and egg yolks—the batter should remain *very* lumpy.

4 Dredge the shrimp very lightly in flour, tapping to remove the excess, then dip in the batter and immediately put in the oil—you can cook 4 to 6 shrimp at a time, depending on the size of your fryer. Cook for 1 minute, no more.

5 Sprinkle with salt and pepper and serve immediately, with the mustard sauce.

MAKES 4 SERVINGS   TIME: 20 MINUTES

Curried shrimp tempura with cucumber-peanut relish

1 tablespoon honey

½ cup roasted peanuts (salted or unsalted), minced

½ cup seeded and minced cucumber (leave the skin on if it is unwaxed)

Juice of 2 limes

1 tablespoon nam pla (Thai fish sauce), or to taste

1 small chile, fresh or dried, stemmed and minced, or to taste

Neutral oil, such as canola or grapeseed, for deep-frying

½ cup flour, plus more for dredging

1 tablespoon plus 1 teaspoon curry powder

2 egg yolks

12 large shrimp, peeled and deveined

1 tablespoon minced cilantro

1 tablespoon minced mint

Salt and freshly ground black pepper

2 teaspoons roasted sesame or peanut oil

A near-classic Thai dipping sauce, one that is perfect with almost any fried seafood. The final addition of herbs to the sauce and sesame oil to the cooked shrimp makes this nontraditional tempura really special.

1 In a small bowl, combine the honey, nuts, cucumber, lime juice, nam pla, and chile; whisk to blend well, then taste and adjust the seasoning.

2 Heat the oil in a deep-fryer or deep saucepan; use a thermometer to make sure the temperature stays between 350° and 375°F. Do not prepare the shrimp until the oil is ready.

3 Combine 1 cup water and 1 cup ice; let sit for a minute, then measure 1 cup water from this. Use chopsticks to lightly stir in the flour, the 1 tablespoon curry powder, and the egg yolks—the batter should remain *very* lumpy.

4 Sprinkle the shrimp with the remaining 1 teaspoon curry powder. Dredge the shrimp very lightly in flour, tapping to remove excess, dip in the batter, and immediately put in the oil—you can cook 4 to 6 shrimp at a time, depending on the size of your fryer. Cook for 1 minute, no more. Stir the herbs into the dipping sauce, sprinkle the shrimp with salt and pepper, and serve immediately, drizzled with the sesame or peanut oil.

MAKES 4 SERVINGS   TIME: 20 MINUTES

Shrimp tempura salad

1 bunch watercress, thick stems removed, washed and dried

2 cups finely shredded or julienned red cabbage

1½ tablespoons soy sauce, plus a little for drizzling

1 tablespoon hazelnut, walnut, or olive oil

1 tablespoon minced shallots

1 tablespoon sherry vinegar

Freshly ground black pepper

Neutral oil, such as canola or grapeseed, for deep-frying

½ cup flour, plus more for dredging

2 egg yolks

12 large shrimp, peeled (and deveined if you like)

1 tablespoon roughly ground Szechwan peppercorns

Chopped chives for garnish

How to turn tempura into a meal, or at least a main course: Add greens. With the moist dressing and cool, spicy watercress, this dish becomes complex in flavor, yet it is still quite easy to prepare.

1 Toss together the cress and cabbage. Combine the soy sauce, nut or olive oil, shallots, and vinegar; season with pepper but hold back on the salt. Set the dressing aside.

2 Heat the oil in a deep-fryer or deep saucepan; use a thermometer to make sure the temperature stays between 350° and 375°F. Do not prepare the shrimp until the oil is ready.

3 Combine 1 cup water and 1 cup ice; let sit for a minute, then measure 1 cup water from this. Use chopsticks to lightly stir in the flour and egg yolks—the batter should remain *very* lumpy. Combine and beat lightly.

4 Sprinkle the shrimp with a little of the Szechwan pepper. Dredge them very lightly in the flour, tapping to remove the excess, dip them in the batter, and immediately put in the oil—you can cook 4 to 6 shrimp at a time, depending on the size of your fryer. Cook for 1 minute, no more.

5 Toss together the dressing and the vegetables; top with the shrimp. Sprinkle with the remaining Szechwan pepper, a drizzle of soy, and the chives, then serve.

MAKES 4 SERVINGS   TIME: 30 MINUTES

Shrimp tempura with peppered melon and sesame dressing

½ cup haricots verts (or slivered green beans), cut into 1-inch lengths

½ cup carrots cut into matchsticks

2 tablespoons Ricard or other anise-flavored liqueur

2 teaspoons nam pla (Thai fish sauce)

1 tablespoon soy sauce

1 tablespoon fresh lime juice

1 tablespoon red wine vinegar

1 teaspoon ground ginger

2 tablespoons neutral oil, such as canola or grapeseed

1½ tablespoons roasted sesame oil

4 cups mesclun, washed and dried

2 fresh figs, cut into quarters

8 thin slices prosciutto

2 cups thinly sliced cantaloupe, papaya, or honeydew (cut into thin slices about 1 inch long)

½ cup white mushrooms trimmed and slivered (cut into the same thickness as haricots verts)

Neutral oil, such as canola or grapeseed, for deep-frying

½ cup flour, plus more for dredging

2 egg yolks

12 large shrimp, peeled (and deveined if you like)

Salt and freshly ground black pepper

Here, the shrimp are cooked as in the first recipe, but an elaborate salad and dressing are built to support them. Definitely a main course.

1 Bring a pot of water to a boil. Blanch the beans and carrots, just for about 2 minutes—enough to remove their crunch. Drain, plunge into ice water to stop the cooking, and drain again.

2 Whisk together the Ricard or other liqueur, nam pla, soy sauce, lime juice, vinegar, ginger, canola oil, and sesame oil. Set aside. Arrange a portion of the mesclun on each of four plates, along with 2 pieces of fig, 2 slices of prosciutto, a little melon, and some of the blanched vegetables and raw mushrooms; sprinkle with plenty of black pepper.

3 Heat the frying oil in a deep-fryer or deep saucepan; use a thermometer to make sure the temperature stays between 350° and 375°F. Do not prepare the shrimp until the oil is ready.

4 Combine 1 cup water and 1 cup ice; let sit for a minute, then measure 1 cup water from this. Use chopsticks to lightly stir in the flour and egg yolks—the batter should remain *very* lumpy. Combine and beat lightly.

5 Dredge the shrimp very lightly in flour, tapping to remove excess, then dip in the batter and immediately put in the oil—you can cook 4 to 6 shrimp at a time, depending on the size of your fryer. Cook for 1 minute, no more.

6 Sprinkle the shrimp with salt and pepper and add them to the prepared plates. Drizzle the dressing over all and serve.

MAKES 4 SERVINGS   TIME: 40 MINUTES

Poached lobster

SIMPLY poached lobster is one of the greatest of seafood pleasures, and we believe that with our simplest technique we've made it not only foolproof but perhaps even humane. In any case, it's a great technique to build on—everyone eventually gets tired of plain boiled lobster—and we do so, with a flavorful butter sauce, a fragrant sweet-wine sauce, and two powerful sauces, one based on anchovies, the other on tamarind. The briny flavor of lobster not only stands up to these sauces but seems made for them as well.

KEYS TO SUCCESS

We've found that by starting the lobster in cold water, you lull it to sleep as the water warms, avoiding the unpleasantness of it kicking and screaming as you plunge it into hot water. If you would like to use this method for parboiling, as in the recipes on pages 248 and 250, put the lobsters in cold water, bring it to a boil, and turn off the heat; remove the lobsters 1 minute later.

These recipes are for 1½-pound lobsters; for larger lobsters (which are just as tender and flavorful), increase the cooking time proportionally. A 2-pound lobster, for example, needs to sit in the hot water for 10 minutes to cook, or 3 or 4 to parboil.

Lobster bodies make great stock. If you are not using them in the recipe (as in the fourth and fifth recipes here), save the cooking water and add the bodies, shells, and any remaining meat to it after you finish eating—after just 15 minutes of simmering you'll have a pungent broth that can be frozen and is perfect for risotto, soups, and many other uses.

Poached lobster

Four 1½-pound lobsters

A couple of handfuls of fresh seaweed (optional)

Salt, if you have no seaweed

The simplest way to cook a lobster we know. Yes, the seaweed makes a difference and a fishmonger may have some around (it's sometimes used for packing). If serving the lobster hot, eat it with lemon wedges or melted butter. If serving cold, eat it with mayonnaise (pages 362–366), vinaigrette (pages 356–360), or lemon wedges.

1 Place the lobsters in a large pot and cover with water, then the seaweed, if using, or add a handful of salt. Cover and turn the heat to high.

2 Bring to a boil, turn off the heat, and let sit for 5 minutes. Serve hot, or chill and serve cold.

MAKES 4 SERVINGS   TIME: 15 MINUTES

Poached lobster in court bouillon with butter sauce

1 onion, peeled and roughly chopped

1 carrot, peeled and roughly chopped

1 stalk celery, roughly chopped

1 branch thyme

1 large clove garlic, peeled and cut in half

1 bay leaf

1 cup dry white wine

Four 1½-pound lobsters

8 tablespoons (1 stick) butter

2 tablespoons fresh lemon juice, or to taste

Salt and cayenne pepper

½ cup chopped chervil, parsley, and/or chives

Here, the lobsters are cooked in a fast, flavorful broth, then finished with a creamy, spicy butter sauce. It's a huge step above the first recipe in flavor, but not that much more work.

1 Bring the first 7 ingredients to a boil in a large pot, then turn the heat to medium-low and simmer for 5 minutes. Add 2 cups water and the lobsters, cover, and cook over medium-high heat for 8 to 10 minutes, or until the lobsters are bright red.

2 Remove the lobsters and keep warm in a low oven. Measure out and strain 2 cups of the cooking liquid, then place it in a wide saucepan and reduce over high heat to about ½ cup. Turn the heat to low and stir in the butter, a little bit at a time; season with the lemon juice and salt and cayenne.

3 Crack the shells and remove the lobster meat, trying to keep the pieces large. Turn in the sauce to warm and coat, then garnish with the herbs and serve.

MAKES 4 SERVINGS   TIME: 40 MINUTES

Poached lobster in sweet coriander-orange broth

2 tablespoons butter

1 medium onion, peeled and chopped

1 stalk celery, peeled and chopped

1 carrot, peeled and chopped

2 large shallots, peeled and chopped

2 cloves garlic, peeled and smashed

2 teaspoons fenugreek seeds

1 tablespoon coriander seeds

Zest of 1 orange, removed in strips

2 cups slightly sweet white wine, such as a German Auslese or a French Coteaux du Layon

2 cups chicken, fish, or vegetable stock or lobster-cooking water (see headnote)

Salt and cayenne pepper

Four 1½-pound lobsters

2 tablespoons fresh lemon juice, or to taste

If you like, garnish this complex-flavored dish with a variety of parboiled vegetables, like carrots, turnips, and fennel. And serve it with plenty of white rice; you will want an excuse to eat all of the sauce.

If you want to use lobster-cooking liquid in place of the stock, start by *steaming* the lobsters, following the timing given below but using only 2 to 3 inches of boiling water in the pot. After removing the lobsters, reduce that cooking liquid over high heat until you have 2 cups.

1   Place 1 tablespoon of the butter in a wide skillet or saucepan and turn the heat to medium. Add the onion, celery, carrot, shallots, garlic, fenugreek, coriander, and orange zest and cook, stirring, until the vegetables soften, 5 to 10 minutes. Add the wine, turn the heat to high, and reduce the mixture until just about ½ cup liquid remains. Add the stock and reduce again until about 1 cup liquid remains. Strain, pressing on the solids to extract as much liquid as possible, and set aside. (*You can do this a day in advance if you like; refrigerate.*)

2   Bring a large pot of water to boil and salt it well. Poach the lobsters for 2 minutes, then remove. Pull off the claws (use a towel to prevent burning yourself) and return them to the water for 4 minutes more. Run the tails and bodies under cold water; when the claws are done, run them under cold water as well.

3 Remove the meat from the claws and tails (along with any roe, which will be black); the tails will still be pretty raw, which is how you want them. Cut into serving pieces.

4 Rewarm the sauce, add the lobster pieces to it, and turn until cooked through and hot, 2 to 4 minutes. Transfer the lobster to a warm plate and stir the remaining 1 tablespoon butter into the sauce. Add the lemon juice and salt and cayenne to taste. Spoon over the lobster and serve.

MAKES 4 SERVINGS   TIME: 45 MINUTES

Butter-poached lobster with anchovy broth

1 tablespoon coriander seeds

¼ vanilla bean, chopped

2 teaspoons mace pieces, or 1 teaspoon ground mace

1 clove

½ cinnamon stick or ½ teaspoon ground cinnamon

¼ teaspoon red pepper flakes

1 tablespoon neutral oil, such as canola or grapeseed

3 tablespoons butter

2 onions, peeled and chopped

1 stalk celery, peeled and chopped

1 leek, trimmed, well washed, and chopped

1 carrot, peeled and chopped

Four 1½-pound lobsters

2 minced anchovies

⅓ cup fresh lime juice

Salt and cayenne pepper

This and the following dish make good use of the lobster bodies, which contain tons of flavor and are too often wasted. Serve this sweet-and-salty dish with any good chutney or fruit relish.

1 Combine the coriander, vanilla, mace pieces, clove, cinnamon stick, and red pepper flakes in a small skillet and toast over medium heat, shaking occasionally, until fragrant, about 2 minutes. Grind in a coffee grinder or spice mill, add preground spices if you're using them, and set aside.

2 Bring a large pot of water to a boil. Meanwhile, place the oil and 1 tablespoon of the butter in a large saucepan and turn the heat to medium. Add half the onions, along with the celery, leek, and carrot, and cook, stirring occasionally, until the vegetables soften, 5 to 10 minutes.

3 Meanwhile, poach the lobsters for 2 minutes in the boiling water, then remove. Pull off the claws (use a towel to prevent burning yourself) and return them to the water for 4 minutes more. Run the tails and bodies under cold water; when the claws are done, run them under cold water as well.

4 Roughly chop the lobster bodies and add them to the vegetables. Cook, stirring, for another 5 minutes, then add 4 cups water. Bring to a boil, then adjust the heat and simmer for 30 minutes. Strain the stock, pressing to extract as much liquid as possible.

5 Heat the remaining 2 tablespoons butter in a skillet and add the remaining onions, along with the anchovies. Cook until the onions are tender, 5 to 10 minutes, then stir in 1 tablespoon of the spice mix, along with the lime juice. Add the strained stock and cook for another 20 minutes. Strain again, then season with salt and cayenne.

6 Crack the lobster shells and remove the meat from the claws and tails (along with any roe, which will be black); the tails will still be pretty raw, which is how you want them. Cut into serving pieces. Measure the broth: You want about 2 cups—if there is much more, reduce it over high heat; if not, just warm it. Heat the lobster in the broth, 2 to 4 minutes. Place the lobster in four bowls, add the broth, and serve.

MAKES 4 SERVINGS   TIME: 1 HOUR

Poached lobster with tamarind sauce

1 tablespoon neutral oil, such as canola or grapeseed

3 tablespoons butter

1 onion, peeled and chopped

1 stalk celery, chopped

1 leek, trimmed, well washed, and chopped

1 carrot, peeled and chopped

Four 1½-pound lobsters

1 bay leaf

3 branches thyme

2 cloves garlic, peeled and smashed

¼ cup tomato paste

1 cup tamarind puree (see Note)

1 tablespoon cumin seeds

1 tablespoon coriander seeds

1 small dried chile, stemmed

¼ cup roasted peanuts (preferably unsalted, but don't worry about it)

2 tablespoons peeled and chopped ginger

½ cup canned unsweetened coconut milk

Salt

This version has more broth than the previous one; it's almost a stew. To make the dish even fancier, garnish it with lightly steamed or sautéed scallions and shiitake mushrooms.

1 Bring a large pot of water to a boil. Meanwhile, place the oil and 1 tablespoon of the butter in a large saucepan and turn the heat to medium. Add the onion, celery, leek, and carrot and cook, stirring occasionally, until the vegetables soften, 5 to 10 minutes.

2 Meanwhile, poach the lobsters in the boiling water for 2 minutes, then remove. Pull off the claws (use a towel to prevent burning yourself) and return them to the water for 4 minutes more. Run the tails and bodies under cold water; when the claws are done, run them under cold water as well.

3 Roughly chop the lobster bodies and add them to the vegetables. Cook, stirring, for another 5 minutes, then add the bay leaf, thyme, garlic, and tomato paste. Cook, stirring, for 2 more minutes, then add 4 cups water. Bring to a boil, then adjust the heat and simmer for 30 minutes.

4 Crack the lobster shells and remove the meat from the claws and tails (along with any roe, which will be black); the tails will still be pretty raw, which is how you want them. Cut into serving pieces.

5 Combine the tamarind puree, cumin, coriander, chile, peanuts, ginger, and coconut milk in a blender or food processor and process to a paste. When the stock has simmered for 30 minutes, stir this into it; cook for another 20 minutes, or until the mixture is quite thick. Strain, pressing on the solids to extract as much liquid as possible.

6 Measure the sauce: You want about 2 cups; if there is much more, reduce it over high heat; if not, just warm it. Heat the lobster in the sauce, 2 to 4 minutes. Place the lobster in four bowls. Add the remaining 2 tablespoons butter to the sauce, along with salt to taste. Spoon over the lobster and serve.

Note *To make tamarind puree:* Combine 2 cups tamarind pulp in a saucepan with 1 cup water and turn the heat to medium. Cook, whisking lightly, breaking up the lumps, and adding more water whenever the mixture becomes dry, until you've added a total of about 2 cups. The process will take about 10 minutes; the result should still be quite thick, but fairly smooth. Strain, then measure out 1 cup for this recipe. The remainder will keep, refrigerated, for several weeks.

MAKES 4 SERVINGS   TIME: 1½ HOURS, SOMEWHAT UNATTENDED

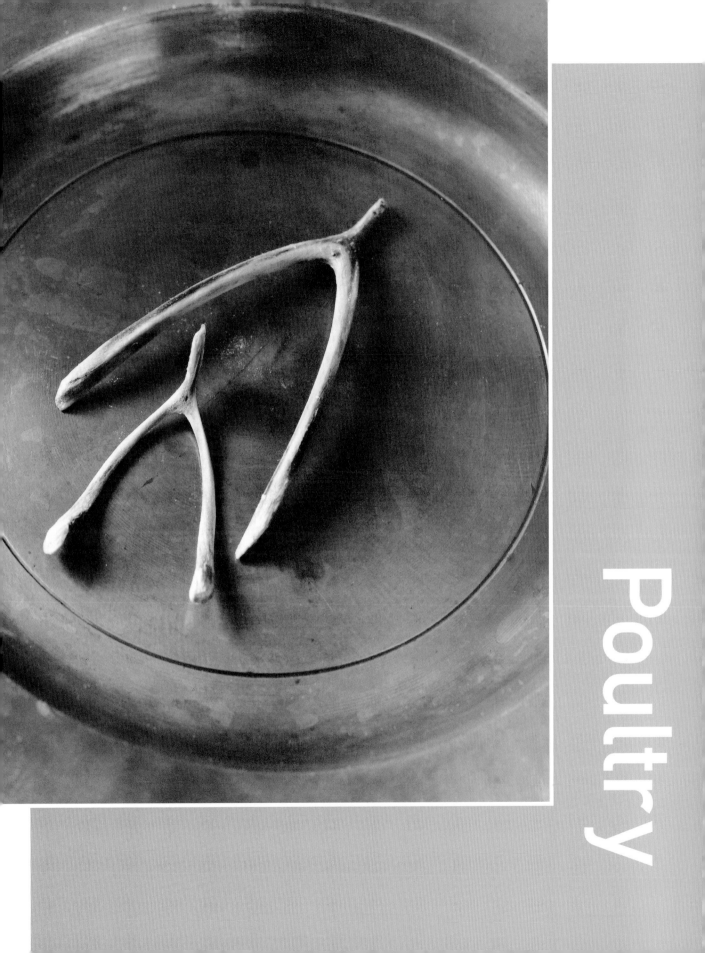

Poultry

Roast chicken

IT'S often said that the sign of a good cook is his or her skill at roasting a chicken, and certainly this basic task is not as easy as it might seem. On the other hand, it's not that difficult once you know a few "secrets," chief among them being high oven heat.

If you have a great chicken—which is not easy to come by—the process is even easier: Take some salt and pepper, roast the chicken, and serve it. But since we have trouble finding a great chicken, we're assuming you will too. So we take a couple of extra measures to make sure that the roasted bird tastes great: We brine it lightly beforehand, and we cook it with plenty of seasonings, including butter. This avoids both mushy texture and predictable blandness.

Our first chicken features garlic, butter, and thyme, a classic French combination; next, we go to a soy glaze, which makes the skin dark and incredibly crisp; and from there, we go to a traditional French peasant preparation, using chicken livers and hearts for depth of flavor; a contemporary combination of olives and vanilla; and, finally, the classic chicken with truffles, which cannot be bettered.

KEYS TO SUCCESS

We brine these birds for 1 to 2 hours; you can skip this step if you like, especially if you're using kosher chickens, which have already been salted.

We brown the birds on top of the stove before putting them in the oven. This step, which guarantees a perfectly browned bird—it's browned before you start roasting it, really—can also be skipped, but you'll have to watch the bird a little more carefully while it's roasting, adjusting the heat so that it browns evenly.

Let the chicken rest for about 5 minutes before carving so its juices retreat back into the meat.

Roast chicken with butter and thyme

½ cup kosher salt (or ¼ cup regular salt), plus more to taste

¼ cup sugar

One 3-pound chicken

3 heads garlic, cut in half

10 sprigs thyme

10 tablespoons (1¼ sticks) butter, softened

Freshly ground black pepper

2 tablespoons neutral oil, such as canola or grapeseed

A fast stuffing ensures a moist, flavorful bird, with enough pan juices to grace potatoes, rice, or bread.

1 Combine the ½ cup salt and the sugar in a large container with 4 cups cold water and stir to dissolve. Add the chicken and soak for 1 to 2 hours at room temperature (if the weather is hot, refrigerate).

2 Preheat the oven to 450°F. Drain the chicken and pat dry. Make a ball of the garlic, thyme, 8 tablespoons (1 stick) of the butter, and salt and pepper to taste and insert it into the chicken's cavity. Season the chicken with salt and pepper and truss it.

3 Combine the remaining 2 tablespoons butter and the oil in a large ovenproof skillet or roasting pan and turn the heat to medium-high. When the butter melts, brown the chicken on both sides, coloring one leg and half the breast at a time; move the chicken occasionally to prevent sticking, and regulate the heat so the skin browns but does not burn—it will take about 5 minutes per side. Put the chicken on its back and put the pan in the oven.

4 Roast for 35 to 45 minutes, basting occasionally with the pan juices, until the bird is nicely browned and an instant-read thermometer inserted into its thigh reads 155°F. Remove the bird from the oven, let rest for a couple of minutes, and carve; serve with the pan juices.

MAKES 4 SERVINGS   TIME: 2 TO 3 HOURS, LARGELY UNATTENDED

Poultry

Roast chicken with ginger and soy-whiskey glaze

½ cup kosher salt (or ¼ cup regular salt), plus more to taste

1¼ cups sugar

One 3-pound chicken

1 cup roughly chopped ginger (don't bother to peel)

Freshly ground black pepper

1 cup soy sauce

¼ cup rye, Scotch, or other whiskey

4 cloves garlic, peeled and smashed

¼ cup peanut or neutral oil, such as canola or grapeseed

Reminiscent of Peking duck, this crisp-skinned bird gives great reward for little effort.

1 Combine the ½ cup salt and ¼ cup of the sugar in a large container with 4 cups cold water and stir to dissolve. Add the chicken and soak for 1 to 2 hours at room temperature (if the weather is hot, refrigerate).

2 Preheat the oven to 450°F. Drain the chicken and pat dry. Stuff about ¾ cup of the ginger into the chicken's cavity, season the bird with salt and pepper, and truss it. Combine the remaining ginger with the soy sauce, whiskey, the remaining 1 cup sugar, and the garlic in a saucepan and bring to a boil; simmer while you brown the chicken, then strain.

3 Heat the oil in a large ovenproof skillet or roasting pan and turn the heat to medium-high. When the oil is hot, brown the chicken on both sides, coloring one leg and half the breast at a time; move the chicken occasionally to prevent sticking, and regulate the heat so the skin browns but does not burn—it will take about 5 minutes per side. Put the chicken on its back, baste it with the soy mixture, and put the pan in the oven.

4 Roast for 35 to 45 minutes, basting every 10 minutes with the soy glaze, until the bird is dark brown and an instant-read thermometer inserted into its thigh reads 155°F. Remove the bird from the oven, let rest for a couple of minutes, and carve; serve with the pan juices.

Simple to Spectacular

MAKES 4 SERVINGS   TIME: 2 TO 3 HOURS, LARGELY UNATTENDED

Roast chicken with rôti d'Abat

½ cup kosher salt (¼ cup regular salt), plus more to taste

¼ cup sugar

One 3-pound chicken

1 head garlic, cut in half

5 sprigs thyme

Freshly ground black pepper

6 tablespoons butter

2 tablespoons neutral oil, such as canola or grapeseed

1 large onion, peeled and chopped

1 large or 2 medium carrots, peeled and chopped

2 stalks celery, chopped

3 chicken livers

3 chicken hearts (or another liver)

2 tablespoons chopped shallots

2 tablespoons parsley leaves

1 egg

¼ cup milk

4 slices sourdough or other good white bread

1 cup One-Hour Chicken Stock (page 3), or any chicken stock

Here, the feature is not so much the chicken, but the very special bread accompaniment, savory French toasts coated with a rich, fragrant combination of chicken livers and seasonings, then sautéed in butter.

1 Combine the ½ cup salt and the sugar in a large container with 4 cups cold water and stir to dissolve. Add the chicken and soak for 1 to 2 hours at room temperature (if the weather is hot, refrigerate).

2 Preheat the oven to 450°F. Drain the chicken and pat dry. Put the garlic and thyme in the chicken's cavity, season the bird with salt and pepper, and truss it.

3 Combine 2 tablespoons of the butter with the oil in a large skillet and turn the heat to medium-high. When the butter melts, brown the chicken on both sides, coloring one leg and half the breast at a time; move the chicken occasionally to prevent sticking, and regulate the heat so the skin browns but does not burn— it will take about 5 minutes per side.

4 Make a bed of the onion, carrots, and celery in a roasting pan; dot with 2 tablespoons of the butter, sprinkle with salt and pepper, and put in the chicken. Put the pan in the oven.

5   Roast for 35 to 45 minutes, basting occasionally with the pan juices, until the bird is nicely browned and an instant-read thermometer inserted into its thigh reads 155°F.

6   While the bird is roasting, finely chop together the livers and hearts with the shallots and parsley; season well with salt and pepper. Beat together the egg and milk and soak the bread in this mixture for a couple of minutes. Spread the liver mixture on one side of each bread slice.

7   Melt 1 tablespoon of the remaining butter in a nonstick skillet over medium heat, add the bread, coated side down, and carefully sauté until browned; turn and lightly brown the uncoated side. Keep warm until the chicken is done.

8   When the chicken is cooked, remove it from the oven and set it on a cutting board. Put the roasting pan on the stove over high heat and stir in the stock; cook, stirring and scraping, for a couple of minutes, until the stock is slightly reduced and the vegetables and pan juices incorporated. Stir in the remaining 1 tablespoon butter until melted.

9   Carve the chicken and serve it with the toasts and sauce.

MAKES 4 SERVINGS   TIME: 2 TO 3 HOURS, LARGELY UNATTENDED

Roast chicken with olive and vanilla sauce

½ cup kosher salt (or ¼ cup regular salt), plus more to taste

¼ cup sugar

One 3-pound chicken

1 head garlic, cut in half

5 sprigs thyme

4 tablespoons butter

2 tablespoons extra-virgin olive oil

Freshly ground black pepper

3 vanilla beans

1 cup pitted black olives, such as Kalamata or Niçoise, finely chopped or pureed

1 teaspoon cumin

1 teaspoon cardamom

1 teaspoon coriander

½ cup any stock, or a little more

1 cup plain yogurt

½ cup mint leaves

This olive and vanilla sauce is dense, rich, and exotic. The yogurt-cucumber sauce, which takes just a couple of minutes to make, coolly offsets it in flavor, color, and temperature. A winning combination—and the vanilla-roasted chicken is pretty special too.

1 Combine the ½ cup salt and the sugar in a large container with 4 cups cold water and stir to dissolve. Add the chicken and soak for 1 to 2 hours at room temperature (if the weather is hot, refrigerate).

2 Preheat the oven to 450°F. Drain the chicken and pat dry. Put the garlic, thyme, and 2 tablespoons of the butter in the chicken's cavity, season the bird with salt and pepper, and truss it.

3 Combine the remaining 2 tablespoons butter with the oil in a large ovenproof skillet or roasting pan and turn the heat to medium-high. When the butter melts, brown the chicken on both sides, coloring one leg and half the breast at a time; move the chicken occasionally to prevent sticking, and regulate the heat so the skin browns but does not burn—it will take about 5 minutes per side. Split one of the vanilla beans; scrape out the seeds and spread them on the chicken's breast, and insert the pod into the cavity. Put the chicken on its back and put the pan in the oven.

245

4 Roast for 35 to 45 minutes, basting occasionally with the pan juices, until the bird is nicely browned and an instant-read thermometer inserted into its thigh reads 155°F.

5 Meanwhile, to make the olive sauce, combine the olives, cumin, cardamom, coriander, and stock in a small saucepan. Split the remaining 2 vanilla beans and add them; bring to a boil, turn off the heat, and keep warm; if the sauce becomes too thick, thin with a little more stock. Just before serving, season to taste.

6 To make the yogurt sauce, combine the yogurt and mint leaves in a blender; puree. Season with salt and pepper.

7 When the chicken is done, remove it from the oven, let rest for a couple of minutes, and carve; serve with the two sauces.

MAKES 4 SERVINGS   TIME: 2 TO 3 HOURS, LARGELY UNATTENDED

Simple to Spectacular

Roast chicken with truffles

½ cup kosher salt (or ¼ cup regular salt), plus more to taste

¼ cup sugar

One 3-pound chicken

1 head garlic, cut in half

5 sprigs thyme

7 tablespoons butter

1 black truffle, thinly sliced

Freshly ground black pepper

2 tablespoons neutral oil, such as canola or grapeseed

2 pounds potatoes, peeled and cut into 1-inch chunks

2 tablespoons canned truffle juice (optional)

3 tablespoons Jus Rôti (page 4) or chicken stock

One of the grandest dishes you can make without working like crazy. It's really quite simple, once you assemble the ingredients.

That, of course, is the hard part, and it's worth knowing that you can make a reasonable facsimile of this by substituting mushrooms for the truffle and chicken stock for the Jus Rôti.

1 Combine the ½ cup salt and the sugar in a large container with 4 cups cold water and stir to dissolve. Add the chicken and soak for 1 to 2 hours at room temperature (if the weather is hot, refrigerate).

2 Preheat the oven to 450°F. Drain the chicken and pat dry. Put the garlic, thyme, and 2 tablespoons of the butter in the chicken's cavity. Use your fingers to loosen the chicken's skin all over and slide the truffle slices between the skin and meat all over the bird. Season the chicken with salt and pepper and truss it.

3   Combine the oil and 2 tablespoons of the butter in a large skillet and turn the heat to medium-high. When the butter melts, brown the chicken on both sides, coloring one leg and half the breast at a time; move the chicken occasionally to prevent sticking, and regulate the heat so the skin browns but does not burn—it will take about 5 minutes per side.

4   Transfer the chicken to a clean skillet or roasting pan and surround with the potatoes; dot the potatoes with the remaining 3 tablespoons butter. Roast for 35 to 45 minutes, basting occasionally with the pan juices, until the bird is nicely browned and an instant-read thermometer inserted into its thigh reads 155°F.

5   Remove the bird from the oven, transfer it to a cutting board, and let it rest while you finish the sauce. Transfer the potatoes to a platter and keep warm. Drain the roasting pan of all but a little of the fat; reserve the fat. Put the pan on the stove over high heat, then stir in the truffle juice, if using, and jus rôti; scrape up any stuck bits from the pan's bottom, incorporating them into the sauce. Stir in a tablespoon or two of the reserved fat.

6   Carve the chicken and put on the platter with the potatoes, then spoon the sauce over all.

MAKES 4 SERVINGS   TIME: 2 TO 3 HOURS, LARGELY UNATTENDED

Simple to Spectacular

Sautéed and roasted chicken

THESE chicken preparations combine two techniques, sautéing and roasting. We use the top of the stove for browning and the oven to finish the cooking. But because we use high heat throughout—you must keep the oven temperature at 500°F for this technique to work—the chicken develops a dark, crisp crust, stays moist within, and cooks very quickly. In fact, the basic technique here will allow you to cook a 3-pound chicken in less than half an hour (larger birds, of course, will require more time)—and the results will be gorgeous.

The procedure allows plenty of opportunities to integrate different flavors and ingredients, at the beginning, middle, or end. And the basic recipe can be varied in more ways than you can imagine.

KEYS TO SUCCESS

It may go without saying, but the first rule here is to use a good chicken—a kosher chicken or a reliable free-range or "natural" chicken is best.

The timing is fairly precise. You must remove the white meat from the oven as soon as it is done, and set it aside while the leg pieces finish cooking. There is no trick to this, as you'll see, but it's the only way to prevent the white meat from overcooking or avoid serving the dark meat underdone.

We strongly suggest that you learn to cut up whole chickens for sautéing, for a couple of reasons. One, it's less expensive. Two, our method of cutting the chicken gives you evenly sized pieces that cook at a more uniform rate than those cut up by supermarket butchers. And, three, you can save the scraps for stock—a good habit to get into.

Sautéed and roasted chicken with natural juices

One 3-pound chicken, cut into 8 pieces for sautéing

Salt and freshly ground black pepper

2 tablespoons extra-virgin olive oil

2 tablespoons butter (or use all olive oil if you prefer)

Start with a good chicken and use this technique, and you will be amazed at the results—even though this dish has very few ingredients. With bread and salad, a complete and simple meal; with herbed rice and a cooked vegetable, it's a little more elaborate but still easy enough to prepare on a weeknight.

1 Set an oven rack as low in the oven as possible (if you can roast on the floor of the oven, so much the better) and preheat the oven to 500°F. Place a large oven-proof skillet or casserole over high heat for about 2 minutes. Meanwhile, season the chicken all over with salt and pepper.

2 Add the olive oil and 1 tablespoon of the butter to the skillet. When the butter melts, add the chicken, skin side down. Cook, undisturbed, until the chicken is nicely browned, about 5 minutes. Turn the chicken and transfer the pan to the oven.

3 After 10 minutes, check the breast and wing pieces for doneness; when cooked, the meat will be firm and its juices will run clear, or nearly so, when pierced with a thin-bladed knife. Transfer the pieces to a platter and return the dark meat to the oven. Roast for 5 to 10 minutes more, until the thigh meat is firm and its juices run clear. Transfer the leg-thigh pieces to the platter.

4 Pour out and discard almost all of the pan juices, and place the skillet over high heat on top of the stove. Add 1 cup water and cook, stirring and scraping, for about 5 minutes, or until the liquid is reduced by about half and thickened somewhat. Turn the heat to medium-low and add the remaining 1 tablespoon butter. Cook, stirring, for a minute, then add the chicken pieces and turn in the sauce to reheat. Serve immediately.

MAKES 4 SERVINGS   TIME: 30 MINUTES

Simple to Spectacular

Poulet au vinaigre (chicken with vinegar)

One 3-pound chicken, cut into 8 pieces for sautéing

Salt and freshly ground black pepper

2 tablespoons extra-virgin olive oil

2 tablespoons butter (or use all olive oil if you prefer)

8 cloves garlic, lightly crushed (don't bother to peel them)

6 to 8 sprigs thyme

½ cup sherry vinegar or other good vinegar

Not much more difficult than the preceding recipe, but markedly more complex in flavor. This is a peasant dish that was popularized by the famous French chef Paul Bocuse. We like sherry vinegar here, but you can use any good vinegar you like. Serve with bread, and be sure to eat the garlic.

1 Set an oven rack as low in the oven as possible (if you can roast on the oven floor, so much the better) and preheat the oven to 500°F. Place a large oven-proof skillet or casserole over high heat for about 2 minutes. Meanwhile, season the chicken with salt and pepper. Add the olive oil and 1 tablespoon of the butter to the skillet. When the butter melts, add the chicken, skin side down, along with the garlic and thyme. Cook, undisturbed, until the chicken is nicely browned, about 5 minutes. Turn the chicken and transfer the pan to the oven.

2 After 10 minutes, check the breast and wing pieces for doneness; when cooked, the meat will be firm and its juices will run clear, or nearly so, when pierced with a thin-bladed knife. Transfer the pieces to a platter and return the dark meat to the oven. Roast for 5 to 10 minutes more, until the thigh meat is firm and its juices run clear. Transfer the leg-thigh pieces to the platter, along with the garlic and thyme. Remove the skins from the garlic and discard.

3 Pour out almost all of the pan juices and place the skillet over high heat. Add the vinegar and cook, stirring and scraping, for about 1 minute, or until the powerful vinegar smell has subsided a bit. Add 1 cup water and cook, stirring, until the liquid is reduced by about half and thickened somewhat. Turn the heat to medium-low and add the remaining 1 tablespoon butter. Cook, stirring, for a minute, then add the chicken pieces and turn in the sauce to reheat. Serve immediately.

MAKES 4 SERVINGS   TIME: 30 MINUTES

Sautéed and roasted chicken with vegetables and lime

One 3-pound chicken, cut into 8 pieces for sautéing

Salt and freshly ground black pepper

2 tablespoons peanut or neutral oil, such as canola or grapeseed

2 cloves garlic, lightly crushed (don't bother to peel them)

5 limes

8 ounces thick asparagus spears, trimmed, peeled, and cut into 2-inch lengths

4 ounces shiitake mushrooms, stems removed, washed, and roughly chopped

2 tablespoons julienned ginger

¼ cup soy sauce

¼ cup chopped cilantro, for garnish

This Asian-flavored dish differs from the preceding two not only in flavor but in preparation time (it's also lower in fat). Both the julienne of ginger and the segmented lime are important components that take a little bit of work. Once those are done, though, the recipe proceeds quickly. Serve with Steamed Sticky Rice (page 103) or other rice.

1 Set an oven rack as low in the oven as possible (if you can roast on the floor of the oven, so much the better) and preheat the oven to 500°F. Place a large ovenproof skillet or casserole over high heat for about 2 minutes. Meanwhile, season the chicken all over with salt and pepper.

2 Add the oil to the skillet. When it is hot, add the chicken, skin side down, along with the garlic. Cook, undisturbed, until the chicken is nicely browned, about 5 minutes. Turn the chicken and transfer the pan to the oven.

3 While the chicken is cooking, juice 3 of the limes. Peel the other 2 limes and segment them as you would a grapefruit.

Simple to Spectacular

4 After 10 minutes, check the breast and wing pieces for doneness; when cooked, the meat will be firm and its juices will run clear, or nearly so, when pierced with a thin-bladed knife. Transfer the pieces to a platter, and add the asparagus, mushrooms, and ginger to the dark meat; stir and return to the oven. Roast for 10 minutes more, stirring once or twice, until the asparagus and mushrooms are tender and chicken is done.

5 Remove the pan from the oven; remove the skins from the garlic and discard. Return the breast meat to the skillet and place on top of the stove over medium-high heat. Add the soy sauce and ½ cup water to the pan and stir; cook for 1 minute, or until bubbly. Add the lime juice and cook for another minute. Add the lime pieces and stir; garnish with the cilantro and serve.

MAKES 4 SERVINGS   TIME: 40 MINUTES

Alsatian chicken with creamy Riesling-onion sauce

One 3-pound chicken, cut into 8 pieces for sautéing

Salt and freshly ground black pepper

2 tablespoons extra-virgin olive oil

2 tablespoons butter (or use all olive oil if you prefer)

2 large onions (about 1½ pounds), peeled and roughly chopped

15 cloves garlic, peeled and roughly chopped

2 cups Riesling or other off-dry white wine

2 sprigs rosemary

1 cup One-Hour Chicken Stock (page 3) or any chicken stock

¼ cup minced parsley, for garnish

Here, you start by browning the chicken, as in the preceding recipes, but ultimately bury it in a moist mixture of onions, garlic, and not-too-dry white wine. When the chicken is done, you puree the onion mixture, which becomes a supremely creamy sauce that contains no cream. Serve with Steamed Sticky Rice (page 103) or Spaetzle with Butter (page 95).

1 Set an oven rack as low in the oven as possible (if you can roast on the floor of the oven, so much the better) and preheat the oven to 500°F. Place a large deep ovenproof casserole over high heat for about 2 minutes. Meanwhile, season the chicken all over with salt and pepper.

2 Add the olive oil and 1 tablespoon of the butter to the pot. When the butter melts, add the chicken, skin side down. Cook, undisturbed, until the chicken is nicely browned, about 5 minutes. Remove the chicken, turn the heat to medium, and add the onions and garlic. Cook, stirring, just until the onions become translucent, 5 to 10 minutes.

3 Add all but a tablespoon of the wine and the rosemary and bring to a boil. Return the chicken to the pot and bury it in the onions. Place in the oven.

4   After 10 minutes, check the breast and wing pieces for doneness; when cooked, the meat will be firm and its juices will run clear, or nearly so, when pierced with a thin-bladed knife. Transfer the pieces to a platter and return the dark meat to the oven. Roast for about 10 minutes more, or until the leg meat is just beginning to separate from the bone; transfer the leg-thigh pieces to the platter.

5   Add the chicken stock to the onion mixture, along with salt and pepper to taste; bring to a boil, then remove from the heat and cool slightly.

6   Carefully puree the onion mixture in a blender, then return to the pot. Add the chicken and the remaining 1 tablespoon wine. Reheat if necessary, garnish with the parsley, and serve.

MAKES 4 SERVINGS   TIME: 40 MINUTES

Curried chicken with dried fruit and yogurt

3 tablespoons peanut or neutral oil, such as canola or grapeseed

One 3-pound chicken, cut into 8 pieces for sautéing and skin removed; the back, neck, wing tips, and other trimmings reserved

1 small stalk celery, roughly chopped

1 small onion, peeled and roughly chopped

1 stalk lemongrass, trimmed and roughly chopped

1 small carrot, peeled and roughly chopped

1 leek (white part only), well washed and roughly chopped

2 cloves

4 cardamom pods

10 coriander seeds

1 teaspoon paprika

2 teaspoons curry powder

½ teaspoon cumin

1 teaspoon cinnamon

2 cups yogurt

½ pound mixed dried fruit and nuts: figs, dates, apricots, peanuts, and walnuts, for example

1 tablespoon fresh lemon juice, or to taste

Salt and freshly ground black pepper

Again the basic cooking techniques remain the same, but here the flavors are a real departure, and the simple garnish adds elegance. It's best to allow the chicken to marinate overnight, but if you're pressed for time, an hour will do the trick.

1 Preheat the oven to 500°F. Add 1 tablespoon of the oil to an ovenproof skillet and turn the heat to high; add the reserved chicken trimmings and cook, stirring, until they begin to brown, about 5 minutes. Place the skillet in the oven; roast until the pieces are good and brown, about 10 minutes. Add the celery, onion, lemongrass, carrot, and leek and roast, stirring occasionally, until the vegetables are well browned, about 20 minutes.

2 Return the skillet to the top of the stove and add water to cover, about 2 cups. Bring to a boil over medium heat, then stir and scrape the sides and bottom of the pan for 1 minute. Cook, stirring occasionally, until the liquid is reduced to about ½ cup, about 1 hour. When the stock is done, strain it. You can cover and refrigerate for a day if you like.

3   Meanwhile, place the cloves, cardamom, and coriander in a dry skillet over medium heat and toast, shaking the pan, until the mixture is aromatic, just a minute or two. Grind to a powder in a spice or coffee grinder, along with the remaining spices. Sprinkle the chicken with 2 teaspoons of the spice mix (reserve the rest); mix the chicken with ¾ cup of the yogurt. Cover and refrigerate for at least 1 hour, and up to a full day.

4   When you're ready to cook, set an oven rack as low in the oven as possible (if you can roast on the floor of the oven, so much the better) and preheat the oven to 500°F. Place a large ovenproof skillet over high heat for about 2 minutes.

5   Add the remaining 2 tablespoons oil to the skillet, then add the chicken, flesh side down; reserve any marinade. Cook, undisturbed, until the chicken is nicely browned, about 5 minutes. Turn and cook for 5 minutes on the other side, then place the skillet in the oven.

6   Meanwhile, mince or julienne the dried fruit and nuts and mix them with the remaining 1¼ cups yogurt. Season with the lemon juice and set aside.

7   After 5 minutes of roasting, check the breast and wing pieces for doneness; when cooked, the meat will be firm and its juices will run clear, or nearly so, when pierced with a thin-bladed knife. Transfer the pieces to a platter and return the skillet to the oven. Roast for 5 to 10 minutes more, until the thigh meat is firm and the juices run clear. Transfer the leg-thigh pieces to the platter.

8   Meanwhile, reheat the chicken stock if necessary. Whisk the reserved marinade into the stock. Pour out almost all of the pan juices from the skillet and place it over high heat on top of the stove. Add the chicken stock and cook, stirring and scraping, for about 2 minutes. Season to taste with salt and pepper and return the chicken to the pan; turn the chicken pieces in the sauce to reheat.

9   To serve, place a couple of chicken pieces on each plate, along with a spoonful of the yogurt mixture and a sprinkling of the spice powder. Pass the remaining yogurt sauce at the table.

MAKES 4 SERVINGS

TIME: AT LEAST 1½ HOURS, PREFERABLY LONGER, LARGELY UNATTENDED

Sautéed chicken chunks

YOU might call these stir-fries, and indeed the technique is the same, but since not all the ingredients are Asian, it seems odd to do so. Still, all the recipes but one feature fast-cooked boneless chicken with vegetables.

That one, the last recipe in the group, is Chicken Pot Pie, in which the chicken itself is cooked much as it is in the other recipes, but is then transferred to a dish with other ingredients and topped with a crust; this is all a bit of a production. The first four recipes, however, are ideal weeknight dishes—chicken with onions, which is great with rice or bread; chicken with eggplant, which would work as a pasta sauce; chicken with coconut milk, a perfect foil for rice noodles; and chicken with Moroccan spices and couscous, a little more elaborate but still doable in about 30 minutes.

KEYS TO SUCCESS

These are chicken breast recipes first and foremost, but there is no reason you could not use boneless chicken thighs, or turkey, pork, shrimp, or scallops, for that matter, in any of them. Cooking times will be about the same—a little longer for dark meat chicken, turkey, or pork, a little shorter for seafood.

As usual, our advice is to steer clear of mass-produced supermarket chicken. Most kosher, free-range, or organic chickens are a much better bet.

Note that the amount of chicken in these recipes is relatively small, 1 pound total for 4 people. We feel that with the vegetables and a side dish, that's enough. If you want to increase all the amounts by fifty percent, or even double the recipes, that's fine, but we recommend that you then cook in batches, or the chicken will not brown.

Sautéed chicken chunks with onions

2 tablespoons extra-virgin olive oil

2 tablespoons butter (or use all oil)

1 large onion, peeled and sliced

1 pound boneless, skinless chicken breasts, cut into ½- to 1-inch dice

Salt and freshly ground black pepper

¼ cup torn parsley leaves

With crisp bread and a salad, a fine meal in under half an hour. Note that the sauce is made with water; use chicken stock if you have some around.

1 Put the oil and butter in a large skillet and turn the heat to medium-high. When the butter melts, add the onion and turn the heat to high. Cook, stirring frequently but not constantly, until the onion is brown and crisp, about 10 minutes. Remove with a slotted spoon and set aside.

2 Season the chicken well with salt and pepper. Turn the heat under the skillet to high and add the chicken; brown well on all sides, a total of about 5 minutes. Return the onions to the pan, along with ½ cup water, and cook, stirring, until saucy. Stir in the parsley and serve.

MAKES 4 SERVINGS   TIME: 20 MINUTES

Sautéed chicken chunks with eggplant

1 lemon

1 pound boneless, skinless chicken breasts, cut into ½- to
1-inch dice

2 bell peppers

1 pound eggplant

¼ cup extra-virgin olive oil

Salt and freshly ground black pepper

½ cup roughly chopped basil

Bright, sunny flavors abound here. Serve this with bread, or, to make it into a pasta sauce, use 2 cups peeled, chopped, and diced tomatoes (canned are fine) in place of the water and cook an extra 5 minutes; thin with a little water if necessary.

1 Cut the lemon in half and segment it as you would a grapefruit, discarding the seeds and reserving the juice. Marinate the chicken with those segments and the juice while you prepare the vegetables.

2 Peel the peppers (use a regular vegetable peeler), then core, seed, and cut into ⅛-inch strips. Peel the eggplant and cut it into ½-inch chunks.

3 Put 2 tablespoons of the oil in a large skillet, preferably nonstick, and turn the heat to medium-high. A minute later, add the peppers and eggplant and turn the heat to high. Cook, stirring frequently but not constantly, until the vegetables are tender and begin to brown, about 10 minutes.

4 Meanwhile, heat the remaining 2 tablespoons oil in a separate skillet. Season the chicken well with salt and pepper. Turn the heat under the skillet to high and add the chicken; brown well on all sides, a total of about 5 minutes.

5 Stir the cooked vegetables into the chicken. Add ½ cup water and cook, stirring, until saucy. Stir in the basil and serve.

MAKES 4 SERVINGS   TIME: 30 MINUTES

Simple to Spectacular

Curried sautéed chicken chunks with coconut milk

1 pound boneless, skinless chicken breasts, cut into ½- to 1-inch dice

1 teaspoon Curry Powder (page 344) or commercial curry powder (See note page xii.)

Salt

1 teaspoon minced fresh chile or red pepper flakes

1 tablespoon minced lemongrass

3 tablespoons butter or neutral oil, such as canola or grapeseed

1 cup canned unsweetened or fresh coconut milk

2 tablespoons nam pla (Thai fish sauce)

1 cup salted peanuts or cashews

½ cup roughly chopped cilantro

Probably our favorite simple chicken recipe. If you're making this for the sticky rice packages on page 106, reduce the coconut milk to ½ cup. In any case, cook the chicken a little more slowly than in the other recipes, in order not to burn the spices.

1 Toss the chicken with the curry powder, salt to taste, chile, and lemongrass.

2 Place the butter in a medium skillet, preferably nonstick, and turn the heat to medium-high. When it melts, add the chicken. Cook the chicken, stirring occasionally, until it loses its raw color. Add the coconut milk and turn the heat to medium.

3 Cook for another 2 to 3 minutes until cooked through, then stir in the nam pla and nuts and cook for another 30 seconds. Garnish with the cilantro and serve.

MAKES 4 SERVINGS   TIME: 30 MINUTES

Sautéed chicken chunks with harissa and couscous

1 pound boneless, skinless chicken breasts, cut into ½- to 1-inch dice

1 teaspoon cumin

½ teaspoon cardamom

Salt and freshly ground black pepper

2 cups One-Hour Chicken Stock (page 3) or any chicken stock

1 cup couscous

¼ cup raisins

2 tablespoons harissa, or more to taste

⅓ cup plus 2 tablespoons extra-virgin olive oil

8 ounces zucchini, washed, trimmed, and cut into ¼-inch-thick slices

1 cup cooked (or canned) chickpeas (rinse if canned)

1 large tomato, peeled, seeded, and diced (about 1 cup; use drained canned tomatoes if you wish)

½ cup shredded mint

Harissa is a delicious North African spice paste—sold in cans everywhere you can buy Middle Eastern ingredients—hot but not fiery. It keeps nearly forever. This is a solid one-pot meal, and an impressive one as well.

1 Toss the chicken with the cumin, cardamom, and salt and pepper to taste and let sit while you prepare the couscous.

2 Bring 1½ cups of the stock to a boil. Combine the couscous, raisins, 1 tablespoon of the harissa, the ⅓ cup olive oil, and salt and pepper to taste in a bowl. Pour the boiling stock over the couscous, stir, and seal the top of the bowl with plastic wrap. Set aside for at least 15 minutes.

3 Meanwhile, put the remaining 2 tablespoons oil in a large skillet and turn the heat to high. A minute later, add the chicken and cook until it begins to brown, about 2 minutes. Add the zucchini and toss, still over high heat, until it begins to brown, 2 to 3 minutes. Stir in the chickpeas and the remaining 1 tablespoon harissa and ½ cup stock, along with the tomato. Bring to a boil, turn the heat to low, and simmer for 2 minutes; the mixture should be brothy. Taste and add more salt, pepper, and/or harissa to taste.

4 Serve on top of the couscous, garnished with the mint.

MAKES 4 SERVINGS   TIME: 30 MINUTES

Chicken pot pie

Salt and freshly ground black pepper

1 cup shelled fresh or thawed frozen peas

2 tablespoons extra-virgin olive oil

4 tablespoons butter (or use all oil)

2 carrots, peeled and cut into ¼-inch rounds

8 ounces potatoes, preferably fingerlings, peeled and cut into ¼-inch-thick rounds

16 pearl onions, peeled

1 pound boneless, skinless chicken breasts, cut into ½- to 1-inch dice

4 ounces white mushrooms, trimmed and cut into halves or quarters if large, left whole if small

2 cloves garlic, peeled and lightly crushed

1 teaspoon thyme leaves

1 cup Jus Rôti (page 4), One-Hour Chicken Stock (page 3), or other chicken stock

2 egg yolks, beaten

6 rounds puff pastry or other dough, 7 to 8 inches in diameter

You can make individual pot pies, as we do here, or one big one; in that case, plan on doubling the baking time. These are as good warm as they are hot.

1 Preheat the oven to 400°F. Bring a small pot of water to a boil and salt it. Boil the peas until tender and bright green, 2 to 3 minutes. Drain, plunge into a bowl of ice water to stop the cooking, and drain again. Set aside. Put a tablespoon each of the oil and butter in a medium ovenproof skillet and turn the heat to high. When the butter melts, add the carrots, potatoes, and onions and stir. Season with salt and pepper and put in the oven. Roast until the potatoes are tender, about 15 minutes.

2 Meanwhile, put the remaining 1 tablespoon oil and another tablespoon of butter in a skillet and turn the heat to high. When the butter melts, add the chicken and mushrooms, along with the garlic and thyme. Cook, stirring occasionally, until the chicken and mushrooms are nicely browned, just over 5 minutes. Add the jus rôti and cook for 10 seconds. Turn off the heat and stir in the remaining 2 tablespoons butter. Add the cooked vegetables and let cool to room temperature. (To hasten the cooling, spread on a plate or board in one layer.)

3 Put the mixture in 6 individual ovenproof 6-inch bowls and brush the edges of the bowls with the egg yolks. Top each with a circle of pastry, draping the crust over the rim. Brush the tops of the pastry with the egg wash and bake for 12 to 15 minutes, or until golden.

MAKES 6 SERVINGS   TIME: ABOUT 1¼ HOURS

Chicken in foil

THE traditional name for this style of cooking is *en papillote*, and the traditional package is made of parchment paper. But aluminum foil is much easier and more available and efficient, so it is the envelope of choice. Here, you are cooking in a very tightly closed container, effectively creating a small, weak pressure cooker. The cooking times are short and the process is simple. One bonus of using this method—in which all of the cooking is done on the stovetop—is that the foil puffs up, making it look like a Jiffy Pop.

This is not really a simple-to-complex entry, since every recipe is about the same amount of work. Rather, it is frugal to expensive: We start with chicken and herbs, then vary and add ingredients until we wind up with chicken and foie gras—in between, the flavors vary greatly, the technique not at all. Master this method and you will be able to vary it infinitely.

KEYS TO SUCCESS

It's easiest to start with a wide (18-inch) roll of heavy-duty aluminum foil; these are sold in all supermarkets. Make sure the pieces of foil you use have no holes.

Make the packages up to 3 hours in advance of cooking if you like; store them in the refrigerator.

Some steam will escape from the packages, and that's normal. If, however, liquid escapes, or huge volumes of steam, you have not sealed them tightly enough.

The first time you make these, you might overcook by a minute or two; once the packages are opened, it's difficult to close them back up. Our timing is correct for our ovens, but it might pay to be cautious until you get the hang of this.

These recipes serve 2; if doubling the recipes, you will have to make two separate packages to serve 4.

Chicken breasts in foil with rosemary and olive oil

3 tablespoons extra-virgin olive oil

20 spinach leaves, trimmed, washed, and dried

2 boneless, skinless chicken breast halves (about 12 ounces)

Salt and freshly ground black pepper

2 sprigs rosemary, plus ½ teaspoon minced rosemary

Minced zest and juice of ½ lemon

Simple, fast, flavorful, and very moist.

1 Tear off two sheets of aluminum foil, each about 18 inches square, and place one on top of the other. Use 1 tablespoon of the olive oil to smear a patch in the center of the foil, large enough to hold the chicken pieces side by side. Make a bed of the spinach in the center, then top with the chicken breasts, salt and pepper to taste, the rosemary sprigs and leaves, and another tablespoon of oil. Sprinkle the lemon zest and juice over the chicken.

2 Fold the foil over the chicken onto itself and crimp the edges as tightly as possible by making 1- or 2-inch folds, one after the other, each sealing the other. Seal the package very tightly, but leave plenty of room around the chicken. (*You can prepare the recipe up to 3 hours in advance to this point; refrigerate the package.*)

3 Place a skillet large enough to hold the package over high heat. A minute later, add the remaining oil, then pour out all but a film. Put the package in the skillet; it will sizzle. About 2 minutes later, the package will expand like a balloon; be careful of escaping steam. Cook for 5 minutes longer from that point.

4 Remove the package from the heat, again taking care to avoid any escaping steam. Let rest for 1 minute, then cut a slit down the length of the top with a knife. Use a knife and fork to open up the package, then spoon the chicken, spinach, and juices onto a plate and serve.

MAKES 2 SERVINGS   TIME: ABOUT 20 MINUTES

Chicken breasts in foil with tomato, olives, and Parmesan

2 tablespoons extra-virgin olive oil

2 thick slices tomato

2 boneless, skinless chicken breast halves (about 12 ounces)

Salt and freshly ground black pepper

½ cup freshly grated Parmesan

1 teaspoon thyme leaves, plus 2 sprigs thyme

10 small black olives, pitted

This is much saucier than the preceding recipe, and rich with Parmesan. Serve it with bread.

1 Tear off two sheets of aluminum foil, each about 18 inches square, and place one on top of the other. Use 1 tablespoon of the olive oil to smear a patch in the center of the foil, large enough to hold the chicken. Make a bed of the tomato slices in the center, then top with the chicken breasts, salt and pepper to taste, the Parmesan, and thyme leaves. Add the olives and thyme sprigs.

2 Fold the foil over the chicken onto itself and crimp the edges as tightly as possible by making 1- or 2-inch folds, one after the other, each sealing the other. Seal the package very tightly, but leave plenty of room around the chicken. (*You can prepare the recipe up to 3 hours in advance to this point; refrigerate the package.*)

3 Place a skillet large enough to hold the package over high heat. A minute later, add the remaining oil, then pour out all but a film. Put the package in the skillet; it will sizzle. About 2 minutes later, the package will expand like a balloon; be careful of escaping steam. Cook for 5 minutes longer from that point.

4 Remove the package from the heat, again taking care to avoid any escaping steam. Let rest for 1 minute, then cut a slit down the length of the top with a knife. Use a knife and fork to open up the package, then spoon the chicken, garnish, and juices onto a plate and serve.

MAKES 2 SERVINGS   TIME: ABOUT 20 MINUTES

Simple to Spectacular

Chicken breasts in foil with mushrooms, shallots, and sherry

2 tablespoons butter, softened

6 to 8 asparagus spears (about 8 ounces), trimmed and peeled

2 boneless, skinless chicken breast halves (about 12 ounces)

Salt and freshly ground black pepper

½ cup stemmed, trimmed, and roughly chopped shiitakes or other mushrooms

2 tablespoons minced shallots

2 tablespoons dry (fino) sherry

3 tablespoons heavy cream

1 tablespoon any oil

A traditional French grouping of flavors, in which a mushroom-cream sauce is produced more or less automatically. Serve with rice, bread, or buttered noodles.

1 Tear off two sheets of aluminum foil, each about 18 inches square, and place one on top of the other. Use the butter to smear a patch in the center of the foil, large enough to hold the chicken. Make a bed of the asparagus in the center, then top with the chicken breasts, salt and pepper to taste, the mushrooms, shallots, sherry, and cream.

2 Fold the foil over the chicken onto itself and crimp the edges as tightly as possible by making 1- or 2-inch folds, one after the other, each sealing the other. Seal the package very tightly, but leave plenty of room around the chicken. *(You can prepare the recipe up to 3 hours in advance to this point; refrigerate the package.)*

3 Place a skillet large enough to hold the package over high heat. A minute later, add the oil, then pour out all but a film. Put the package in the skillet; it will sizzle. About 2 minutes later, the package will expand like a balloon; be careful of escaping steam. Cook for 5 minutes longer from that point.

4 Remove the package from the heat, again taking care to avoid any escaping steam. Let rest for 1 minute, then cut a slit down the length of the top with a knife. Use a knife and fork to open up the package, then spoon the chicken and mushrooms with their sauce onto a plate and serve.

MAKES 2 SERVINGS   TIME: ABOUT 20 MINUTES

Thai-style **chicken breasts in foil**

3 tablespoons peanut or neutral oil, such as canola or grapeseed

6 to 8 thin slices lotus root or peeled jicama

2 boneless, skinless chicken breast halves (about 12 ounces)

½ teaspoon red pepper flakes

8 thin slices peeled green (unripe) mango

2 lime leaves, minced (or minced zest of 1 lime)

2 tablespoons chopped scallions

¼ cup canned unsweetened coconut milk

1 teaspoon nam pla (Thai fish sauce)

This mélange of Thai ingredients produces a stunning aroma when the package is opened. You might substitute roasted sesame oil for some of the peanut oil for even more flavor. Best with rice.

1 Tear off two sheets of aluminum foil, each about 18 inches square, and place one on top of the other. Use 1 tablespoon of the oil to smear a patch in the center of the foil, large enough to hold the chicken. Make a bed of the lotus root or jicama in the center, then top with the chicken breasts, red pepper flakes, mango, lime leaves, scallions, coconut milk, nam pla, and another tablespoon of oil.

2 Fold the foil over the chicken onto itself and crimp the edges as tightly as possible by making 1- or 2-inch folds, one after the other, each sealing the other. Seal the package very tightly, but leave plenty of room around the chicken. *(You can prepare the recipe up to 3 hours in advance to this point; refrigerate the package as is for up to three hours before proceeding.)*

3 Place a skillet large enough to hold the package over high heat. A minute later, add the remaining oil, then pour out all but a film. Put the package in the skillet; it will sizzle. About 2 minutes later, the package will expand like a balloon; be careful of escaping steam. Cook for 5 minutes longer from that point.

4 Remove the package from the heat, again taking care to avoid any escaping steam. Let rest for 1 minute, then cut a slit down the length of the top with a knife. Use a knife and fork to open up the package, then spoon the chicken and garnishes onto a plate and serve.

MAKES 2 SERVINGS   TIME: ABOUT 20 MINUTES

Chicken breasts in foil with foie gras and porcini

2 tablespoons extra-virgin olive oil

2 cloves garlic, peeled and crushed

¼ pound fresh porcini or shiitake mushrooms, trimmed and sliced

Salt and freshly ground black pepper

1 tablespoon butter

1 cup shredded cabbage

2 boneless, skinless chicken breast halves (about 12 ounces)

4 ounces foie gras, cut into chunks

3 tablespoons Jus Rôti (page 4) or any good chicken stock

The ultimate in luxury, really delicious—but easy as well.

1 Place half the olive oil in a medium skillet and turn the heat to high. A minute later, add the garlic, mushrooms, and salt and pepper to taste. Cook, stirring frequently, until the mushrooms are tender and browned all over, 5 to 10 minutes.

2 Tear off two sheets of aluminum foil, each about 18 inches square, and place one on top of the other. Use the butter to smear a patch in the center of the foil, large enough to hold the chicken. Make a bed of the cabbage in the center, then top with the chicken breasts, salt and pepper to taste, the foie gras, mushrooms and garlic, and jus rôti or stock.

3 Fold the foil over the chicken onto itself and crimp the edges as tightly as possible by making 1- or 2-inch folds, one after the other, each sealing the other. Seal the package very tightly, but leave plenty of room around the chicken.

4 Place a skillet large enough to hold the package over high heat. A minute later, add the remaining oil, then pour out all but a film. Put the package in the skillet; it will sizzle. About 2 minutes later, the package will expand like a balloon; be careful of escaping steam. Cook for 5 minutes longer from that point.

5 Remove the package from the heat, again taking care to avoid any escaping steam. Let rest for 1 minute, then cut a slit down the length of the top with a knife. Use a knife and fork to open up the package, then spoon the chicken and garnish onto a plate and serve.

MAKES 2 SERVINGS   TIME: ABOUT 20 MINUTES

Simple to Spectacular

Meat

Seared steaks

THESE are steaks cooked on the stovetop, not the grill, with sauces built in the pan based on the juices the steaks leave behind. Unlike the tenderloin steaks on pages 283–290, these steaks—you can use sirloin or rib-eye—contain plenty of flavor of their own, so our preparations are gutsy and strong.

We start with a few fast weeknight preparations, ranging from one based on soy, ginger, and butter—a uniquely American combination—to a classic French steak au poivre with mustard (talk about powerful!) to a peasant dish of steak with red wine and loads of garlic. On the more spectacular side, we offer a lovely lemon-shallot compote and a knockout dish featuring every type of celery we could think of, plus Jean-Georges' innovative, eggless "béarnaise" sauce.

KEYS TO SUCCESS

You can use either sirloin strip (sometimes called New York sirloin or strip) or boneless rib-eye here; those are the most flavorful steaks, and they're quite tender as well. If you can get dry-aged prime steaks, so much the better.

These recipes are designed to serve 4, but it's up to you to determine how big the steaks are. You can use four 6- to 8-ounce steaks, or they can be even bigger, up to 10 ounces or so. If you want to reduce portion size, cook two 8- to 10-ounce steaks and divide them in half; 4-ounce steaks will cook too quickly.

After the initial browning, the meat is set aside while you prepare the sauce. Be sure to add any juices that accumulate around the steaks to the sauce before finishing the dish.

Steak with butter and ginger sauce

1½ to 2 pounds boneless rib-eye or sirloin steaks, about 1 inch thick

3 tablespoons butter

2 tablespoons minced ginger

2 tablespoons soy sauce

A super-fast dish with remarkable flavor, and one that has the potential to become a real classic.

1 Preheat a large heavy skillet over medium-high heat until it begins to smoke. Add the steaks and cook until nicely browned, 1 to 2 minutes. Turn and brown the other side, another minute or two. Remove the skillet from the heat and transfer the steaks to a plate.

2 When the skillet has cooled slightly, return it to the stove over medium heat. Add the butter and, when it melts, the ginger. About 30 seconds later, add the soy sauce and 2 tablespoons water and stir to blend. Return the steaks to the skillet, along with any accumulated juices.

3 Turn the heat to medium and cook the steaks for a total of about 4 minutes more, turning 3 or 4 times. (If at any time the pan threatens to dry out entirely, add another couple tablespoons of water.) At this point, the steaks will be medium-rare; cook for a little longer if you like, and serve, with the pan juices spooned over.

MAKES 4 SERVINGS   TIME: 20 MINUTES

Steak au poivre with mustard sauce

1½ to 2 pounds boneless rib-eye or sirloin steaks, about
1 inch thick

Salt

4 teaspoons cracked black pepper, more or less

2 tablespoons butter

2 tablespoons neutral oil, such as canola or grapeseed

1 tablespoon Cognac

¼ cup Dijon mustard

½ cup heavy cream

A typical Parisian dish, with super-intense flavors. You can finish with chicken stock instead of cream if you prefer.

1 Sprinkle the steaks with salt and press about a teaspoon of pepper into each side of the steaks. Put the butter and oil in a 10- or 12-inch skillet and turn the heat to medium-high. When the butter melts, turn the heat to high and add the steaks. Cook until almost done, 3 to 4 minutes per side for rare. Turn off the heat and transfer the steaks to a warm platter in a low oven.

2 Add the Cognac to the pan, turn the heat to low, and stir, then add the mustard and cream. Bring to a boil, then reduce the heat to low.

3 Add the steaks and any accumulated juices to the sauce, turn once or twice, and serve.

MAKES 4 SERVINGS   TIME: 20 MINUTES

Simple to Spectacular

Louis Outhier's steak with red wine and garlic

1½ to 2 pounds boneless rib-eye or sirloin steaks, about
1 inch thick

Salt and freshly ground black pepper

2 tablespoons neutral oil, such as canola or grapeseed

5 tablespoons butter

8 cloves garlic, peeled and sliced

2 cups plus 2 tablespoons sturdy red wine

½ cup chopped parsley

Chef Outhier was Jean-Georges' first mentor, and this was his favorite dish to have after a hard night of cooking. It's a real bistro dish—there's nothing fancy about it, but the flavors are solidly appealing.

1   Sprinkle the steaks with salt and pepper. Put the oil and 2½ tablespoons of the butter in a 10- or 12-inch skillet and turn the heat to medium-high. When the butter melts, turn the heat to high and add the steaks. Cook until almost done, 3 to 4 minutes per side for rare. Turn off the heat and transfer the steaks to a warm platter in a low oven.

2   Pour the fat out of the pan and return to the stove, over medium heat. Add 2 tablespoons of the remaining butter to the pan; when it melts, add the garlic and turn the heat up a bit. When the garlic begins to brown, about 5 minutes, add 2 cups of the wine and turn the heat to high. Reduce by about two-thirds, until the mixture is thick and saucy; season with a little salt and plenty of pepper, then stir in the remaining ½ tablespoon butter. When it melts, add the parsley and the remaining 2 tablespoons wine.

3   Add the steaks and any accumulated juices to the sauce, turn once or twice, and serve.

MAKES 4 SERVINGS   TIME: 30 MINUTES

Simple to Spectacular

Steak with shallot and lemon compote

Salt

12 shallots, peeled

⅓ cup plus 2 tablespoons neutral oil, such as canola or grapeseed

Minced zest and juice of 3 lemons

12 coriander seeds

6 peppercorns

1 bay leaf

1 branch thyme

1 teaspoon sugar

2 cloves garlic, peeled

1 stalk celery

1 sprig parsley

Freshly ground black pepper

4 scallions, trimmed and cut into 2-inch lengths

1½ to 2 pounds boneless rib-eye or sirloin steaks, about 1 inch thick

2 tablespoons butter

An exotic jam of shallots, lemons, and spices cuts through and offsets the richness of the steaks.

1   Bring a small pot of water to a boil and salt it; cook the shallots for 3 minutes, then drain. Combine the shallots, the ⅓ cup oil, the lemon zest and juice, coriander, peppercorns, bay leaf, thyme, sugar, garlic, celery, parsley, a sprinkling of salt and pepper, and ¼ cup water in a small saucepan. Bring to a boil, cover, and simmer for 30 minutes. When the compote is done, taste and adjust the seasoning, then add the scallions and keep it warm.

2   Season the steaks with salt and pepper. Put the butter and the remaining 2 tablespoons oil in a 10- or 12-inch skillet and turn the heat to medium-high. When the butter melts, turn the heat to high and add the steaks. Cook until almost done, 3 to 4 minutes per side for rare. Serve the steaks with some of the compote spooned over them.

MAKES 4 SERVINGS   TIME: 40 MINUTES

Steak with four celery flavors and eggless "béarnaise"

1 knob celeriac (celery root), peeled and cut into 12 wedges

¼ cup extra-virgin olive oil

1 teaspoon thyme leaves

1 clove garlic, peeled and chopped

Salt and freshly ground black pepper

1½ to 2 pounds boneless rib-eye or sirloin steaks, about
1 inch thick

1 teaspoon Celery Salt (page 338), or use commercial celery
salt

4 stalks celery, trimmed, leaves reserved, and chopped

½ cup peeled and minced shallots

1 cup white wine vinegar, preferably Champagne

1 branch tarragon

1 tablespoon cracked black pepper

1 tablespoon chopped tarragon

2 tablespoons butter

There's a lot of celery here, but the flavors remain fairly subtle, especially compared to the combination of shallots, vinegar, and tarragon that begins as if you were making a béarnaise sauce, but finishes without the addition of egg. The result is a sharp-tasting relish that works perfectly with steak.

1 Preheat the oven to 450°F. Put the celery root on a baking sheet and drizzle with 2 tablespoons of the oil; sprinkle with the thyme, garlic, and salt and pepper. Cover with foil and roast for 15 minutes; uncover, turn, and cook for another 15 minutes, or until the wedges are browned and tender.

2 Meanwhile, sprinkle the steaks with the celery salt; let sit while you continue to cook. Bring a pot of water to a boil and salt it; cook the celery stalks for about 2 minutes, or until barely tender. Remove (leave the hot water simmering on the stove) and plunge into a bowl of ice water; drain and set aside.

3 Combine the shallots, vinegar, tarragon branch, and pepper in a small sauce-pan and cook until almost dry. Remove the tarragon stem and stir in the chopped tarragon; keep warm.

4 When you're ready to eat, put the butter and the remaining 2 tablespoons oil in a 10- or 12-inch skillet and turn the heat to medium-high. When the butter melts, turn the heat to high and add the steaks. Cook until almost done, about 4 minutes per side for rare. Meanwhile, quickly reheat the celery stalks in the hot water.

5 Serve the steaks with the celery root and the shallot sauce on the side, each gar-nished with a celery stalk and some celery leaves.

MAKES 4 SERVINGS   TIME: 1 HOUR

THESE are filet mignons—cross-cut pieces of beef tenderloin—but you can use sirloin steak in any of these recipes except the last one. Sirloin is more flavorful, but the mild flavor of tenderloin takes well to sauces and spices, and its leanness makes it easy to cook in a skillet. It's a quick-cooking cut, and one that is always tender.

The first recipe is completely basic; we add a touch of class by dipping the steaks in herbs right before serving. From there, we go to an updated steak au poivre; one made with one of Jean-Georges' favorite "new" sauces, containing chicory; a Thai-style steak; and, finally, steak stuffed with bone marrow, a classic luxury.

KEYS TO SUCCESS

Keep the heat fairly high and the cooking time fairly short, to sear the outside of the steaks while leaving the inside rare; because tenderloin has so little fat, it will not generate a lot of smoke.

The steaks should weigh 6 to 8 ounces and be at least an inch thick, or they will overcook.

Herb-dipped **tenderloin steaks**

1 tablespoon butter

1 tablespoon neutral oil, such as canola or grapeseed

4 tenderloin steaks (each about 6 to 8 ounces)

1 cup mixed tender herb leaves, such as basil, chives, chervil, parsley, and tarragon

Salt and coarsely ground black pepper

Use any herbs you like here, as long as they are tender (don't, for example, use rosemary or bay leaves).

1   Put the butter and oil in a large skillet and turn the heat to medium-high. When the butter melts, add the steaks and turn the heat to high. Sear on the first side for about 3 minutes, then turn and sear on the second side for 2 to 3 minutes. Lower the heat and cook until the steaks reach your chosen level of doneness, about 8 minutes total for medium-rare.

2   While the steaks are cooking, chop the herbs together and put them on a plate.

3   When the steaks are done, season them well, then dip one side of each into the herbs. Serve, dipped side up, with additional salt and coarsely cracked pepper on the side.

MAKES 4 SERVINGS   TIME: 15 MINUTES

Green peppercorn steak au poivre

3 tablespoons butter

1 tablespoon neutral oil, such as canola or grapeseed

4 tenderloin steaks (each about 6 to 8 ounces)

Salt and coarsely ground black pepper

2 tablespoons minced shallots

2 tablespoons canned green peppercorns

1 tablespoon Dijon mustard

2 tablespoons cream

This mustard-laced sauce is silky smooth, a classic that deserves resurrection. You might use even more butter in this dish, up to 5 tablespoons or so, for extra richness. Use only green peppercorns that have been packed in brine, not the dried kind.

1 Preheat the oven to 200°F. Put 2 tablespoons of the butter and oil in a large skillet and turn the heat to medium-high. When the butter melts, add the steaks and turn the heat to high. Sear on the first side for about 3 minutes, then turn and sear on the second side for 2 to 3 minutes. Lower the heat and cook until just short of your chosen level of doneness, about 7 minutes total for medium-rare. Keep warm in the oven while you make the sauce.

2 Pour out any fat from the skillet leaving the brown bits in there. Add the remaining butter and shallots and cook over medium-high heat, stirring occasionally, until the shallots are soft, about 3 minutes. Add the green peppercorns and cook for 30 seconds. Add the mustard and cream and cook, stirring, for 30 seconds.

3 Pour the sauce over the steaks and serve.

MAKES 4 SERVINGS   TIME: 20 MINUTES

Simple to Spectacular

Tenderloin steaks with chicory sauce

⅓ cup chicory

Salt and freshly ground black pepper

1 bunch Swiss chard, about 1 pound

1 small onion, peeled and sliced into rings

6 tablespoons butter

½ cup One-Hour Chicken Stock (page 3) or other chicken stock

vinegar

1 tablespoon neutral oil, such as canola or grapeseed

4 tenderloin steaks (each about 6 ounces)

3 teaspoons sherry vinegar

A strong combination of flavors—bitter from the chicory (which is sometimes used as a coffee substitute), sweet from the onion, tart from the vinegar. And the chard adds yet another dimension.
You can buy chicory at almost any good coffee vendor.

1 Bring ½ cup water to a boil in a small saucepan and steep the chicory in it for 10 minutes. Strain through a cloth-lined strainer, pressing hard on the chicory to extract its juice.

2 Bring a large pot of water to a boil and salt it. Separate the chard leaves and stems. Cut the stems into 1-inch lengths and roughly chop the leaves, then wash them, keeping the stems and leaves separate. Put the leaves in the boiling water and cook until tender, about 2 minutes. Remove the leaves and plunge into cold water to stop the cooking; drain. Cook the stems in the water until tender, about 10 minutes. Remove and plunge into cold water; drain.

3 Put the onion in the water and cook for about 10 minutes, until tender and sweet. Drain and plunge into cold water; drain again.

4 Combine the onion, chicory liquid, 4 tablespoons of the butter, and the stock in a blender and blend until smooth; the mixture will be the color of coffee with cream. Put in a small saucepan and keep warm over low heat.

285

5 Put 1 tablespoon of the butter in a skillet and turn the heat to medium. When it melts, add the chard and cook, stirring occasionally, until reheated. Add 1 teaspoon of the vinegar, season with salt and pepper, and keep warm.

6 Meanwhile, cook the steaks: Put the remaining 1 tablespoon butter and the oil in a large skillet and turn the heat to medium-high. When the butter melts, add the steaks and turn the heat to high. Sear on the first side for about 3 minutes, then turn and sear on the second side for 2 to 3 minutes. Lower the heat and cook until the steaks reach your chosen level of doneness, 7 to 8 minutes total for medium-rare. Season with salt and pepper and let rest for a minute.

7 Season the chicory sauce with salt and pepper and the remaining vinegar. Slice the steaks. For each serving, put some chard on a plate, top with some of the steak, and spoon a little of the sauce over the meat.

MAKES 4 SERVINGS   TIME: 45 MINUTES

Spice-rubbed tenderloin steaks

1 stalk lemongrass

2 small chiles, stemmed and seeded

2 shallots, peeled and chopped

2 cloves garlic, peeled and chopped

½ cup packed cilantro (stems and all), chopped, plus minced cilantro for garnish

2 tablespoons nam pla (Thai fish sauce)

3 tablespoons canned unsweetened coconut milk

4 tenderloin steaks (each about 6 ounces)

8 ounces medium rice noodles (rice stick)

Salt and freshly ground black pepper

8 ounces snow peas or green beans, trimmed

3 tablespoons butter

1 tablespoon neutral oil, such as canola or grapeseed

¼ cup Jus Rôti (page 4), One-Hour Chicken Stock (page 3), or other stock

This is a one-dish meal, reminiscent of Vietnamese pho—the hearty soup staple—but considerably more elegant. Be sure to cook the steak over slightly lower heat than in the other recipes so as not to burn the marinade.

1 Trim both ends of the lemongrass and remove the outer sheaths in layers until you get to the tender inner core. Finely mince. Combine the lemongrass, chiles, shallots, garlic, and chopped cilantro in a blender with the nam pla and coconut milk and blend until smooth. Marinate the steaks in this mixture for an hour, more or less.

2 Soak the noodles in warm water to cover until they are soft, 10 to 15 minutes.

3 Meanwhile, bring a small saucepan of water to a boil; salt it. Cut the snow peas lengthwise into about the same thickness as the noodles. Blanch them in the boiling water for 15 seconds; drain, then plunge into ice water to stop the cooking. Drain again.

4 Combine 2 tablespoons of the butter and 2 tablespoons water in a large skillet and turn the heat to medium-high. Bring to a boil, then add the noodles and peas until heated through, about 5 minutes; keep warm.

5 Put the remaining 1 tablespoon butter and the oil in a large skillet and turn the heat to medium-high. When the butter melts, add the steaks (reserve the marinade) and turn the heat to medium. Cook on the first side for about 4 minutes, then turn and sear on the second side for 4 to 5 minutes. Continue to cook until the steaks reach your chosen level of doneness, about 10 minutes total for medium-rare. Let rest for a couple of minutes.

6 Heat together the jus rôti and ¼ cup of the reserved marinade. Divide the noodles among four bowls. Slice the steaks and arrange the slices on top of the noodles; top each dish with a couple of spoonfuls of the marinade mixture, garnish with the cilantro, and serve.

MAKES 4 SERVINGS   TIME: 1¼ HOURS, SOMEWHAT UNATTENDED

Simple to Spectacular

Tenderloin steaks with marrow butter

4 ounces marrow, removed from the bones

2 tablespoons butter

1 tablespoon minced shallots

Salt and freshly ground black pepper

1 cup chopped chervil

1 cup chopped chives

Juice of ½ lemon

4 tenderloin steaks (each about 6 to 8 ounces)

2 tablespoons extra-virgin olive oil

2 tablespoons sherry vinegar

4 cups frisée, washed and dried

1 tablespoon neutral oil, such as canola or grapeseed

If you really want to go all out, serve these with potatoes roasted in duck fat. If you don't have a pastry bag, use a closed Ziploc bag with one corner cut from it to pipe the marrow butter into the steaks (squeeze out of that corner). The easiest way to get marrow from the bones? Ask a butcher to do it for you.

1 Cut the marrow into ¼-inch-thick slices. Soak it in cold salted water to cover for 2 hours.

2 Bring a pot of water to a boil and add the marrow; lower the heat and cook very gently for 2 to 3 minutes, then drain and refrigerate for at least 15 minutes. (*You can refrigerate overnight if you like, as long as the marrow is well covered.*)

3 Put 1 tablespoon of the butter in a small skillet and turn the heat to medium. Add the shallots, along with a pinch of salt, and cook, stirring occasionally, until softened, about 5 minutes. Combine the shallots, marrow, half the chervil and chives, salt and pepper to taste, and the lemon juice in the container of a food processor or blender and puree. Taste and adjust the seasoning.

4 Use a thin-bladed knife to cut a horizontal pocket in each of the steaks and use a pastry bag to pipe a portion of the marrow butter into each pocket. Close the openings with toothpicks.

5 Whisk together the extra-virgin olive oil and sherry vinegar, along with a little salt and pepper. Toss with the frisée and remaining herbs.

6 Put the remaining 1 tablespoon butter and the canola oil in a large skillet and turn the heat to medium-high. When the butter melts, add the steaks and turn the heat to high. Sear on the first side for about 3 minutes, then turn and sear on the second side for 2 to 3 minutes. Lower the heat and cook until the steaks reach your chosen level of doneness, 6 to 8 minutes total for medium-rare. Serve a portion of the frisée salad alongside each of the steaks.

MAKES 4 SERVINGS   TIME: 2½ HOURS, LARGELY UNATTENDED

HERE is slow-cooked meat that is big on flavor and extraordinarily tender. Red wine is the norm for cooking short ribs, and their own rich flavor infuses the cooking liquid, making it rich and dark. But citrus combined with light, slightly sweet white wine makes an entirely different broth, as does one based on soy. Once in the oven, short ribs can virtually be ignored, and the results are well worth the long cooking time.

KEYS TO SUCCESS

The number one rule: Don't rush it. Short ribs might be done in as little as 90 minutes, or they might take 4 hours. The meat should just about be falling off the bone and fork-tender before you consider them done. Go take a nap while they're cooking.

If you have time after cooking, remove the ribs from the liquid and refrigerate both separately. Then skim excess fat from the chilled liquid before recombining and reheating. But don't consider this step necessary—short ribs are not as fatty as many other meats used in braising.

Short ribs braised in red wine

2 tablespoons neutral oil, such as canola or grapeseed

3 tablespoons butter

4 pounds short ribs

Salt and freshly ground black pepper

1 large onion, peeled and roughly chopped

1 large carrot, peeled and roughly chopped

1 stalk celery, roughly chopped

4 large cloves garlic, peeled and smashed

1 bottle fruity but sturdy red wine, such as Côtes du Rhone or Zinfandel

3 branches thyme

4 stems parsley

1 bay leaf

½ cup chopped parsley

Quite possibly the best simple beef stew you've ever made or tasted.

1 Put a tablespoon each of the oil and butter in a deep heavy skillet or casserole and turn the heat to high. A minute later, brown the ribs well on all sides, seasoning well with salt and pepper as they cook; this will take about 20 minutes (work in batches if necessary to avoid crowding). Remove the ribs, pour out and discard the fat, and wipe out the pan.

2 Preheat the oven to 350°F. Put the remaining 1 tablespoon oil and another tablespoon of butter in the pan, turn the heat to medium-high, and add the onion, carrot, celery, garlic, a large pinch of salt, and pepper to taste. Cook, stirring, until the onions are soft, about 10 minutes.

3 Add the red wine, thyme, parsley stems, and bay leaf to the pan and bring to a boil; add the ribs, cover, and put in the oven. Cook until the meat is very tender and falling from the bone, about 3 hours; turn the meat once or twice an hour.

4 Transfer the ribs to a platter. Strain the vegetables and liquid, pressing hard on the vegetables to extract all of their juices, into another large pan and refrigerate (see Keys to Success). Reheat, then bring to a boil and stir in the remaining 1 tablespoon butter; whisk until slightly thickened, then add the ribs and half the parsley. Heat the ribs through, adjust seasoning as necessary, and serve, garnished with the remaining parsley.

MAKES 4 SERVINGS   TIME: AS LONG AS 4 HOURS, LARGELY UNATTENDED

Meat

Short ribs braised with mushrooms, pearl onions, and bacon

2 tablespoons neutral oil, such as canola or grapeseed

4 tablespoons butter

4 pounds short ribs

Salt and freshly ground black pepper

1 large onion, peeled and roughly chopped

1 large carrot, peeled and roughly chopped

1 stalk celery, roughly chopped

4 large cloves garlic, peeled and smashed

1 bottle fruity but sturdy red wine, such as Côtes du Rhône or Zinfandel

3 branches thyme

4 stems parsley

1 bay leaf

4 ounces slab bacon, cut into strips 1 inch long and ¼ inch thick

8 ounces pearl onions, peeled

1 teaspoon sugar

1 tablespoon extra-virgin olive oil

8 ounces small mushrooms, trimmed

Minced chives for garnish

The extra flavors go a long way here, turning this into a classic luxury.

1 Put a tablespoon each of the oil and butter in a deep heavy skillet or casserole and turn the heat to high. A minute later, brown the ribs well on all sides, seasoning well with salt and pepper as they cook; this will take about 20 minutes (work in batches if necessary to avoid crowding). Remove the ribs, pour out and discard the fat, and wipe out the pan.

2 Preheat the oven to 350°F. Put the remaining canola oil and another tablespoon of butter in the pan, turn the heat to medium-high, and add the onion, carrot, celery, garlic, a large pinch of salt, and pepper to taste. Cook, stirring, until the onions are soft, about 10 minutes.

3 Add the red wine, thyme, parsley stems, and bay leaf to the pan and bring to a boil; add the ribs, cover, and put in the oven. Cook until the meat is very tender and falling from the bone, about 3 hours; turn the meat once or twice an hour.

4 While the meat is cooking, put the bacon in a skillet and cook over medium heat, stirring occasionally, until crisp, about 10 minutes. Drain on paper towels.

5 Put the pearl onions in a small saucepan with another tablespoon of the butter, water to cover, a pinch of salt, and the sugar and cook over high heat until most of the water evaporates. Reduce the heat to medium and cook until a nice glaze forms; continue to cook, stirring occasionally, until the onions brown a little. Set aside.

6 Put the olive oil in a skillet and turn the heat to medium. Add the mushrooms with a little salt and cook, stirring occasionally, until they give up their juices and brown a little, about 10 minutes. Set aside.

7 When the ribs are done, transfer them to a platter. Strain the vegetables and liquid, pressing hard on the vegetables to extract all of their juices, into another large pan and refrigerate (see Keys to Success) or reheat. Bring to a boil and stir in the remaining 1 tablespoon butter; whisk until slightly thickened, then add the ribs and heat through. Adjust the seasoning as necessary, then stir in the bacon, pearl onions, and mushrooms; cook for another minute or two to reheat. Serve, garnished with chives.

MAKES 4 SERVINGS   TIME: AS LONG AS 4 HOURS, LARGELY UNATTENDED

Short ribs braised with citrus

2 tablespoons neutral oil, such as canola or grapeseed

3 tablespoons butter

4 pounds short ribs

Salt and freshly ground black pepper

4 oranges

4 lemons

4 limes

1 large onion, peeled and roughly chopped

1 large carrot, peeled and roughly chopped

1 stalk celery, roughly chopped

1 tablespoon coriander seeds

4 large cloves garlic, peeled and smashed

1 bottle fruity white wine, such as Vouvray or Gewürztraminer

3 branches thyme

4 stems parsley

1 bay leaf

1 small head white cabbage

¼ cup chopped cilantro, for garnish

This is an unusual group of flavors for a dark beef stew—citrus, coriander, and fruity white wine. The results are equally unusual, and quite delightful.

1 Put a tablespoon each of the oil and butter in a deep heavy skillet or casserole and turn the heat to high. Brown the ribs well on all sides, seasoning well with salt and pepper as they cook; this will take about 20 minutes. Remove the ribs, pour out and discard the fat, and wipe out the pan.

2 Meanwhile, use a vegetable peeler to remove the zest and squeeze the juice from 2 each of the oranges, lemons, and limes.

3 Preheat the oven to 350°F. Put the remaining 1 tablespoon oil and another tablespoon of butter in the pan, turn the heat to medium-high, and add the onion, carrot, celery, the orange, lemon, and lime zest, the coriander, garlic, a large pinch of salt, and pepper to taste. Cook, stirring, until the onions are soft, about 10 minutes.

4 Add the white wine, orange, lemon, and lime juice, thyme, parsley stems, and bay leaf to the pan and bring to a boil; add the ribs, cover, and put in the oven. Cook until the meat is very tender and falling from the bone, about 3 hours; turn the meat once or twice an hour.

5 While the ribs are cooking, remove the central core from the cabbage, then separate the leaves and cut them into 3 or 4 pieces each. Cook them in boiling salted

water until tender, about 5 minutes. Drain, then plunge into ice water to stop the cooking; drain again and set aside. Remove the zest from the remaining fruit with a zester and mince. Cut each fruit in half and section as you would a grapefruit, removing any seeds; do this over a bowl so you catch all the juices.

6 Transfer the ribs to a platter. Strain the vegetables and liquid, pressing hard on the vegetables to extract all of their juices, into another large pan and refrigerate (see Keys to Success) or reheat. Bring to a boil and stir in the remaining 1 tablespoon butter; whisk until slightly thickened, then add the ribs, citrus sections, and cabbage. Heat the ribs through, adjust the seasoning as necessary, and serve, garnished with the citrus zest and cilantro.

MAKES 4 SERVINGS   TIME: AS LONG AS 4 HOURS, LARGELY UNATTENDED

Short ribs braised with Chinese flavors

¼ cup peanut or neutral oil, such as canola or grapeseed

4 pounds short ribs

Salt and freshly ground black pepper

1 large onion, peeled and roughly chopped

4 large cloves garlic, peeled and smashed

¼ cup roughly chopped ginger (don't bother to peel)

2 tablespoons sugar

5 star anise

5 dried chiles

2 tablespoons Szechwan peppercorns

20 cilantro stems, preferably with roots attached, well washed

1 cup dry (fino) sherry

½ cup soy sauce

1 pound bok choy (preferably 4 small heads; or 1 large head, split into quarters)

12 water chestnuts, preferably fresh, peeled, washed, and cut into quarters (canned are okay; rinse them first)

2 tablespoons peeled and finely minced ginger

Minced cilantro for garnish

This is a different kind of classic, but one that is equally venerable as the first two French-style ones. You can consider the additions of bok choy and water chestnuts optional; without them, this is a fairly simple preparation (though no less time-consuming). Almost needless to say, serve this with white rice.

1 Put 2 tablespoons of the oil in a deep heavy skillet or casserole and turn the heat to high. Brown the ribs well on all sides, seasoning well with salt and pepper as they cook; this will take about 20 minutes. Remove the ribs, pour out and discard the fat, and wipe out the pan.

2 Preheat the oven to 350°F. Put the remaining 2 tablespoons oil in the pan, turn the heat to medium-high, and add the onion, garlic, chopped ginger, and sugar. Cook, stirring, until the onion is very brown, 10 to 15 minutes.

3 Add the star anise, chiles, peppercorns, and cilantro stems; cook, stirring, for another minute, then add the sherry, soy sauce, and 3 cups water. Add the ribs, cover, and put in the oven. Cook until the meat is very tender and falling from the bone, about 3 hours; turn the meat once or twice an hour.

4 Just before the meat is done, steam the bok choy on a rack over boiling water until it is tender, 5 to 10 minutes; keep warm.

5 Transfer the ribs to a platter. Strain the vegetables and liquid, pressing hard on the vegetables to extract all of their juices, into another large pan and refrigerate (see Keys to Success) or reheat. Bring to a boil and whisk until slightly reduced, then add the ribs, water chestnuts, and minced ginger. Heat the ribs through, and adjust the seasoning as necessary. Place a portion of the bok choy on each of four plates and top with a portion of the meat and sauce; garnish with cilantro and serve.

MAKES 4 SERVINGS   TIME: AS LONG AS 4 HOURS, LARGELY UNATTENDED

Stewed short ribs with marrow butter

2 tablespoons neutral oil, such as canola or grapeseed	3 branches thyme
3 tablespoons butter	4 stems parsley
4 pounds short ribs	1 bay leaf
Salt and freshly ground black pepper	4 ounces marrow, cut into slices
1 large onion, peeled and roughly chopped	2 tablespoons minced shallots
1 large carrot, peeled and roughly chopped	3 tablespoons roughly chopped basil
1 stalk celery, roughly chopped	3 tablespoons roughly chopped chives
4 large cloves garlic, peeled and smashed	3 tablespoons roughly chopped chervil
1 bottle fruity but sturdy red wine, such as Côtes du Rhône or Zinfandel	3 tablespoons roughly chopped parsley
	2 tablespoons butter, softened
	1 tablespoon fresh lemon juice, or to taste

Here's a pull-out-all-the-stops dish that is best served (why not be consistent?) extravagantly on top of truffled mashed potatoes; if you make the ones on page 125 you can actually skip the gravy. Of course, Simple Mashed Potatoes (page 121) are nearly as good.

1 Put a tablespoon each of the oil and butter in a deep heavy skillet or casserole and turn the heat to high. Brown the ribs well on all sides, seasoning well with salt and pepper as they cook; this will take about 20 minutes. Remove the ribs, pour out and discard the fat, and wipe out the pan.

2 Preheat the oven to 350°F. Put the remaining 1 tablespoon oil and another tablespoon of butter in the pan, turn the heat to medium-high, and add the onion, carrot, celery, garlic, a large pinch of salt, and pepper to taste. Cook, stirring, until the onion is soft, about 10 minutes.

3 Add the red wine, thyme, parsley stems, and bay leaf to the pan and bring to a boil; add the ribs, cover, and put in the oven. Cook until the meat is very tender and falling from the bone, about 3 hours; turn the meat once or twice an hour.

4 Meanwhile, soak the marrow in cold salted water to cover for 2 hours. Bring a pot of water to a boil and add the marrow; cook very gently for 2 to 3 minutes, then drain.

5 Put 1 tablespoon butter in a small skillet and turn the heat to medium. Add the shallots, along with a pinch of salt, and cook, stirring occasionally, until softened, about 5 minutes. Put this in a small food processor with 2 tablespoons of each of the herbs, the marrow, and the softened butter and puree. Add salt and pepper and lemon juice to taste.

6 Transfer the ribs to a platter. Strain the vegetables and liquid, pressing hard on the vegetables to extract all of their juices, into another large pan and refrigerate (see Keys to Success) or reheat. Bring to a boil and stir in the marrow butter; whisk until slightly thickened, then add the ribs. Heat the ribs through, adjust the seasoning as necessary, and serve, garnished with the remaining herbs.

MAKES 4 SERVINGS   TIME: AS LONG AS 4 HOURS, LARGELY UNATTENDED

Braised veal

START with boneless veal, cut it into chunks, and then braise it. Unlike other meats, veal—thanks to its youth—braises quickly and remains tender. And because it has a high percentage of collagen, or connective tissue, it creates a silky broth. This is a real advantage, because you get all the assets of a long-braised meat dish in less than half the normal time.

A simple veal stew can be seasoned with almost anything: we begin with a little tomato paste and tarragon, continue with a Swiss-style combination of mushrooms and crème fraîche, then move to a Vietnamese-style stew with tamarind, and finally become really creative, using vanilla with Thai spices and, lastly, an asparagus puree. Most take under an hour, none much longer.

KEYS TO SUCCESS

Veal shoulder is the best cut for this group of recipes—it's inexpensive and easy to cut up.

Browning is an important step here; if your skillet isn't big enough to accommodate all the meat in one layer, brown it in batches. And take your time; it will pay off with more intense flavor and better color in the end.

Simple to Spectacular

Veal stew with tarragon

2 tablespoons neutral oil, such as canola or grapeseed

2 tablespoons butter (or use all oil)

1½ to 2 pounds boneless veal shoulder, cut into ½-inch chunks

Salt and freshly ground black pepper

¼ cup peeled and minced shallots

¼ cup tomato paste

1 tablespoon minced fresh tarragon, or ½ teaspoon dried tarragon

After about fifteen minutes of initial chopping and browning, you can all but ignore this simple braise until it's done. Serve with buttered egg noodles.

1 Put the oil and butter in a large skillet and turn the heat to medium-high. Season the veal well with salt and pepper. When the butter melts and its foam begins to subside, add the veal, turn the heat to high, and cook, turning only occasionally, until nicely browned, about 10 minutes. (Do this in batches if necessary.) When the veal is just about browned, add the shallots and continue to cook, stirring occasionally, for 3 minutes or so.

2 Add the tomato paste and stir, then add 1 cup water. Cook, stirring occasionally, until slightly thickened, a minute or two. Cover and turn the heat to medium-low; cook, checking every now and then, until the veal is tender, another 40 minutes or so, perhaps longer.

3 Stir in the tarragon, adjust the seasoning, and serve.

MAKES 4 SERVINGS   TIME: 1 HOUR OR MORE, LARGELY UNATTENDED

Veal stew *Zurichoise*

2 tablespoons neutral oil, such as canola or grapeseed

2 tablespoons butter (or use all oil)

1½ to 2 pounds boneless veal shoulder, cut into ½-inch chunks

Salt and freshly ground black pepper

2 cups trimmed and sliced white mushrooms

¼ cup peeled and minced shallots

1 cup dry white wine

1 cup crème fraîche

¼ cup chopped parsley leaves

Zurichoise means with mushrooms and cream. A classic veal stew, best served with rice, noodles, or bread.

1 Put the oil and butter in a large skillet and turn the heat to medium-high. Season the veal well with salt and pepper. When the butter melts and its foam begins to subside, add the veal, turn the heat to high, and cook, turning only occasionally, until nicely browned, about 10 minutes. (Do this in batches if necessary.) Transfer the veal to a plate and pour off any excess liquid it may have given off.

2 Add the mushrooms and shallots to the pan and cook over high heat, stirring occasionally, until the mushrooms begin to brown, about 10 minutes. Add the wine and cook, still over high heat, until it reduces by about half.

3 Turn the heat to medium-low and stir in the crème fraîche and the veal; cover and cook, checking every now and then, until the veal is tender, another 40 minutes or so, perhaps longer.

4 Stir in the parsley, adjust the seasoning, and serve.

MAKES 4 SERVINGS   TIME: 1 HOUR OR MORE, LARGELY UNATTENDED

Simple to Spectacular

Veal stew with pineapple and tomato

2 tablespoons neutral oil, such as canola or grapeseed

2 tablespoons butter (or use all oil)

1½ to 2 pounds of boneless veal shoulder, cut into 2-inch chunks

Salt and freshly ground black pepper

1½ cups fresh pineapple chunks

1 cup roughly chopped onions

2 tablespoons chopped garlic

1 cup chopped tomatoes

1½ cups peeled turnips or daikon radish cut into 1-inch chunks

1 small chile, stemmed, seeded, and minced

½ cup tamarind puree (see Note)

¼ cup chopped cilantro

Here we use the flavors we encountered over and over on a trip to Vietnam: pineapple, chile, tomato, and tamarind. It's a wonderful combination of sweet, sour, and spicy, and it works perfectly with veal.

Note that the veal chunks are bigger in this—and the subsequent recipes—so the cooking time is longer.

1 Put the oil and butter in a large skillet and turn the heat to medium-high. Season the veal well with salt and pepper. When the butter melts and its foam begins to subside, add the veal, turn the heat to high, and cook, turning only occasionally, until nicely browned, about 10 minutes. (Do this in batches if necessary.) Transfer the veal to a plate and pour off any excess liquid it may have given off.

2 Add the pineapple, onions, and garlic to the pan and cook, stirring only occasionally, until the pineapple begins to brown, about 5 minutes. Return the veal to the skillet and add the tomatoes, turnips or daikon, chile, tamarind puree, and 2 cups water. Bring to a boil, then cover and turn the heat to medium-low; cook, checking every now and then, until the veal is tender, at least another hour.

3 Stir in the cilantro, adjust the seasoning, and serve.

Note *To make tamarind puree:* Combine 2 cups tamarind pulp (it's sold in almost every Asian food market and in many supermarkets) in a saucepan with 1 cup water, and turn the heat to medium. Cook, whisking lightly, breaking up the lumps, and adding more water whenever the mixture becomes dry, until you've added a total of about 2 cups. The process will take about 10 minutes; the result should still be quite thick, but fairly smooth. Strain, then measure ½ cup for this recipe. The remainder will keep, refrigerated, for several weeks.

MAKES 4 SERVINGS   TIME: 1½ HOURS OR LONGER, LARGELY UNATTENDED

Veal stew with vanilla

2 tablespoons neutral oil, such as canola or grapeseed

2 tablespoons butter (or use all oil)

1½ to 2 pounds boneless veal shoulder, cut into 2-inch chunks

Salt and freshly ground black pepper

1 carrot, peeled and roughly chopped

1 stalk celery, roughly chopped

6 sprigs thyme

1 stalk lemongrass, trimmed, bruised with the back of a knife, and cut into a few pieces

2 cloves garlic, peeled and crushed

1 small chile, stemmed and seeded

3 lime leaves

1 vanilla bean

4 cups One-Hour Chicken Stock (page 3) or other chicken stock

8 shiitake mushrooms, stems removed and discarded

8 pearl onions, peeled

1 cup sugar snap or snow peas, trimmed

2 tablespoons crème fraîche

3 tablespoons canned unsweetened coconut milk

1 tablespoon fresh lime juice

Vanilla adds a beguiling flavor to a dish with mostly Thai flavors. We think it works well. The garnish in Step 3 can comprise any assortment of small vegetables you like—turnips, carrots, shallots, zucchini, or almost anything else—as long as they are blanched until just tender.

1 Put the oil and butter in a large skillet and turn the heat to medium-high. Season the veal well with salt and pepper. When the butter melts and its foam begins to subside, add the veal, turn the heat to high, and cook, turning only occasionally, until nicely browned, about 10 minutes. (Do this in batches if necessary.)

2 Add the carrot, celery, thyme, lemongrass, garlic, chili, and lime leaves. Split the vanilla bean lengthwise in half, scrape out the seeds, and set them aside; add the pod to the pan. Stir in the chicken stock and bring to a boil, then cover and turn the heat to medium-low; cook, checking every now and then, until the veal is tender, at least another hour.

3 Meanwhile, bring a medium pot of water to the boil. Blanch the shiitakes until tender, about 3 minutes; remove with a slotted spoon and plunge into a bowl of ice water to stop the cooking. Repeat with the onions and then the peas. Drain the cooled vegetables and set aside.

4 When the meat is tender, remove it from the pan. Strain the cooking liquid, pressing on the vegetables to extract as much liquid as possible, into a clean pan. Put the pan over medium heat, whisk in plenty of black pepper, the vanilla seeds, crème fraîche, coconut milk, and lime juice, and bring to a simmer. Stir in the veal and blanched vegetables and heat through; adjust the seasoning and serve.

MAKES 4 SERVINGS   TIME: 1½ HOURS OR LONGER, LARGELY UNATTENDED

Veal stew with asparagus

2 tablespoons neutral oil, such as canola or grapeseed

2 tablespoons butter (or use all oil)

1½ to 2 pounds boneless veal shoulder, cut into 2-inch chunks

Salt and freshly ground black pepper

1 large onion, peeled and roughly chopped

2 carrots, peeled and roughly chopped

2 shallots, peeled and roughly chopped

6 cloves garlic, peeled and lightly crushed

1 stalk celery, roughly chopped

6 thyme sprigs

2 cups One-Hour Chicken Stock (page 3) or other chicken stock

1½ pounds thick asparagus spears, trimmed

4 ounces stemmed shiitake mushrooms, the caps left whole

There are two sauces here, one a veal jus rôti—a dark stock based on light stock—and the other a puree made from the asparagus trimmings. The combination is attractive and intensely flavorful.

1 Preheat the oven to 450°F. Put the oil and butter in a large ovenproof skillet and turn the heat to medium-high. Season the veal well with salt and pepper. When the butter melts and its foam begins to subside, add the veal, turn the heat to high, and cook, turning only occasionally, until nicely browned, about 10 minutes. (Do this in batches if necessary.) Transfer the veal to a plate and pour off any excess liquid it may have given off.

2 Add the onion, carrots, shallots, garlic, celery, and thyme to the pan; cook, stirring occasionally, for a minute, then return the veal to the pan. Put the pan in the oven and roast, stirring occasionally, until the vegetables are nicely browned, about an hour. Add the stock and continue to roast, stirring occasionally, until the liquid is just about evaporated and the veal is very tender, about an hour longer.

3 Use a slotted spoon to transfer the veal to a saucepan, then strain the liquid, pressing on the solids to extract as much juice as possible; add the liquid to the pan with the veal. *(You can prepare the dish in advance to this point; cover and refrigerate for up to a day before proceeding. Reheat as necessary.)*

4 About 30 minutes before serving, remove the tips from the asparagus; blanch them in boiling salted water until bright green, then remove with a slotted spoon and plunge into ice water to stop the cooking. Repeat with the shiitakes (do not drain the water).

5 Chop the asparagus stalks into small pieces and cook in the boiling water until very tender, about 10 minutes. (Again, do not drain the water; keep it hot.) Puree in a blender with as little of the cooking liquid as you need to allow the blender to do its work. Put in a small saucepan and keep warm over the lowest possible heat.

6 When the veal is ready, reheat the asparagus tips and shiitakes in the hot water. Serve the veal with some of its juices, surrounded by the asparagus puree, asparagus tips, and shiitakes.

MAKES 4 SERVINGS   TIME: ABOUT 2 HOURS, SOMEWHAT UNATTENDED

Roast pork loin

A too-often-ignored cut of meat, the pork loin—bone-in, please—roasts perfectly, becoming brown and crisp on the outside while remaining moist, tender, and juicy inside. The first three recipes here are quite traditional: a simple roast pork with rosemary; one with mixed vegetables; and the classic treatment, using lardons—pieces of bacon—to add extra moisture. The fourth recipe features a wonderful citrus gastrique, a caramelized sweet-and-sour sauce, and we finish with a fairly traditional Alsatian pork and cabbage—but smoke the pork, Chinese-style, beforehand.

KEYS TO SUCCESS

Bone-in loin will cook more evenly and remain moister than meat that has been boned. Cut into chops for serving.

If the parts of the bones without meat or fat are browning too quickly, turn the roast, or shield the bones with a piece of aluminum foil.

If the bottom of the roasting pan dries out, splash in a little water or wine—in none of these recipes should the drippings be allowed to burn.

An instant-read thermometer prevents under- or over-cooking. If you remove the roast when the thermometer reads 145°F (test it in two or three places to be sure) and let it rest for a few minutes before carving, its temperature will rise to 155°F, which will leave the center barely pink; that's how you want it.

Roast pork with rosemary

1 tablespoon rosemary leaves, preferably fresh

¼ cup sugar

1 teaspoon salt

½ teaspoon cayenne pepper

One 2½- to 3-pound bone-in pork loin roast

½ cup dry white wine

A simple preparation that could easily become part of your standard repertoire, as it has of ours.

1 Preheat the oven to 450°F. Combine the rosemary, sugar, salt, and cayenne and rub this mixture all over the pork. Put the pork in a large ovenproof casserole or a roasting pan, fat side down, and put in the oven. Roast for 15 minutes, shaking the pan once or twice to prevent the pork from sticking, for about 15 minutes. Turn and splash with the wine.

2 Continue to roast, basting with the pan juices every 15 minutes or so, for about 1 hour and 15 minutes, or until an instant-read thermometer inserted into the center of the meat measures 145°F and the pork is a beautiful brown. Remove from the oven.

3 Let the pork rest for a few minutes, then carve and serve with the pan juices.

MAKES 4 SERVINGS   TIME: ABOUT 1½ HOURS

Simple to Spectacular

Roast pork with vegetables

6 tablespoons butter

¼ cup neutral oil, such as canola or grapeseed

1 large onion, peeled and cut into thick slices

6 large cloves garlic, peeled

Salt and freshly ground black pepper

8 ounces carrots, peeled and cut diagonally into thick slices

2 large tomatoes (1 pound or more), peeled, seeded, and cut into quarters

One 2½- to 3-pound bone-in pork loin roast

6 branches thyme

This takes longer than some of the other recipes, but the results are worth it—you end up with beautifully caramelized vegetables and delicious meat. All you need is a salad and/or a loaf of bread to complete the feast.

1 Put 1 tablespoon each of the butter and oil in a large skillet and turn the heat to high. When the butter foam subsides, sear the onion and garlic on both sides until good and brown, 3 to 4 minutes per side; season, then remove and set aside. Wipe out the skillet, add another tablespoon each of butter and oil and repeat with the carrots; season, remove, and set aside. Again, wipe out the skillet, add another tablespoon each of butter and oil, and repeat with the tomatoes, cooking them on their smooth side only, for about half the time; season, remove the tomatoes (and their juices), and set aside. (*All of this can be done several hours in advance if you like; keep the vegetables at room temperature.*)

2 Preheat the oven to 450°F. Once more, wipe out the skillet, add another tablespoon each of butter and oil, and sear the pork on all sides, browning and seasoning it well.

3 Layer the pork and vegetables in a large ovenproof casserole or a roasting pan. Top with the remaining 2 tablespoons butter and the thyme. Roast, basting every 15 minutes or so, for about 1 hour and 15 minutes, or until an instant-read thermometer inserted into the center of the meat measures 145°F. Remove from the oven.

4 Let the pork rest for a few minutes, then carve the meat and serve with the vegetables and pan juices.

MAKES 4 SERVINGS   TIME: ABOUT 2 HOURS

Roast pork with lardons

2 ounces slab bacon, in one piece

12 sage leaves

One 2½- to 3-pound bone-in pork loin roast

4 tablespoons butter

2 tablespoons neutral oil, such as grapeseed or canola

30 pearl onions, peeled

Salt and freshly ground black pepper

3 tablespoons honey

4 lemons

5 sprigs sage

This is a dish with plenty going for it: It is sweet (onions and honey), sour (lemons), and even homey, what with the sage and bacon.

1 Cut the bacon into 12 long thin pieces and wrap each one in a sage leaf. Using a knife and your fingers, poke 12 holes in the meat and shove these little packages into them.

2 Preheat the oven to 450°F. Combine 2 tablespoons of the butter with the oil in a large ovenproof casserole or a roasting pan. Turn the heat to medium-high and, when the butter foam subsides, brown the onions, stirring occasionally, for about 10 minutes.

3 Season the pork with salt and pepper. Drizzle some of the honey over the pork and put it, fat side down, in the casserole. Add the lemons, sage, and the remaining 2 tablespoons butter. Drizzle the remaining honey over all.

4 Roast, turning the pork after 15 minutes and basting every 15 minutes or so, for about 1 hour and 15 minutes, or until an instant-read thermometer inserted into the center of the meat measures 145°F. Remove from the oven.

5 Let the pork rest for a few minutes, then carve the meat and serve with the onions and pan juices. Cut the lemons open, scoop out the pulp, and serve them on top of the meat.

MAKES 4 SERVINGS   TIME: ABOUT 1½ HOURS

Roast pork with citrus caramel

Minced zest and juice of 1 lemon

Minced zest and juice of 1 lime

Minced zest and juice of 1 orange

½ cup sherry vinegar

½ cup sugar

1 tablespoon cracked black pepper

1 tablespoon butter

1 tablespoon neutral oil, such as canola or grapeseed

One 2½- to 3-pound bone-in pork loin roast

Salt and freshly ground black pepper

A distinctive dish that begins with an unforgettable bitter caramel sauce known as a gastrique. Good with Lentil Pancakes (page 164).

1 Preheat the oven to 450°F. Combine the citrus juices and vinegar and set aside. Combine the sugar, citrus zest, and pepper in a heavy pot and turn the heat to medium-high. Do not stir until the sugar melts; once it has, stir occasionally until nicely browned. Turn off the heat, stand back, and add the citrus-vinegar mixture. Return to medium heat and cook, stirring, until the caramel dissolves. Set aside.

2 Combine the butter and oil in a heavy ovenproof casserole or a roasting pan over medium-high heat. When the butter foam subsides, add the pork and sear it on all sides, seasoning it well. When the pork is browned, add the caramel mixture and turn the pork over a few times in it, ending with the fat side up.

3 Roast, basting the pork every 15 minutes or so, for about 1 hour and 15 minutes, adding a tablespoon or two of water at a time as necessary to keep the liquid syrupy, until an instant-read thermometer inserted into the center of the meat measures 145°F. Remove from the oven.

4 Let the pork rest for a few minutes, then carve the meat and serve with the pan juices.

MAKES 4 SERVINGS   TIME: ABOUT 1½ HOURS

Smoked roast pork with cabbage

1 cup sugar

1 cup Lapsang Souchong or other black tea

1 cup uncooked rice

6 cloves

6 star anise

Peel of 1 orange

One 2½- to 3-pound bone-in pork loin roast

One 2- to 2½-pound red cabbage, cored and thinly shredded

⅓ cup red wine vinegar

Salt and freshly ground black pepper

2 tablespoons butter

1 large onion, peeled and sliced

1 mango, peeled, pit removed, and thinly sliced

1 cup dry red wine

A gorgeous dish, purple, yellow, and brown, and rich in flavor as well. Line whatever pot you use for the smoking with a double thickness of heavy-duty aluminum foil, or use a pot you don't care about. And try your best to use Lapsang Souchong tea, which has already been smoked and will therefore give a more intense flavor to the pork.

1 Line the inside of a wok or a large pot with a double layer of heavy-duty foil (or use a pot you don't care about). Combine the sugar, tea, rice, spices, and orange peel in the bottom; place a rack over this mixture (or you can build a little platform with chopsticks or knives) and lay the pork on the rack. Cover tightly with foil, leaving just one tiny gap, no bigger than ¼ inch. Turn the heat to high and, when the smoke starts to come out, adjust the heat so that smoke escapes slowly. Smoke, undisturbed, for about 1 hour.

2 Meanwhile, soak the cabbage in a mixture of the vinegar and 1 teaspoon salt.

3 When the pork is ready, preheat the oven to 450°F. Put the butter in a large heavy casserole and turn the heat to medium-high. Add the onion and cook, stirring, until it softens; you do not want it to brown. Add the cabbage and season it well. Bury the pork in the cabbage, top with the mango, and pour in the red wine.

4 Bring to a boil, transfer to the oven, and cook, stirring the cabbage occasionally and adding a little more wine or water if necessary, until the pork and cabbage are tender, about 1 hour. Carve the pork and serve.

MAKES 4 SERVINGS   TIME: ABOUT 2½ HOURS, LARGELY UNATTENDED

THESE are venison steaks, not very different in appearance from the beef tender-loin steaks on pages 298–305 (either can be used in either set of recipes). Wild venison, of course, is more strongly flavored than beef, and most people like the difference. If you don't, you can find mild farm-raised venison, or simply use beef tenderloin in these recipes.

Venison and juniper are a natural combination—they both come from the same woods—and we begin there. Then we make good use of a classic Alsatian combination of dried pears and bacon. From there we go to an Asian-flavored preparation, then a lovely (and pink) beet-and-onion sauce. Finally, we make a venison stew as a sauce for the steaks.

KEYS TO SUCCESS

Wild venison varies greatly in flavor, from fairly mild to rather strong and bitter; if you don't know whether you like it or not, you might be better off starting out with farm-raised venison.

Venison is very lean and should not be overcooked; treat it like beef and keep it medium-rare.

Venison with juniper

8 venison medallions (about 1½ pounds)

30 juniper berries, crushed and minced

Salt and freshly ground black pepper

3 tablespoons butter

2 tablespoons neutral oil, such as canola or grapeseed

½ cup gin

Simple enough for a weeknight, elegant enough for guests. Juniper berries are sold in the spice section; when fairly fresh, they are soft enough to mince easily. If yours are dry and hard, coarsely grind them in a coffee or spice mill. The hit of gin at the end really boosts the flavor of juniper.

1 Sprinkle the venison medallions with the juniper and salt and pepper.

2 Put 2 tablespoons of the butter and the oil in a large skillet and turn the heat to medium-high. When the butter foam subsides, add the venison and turn the heat to high. Cook until nicely browned, about 2 minutes; turn, lower the heat to medium, and continue to cook, turning once or twice, until medium-rare, about 6 minutes total.

3 Transfer the meat to a warm platter. Add the gin to the pan, and turn the heat up to high again. Reduce the gin to about 2 tablespoons, then stir in the remaining 1 tablespoon butter. Spoon the sauce over the venison and serve.

MAKES 4 SERVINGS   TIME: 15 MINUTES

Venison medallions with poires au lard

8 dried pear halves, preferably unsulphured

3 ounces good bacon, cut into strips 1 inch long and ¼ inch thick

1 large onion, peeled and sliced

1 small chile, stemmed and minced

2 bay leaves

6 sprigs thyme

2 cups any good chicken stock

3 tablespoons neutral oil, such as canola or grapeseed

8 venison medallions (about 1½ pounds)

Salt and freshly ground black pepper

Chopped parsley for garnish

These delicious pears, which could become a winter staple in your house, are a wonderful accompaniment to any hearty meat dish. You can prepare them in advance and reheat them if you like.

1 Soak the pears overnight (or for at least 2 hours) in water to cover; drain.

2 Preheat the oven to 350°F. Put the bacon in a medium ovenproof skillet and turn the heat to medium-high. Cook, stirring occasionally, until crisp, then remove with a slotted spoon and set aside. Add the onion to the pan and cook until it is lightly browned, then transfer to a shallow baking dish; top with the chile, bay leaves, thyme, and drained pears.

3 Add the stock to the skillet, turn the heat to high, and cook, stirring occasionally, until reduced by about half; pour the stock over the onion mixture. Cover with foil and bake for 40 minutes, undisturbed.

4 About 10 minutes before the pears are done, put the oil in a large skillet and turn the heat to medium-high. One or two minutes later, add the venison and turn the heat to high. Season the meat with salt and pepper and cook until nicely browned, about 2 minutes; turn, lower the heat to medium, and continue to cook, turning once or twice, until medium-rare, about 6 minutes total.

5 Just before the medallions are done, sprinkle the bacon over the top of the pears and run under the broiler to brown lightly.

6 To serve, put 2 pear halves on each plate, along with 2 medallions; spoon some of the pear juice and onions over all, and garnish with parsley.

MAKES 4 SERVINGS   TIME: AT LEAST 3 HOURS, LARGELY UNATTENDED

Venison medallions with shallot-soy sauce

1 cup light soy sauce

½ cup rice vinegar

1 tablespoon honey

2 shallots, peeled and sliced

3 cloves garlic, peeled and sliced

1½ teaspoons peppercorns

6 tablespoons butter

Freshly ground black pepper

¼ cup fresh lime juice, or more to taste

8 ounces shiitake mushrooms, trimmed, stemmed, and diced

4 ounces enoki mushrooms, bottoms trimmed, diced

1 tablespoon minced ginger

2 tablespoons chopped chives

2 tablespoons neutral oil, such as canola or grapeseed

8 venison medallions (about 1½ pounds)

This soy-based sauce is great with any red meat, whether roasted, sautéed, or grilled. For the mushrooms, use an assortment if you can, or simply rely on shiitakes (caps only) or the more common white mushrooms.

1 Combine the first 6 ingredients in a small saucepan and turn the heat to medium-high. Reduce by about one-third; cover and let sit overnight, refrigerated.

2 Strain the sauce, then combine it in a small saucepan with 4 tablespoons of the butter, at least 1 teaspoon ground black pepper, and the lime juice. Bring to a boil, taste, and adjust the seasoning; the sauce should be very strongly flavored. Keep it warm.

3 Put the remaining 2 tablespoons butter in a medium skillet and turn the heat to high. When the foam subsides, add the mushrooms and ginger, and cook, stirring

occasionally, until the mushrooms become tender, then brown and become a little crunchy. Stir in the chives and turn the heat to low to keep warm while you cook the venison.

4 Put the oil in a large skillet and turn the heat to medium-high. One or two minutes later, add the venison, and turn the heat to high. Season the meat and cook until nicely browned, about 2 minutes; turn, lower the heat to medium, and continue to cook, turning once or twice, until medium-rare, about 6 minutes total.

5 To serve, put a puddle of sauce on each plate, top with the venison, and surround the meat with the mushrooms.

MAKES 4 SERVINGS   TIME: OVERNIGHT, LARGELY UNATTENDED

Venison medallions with beet-and-nut soubise

5 tablespoons butter, softened

2 large onions (about 1 pound), peeled and thinly sliced

1½ pounds beets, trimmed, peeled, and thinly sliced

Salt and freshly ground black pepper

4 large venison medallions (about 1½ pounds)

Flour for dredging

2 eggs, lightly beaten in a bowl

2 cups peeled chestnuts, cashews, almonds, or other nuts, very finely chopped

2 tablespoons neutral oil, such as canola or grapeseed

Crunchy, nut-coated venison in a hot-pink sauce—kind of wild. Use a food processor to chop the nuts here, and keep them fairly coarse, not at all powdery. Keep the heat more moderate when you're cooking the venison than in the other recipes in order not to burn the coating.

1 Preheat the oven to 350°F. Smear 2 tablespoons of the butter in the bottom of a shallow casserole or gratin dish. Make a layer of onions and beets, season with salt and pepper, and repeat three or four times. Top with 2 tablespoons butter. Cover with a piece of parchment paper or foil, then cover with a lid or more foil; the seal should be tight. Bake for about 1 hour, undisturbed, until the beets and onions are very tender.

2 Puree the beets and onions carefully in a blender (it's hot), adding a little bit of stock or water if necessary. Taste and adjust the seasoning, then keep warm in the oven (you can turn it off).

3 Season the medallions with salt and pepper. Dredge them lightly in flour, tapping to remove the excess, then run them through the beaten eggs. Finally, press a layer of chopped nuts onto both sides of each medallion.

4 Combine the remaining tablespoon of butter and the oil in a large skillet and turn the heat to medium-high. When the butter foam subsides, add the venison and turn the heat to medium. Cook slowly and carefully, so the nuts brown but do not burn; turn as frequently as is necessary. Total cooking time for medium-rare medallions will be 10 to 15 minutes. To serve, make a puddle of the soubise on each plate and top with a medallion.

MAKES 4 SERVINGS   TIME: 1½ HOURS

Simple to Spectacular

Venison medallions with venison sauce

¼ cup neutral oil, such as canola or grapeseed

2 carrots, peeled and roughly chopped

2 stalks celery, roughly chopped

2 onions, peeled and roughly chopped

4 cloves garlic, peeled and roughly chopped

2 stalks lemongrass, trimmed and roughly chopped

8 juniper berries, crushed with the side of a knife

Salt and freshly ground black pepper

1½ cups red wine vinegar

2 cups dry red wine

1 pound venison stew meat

4 to 6 small venison medallions (1 to 1½ pounds)

1 cinnamon stick

3 juniper berries

½ teaspoon peppercorns

½ teaspoon Szechwan peppercorns

1 star anise

½ teaspoon coriander seeds

½ teaspoon nigella

½ teaspoon cardamom seeds

½ teaspoon ground ginger

5 tablespoons butter

1 teaspoon sugar

1 teaspoon Curry Powder (page 344), or use commercial curry powder

1 tablespoon minced ginger

1 tablespoon minced lemongrass

½ pineapple, peeled, cored, and cut into 8 to 12 chunks

This is really two recipes in one—you first make a venison stew to use as a "sauce" for the venison steaks. It's filled with wonderful, exotic flavors, and is incredibly delicious, so you may think, as we do, that it's worth the effort.

Nigella is sometimes called black onion seed, and they are similar in appearance, but there is no relationship between the two. The tiny triangular black seeds have a sharp, pleasant flavor; if you cannot find them, though, you can leave them out.

1 Put 2 tablespoons of the oil in a medium saucepan and turn the heat to medium-high. A minute later, add half of the carrots, celery, onions, and garlic, along with the chopped lemongrass, crushed juniper berries, a big pinch of salt, and pepper to taste. Cook, stirring occasionally, until the vegetables become tender, 10 to 15 minutes.

2 Add the vinegar and stir; cook over high heat, stirring occasionally, until the mixture is almost dry, then add ½ cup of the wine. Bring to a boil, then turn the heat to medium-low and simmer for 30 minutes, stirring only once or twice. Cool, then strain, pressing on the solids to extract as much liquid as possible.

3 Marinate all the venison in this liquid, refrigerated, for 24 hours. Combine the cinnamon, whole juniper berries, black and Szechwan peppercorns, star anise, coriander, nigella, and cardamom in a dry small skillet over medium heat. Toast, shaking the skillet periodically, until the spices are fragrant, just a minute or two. Stir in the ginger. Grind to a powder, using a spice or coffee mill or mortar and pestle.

4 Remove the meat from the marinade. Strain the liquid, bring it to a boil, and skim anything that rises to the surface; set aside. Dry the stew meat. Put 1 tablespoon each of the butter and oil in a large heavy skillet and turn the heat to medium-high. When the butter foam subsides, add the stew meat, turn the heat to high, and sprinkle the meat with the sugar. Pour off the liquid that comes out of the meat and keep cooking, stirring occasionally, until the meat is nicely browned—this could take as long as 15 minutes; turn the heat down a bit if the meat threatens to scorch.

5 Add 1 teaspoon of the spice mixture, then another tablespoon of butter, and finally the remaining onions, carrots, celery, and garlic and the curry. Cook until the vegetables begin to brown, 2 to 3 minutes, then add the minced ginger, minced lemongrass, and the remaining 1½ cups wine. Let the wine bubble for a minute, then add the marinade, cover, and simmer, not too slowly, for 1 hour or so.

6 Just before serving, put 2 tablespoons of the butter in a nonstick skillet and turn the heat to medium-high; when it melts, add the pineapple and cook, turning occasionally, until nicely browned all over, 8 to 12 minutes. Keep warm.

7 Dry the medallions and rub them with a little of the remaining spice mix, along with some salt and pepper. Put the remaining 1 tablespoon each butter and oil in a large skillet and turn the heat to medium-high. When the butter foam subsides, add the venison and turn the heat to medium. Cook slowly and carefully, so the spice mix does not burn; turn as frequently as is necessary. Total cooking time for medium-rare medallions will be 8 to 12 minutes, depending on their size.

8 To serve, put a medallion on each plate, with a portion of the stew, including some of the vegetables, and a little dusting of the spice mix.

MAKES 4 TO 6 SERVINGS   TIME: 24 HOURS, LARGELY UNATTENDED

Rabbit

RABBIT is naturally more flavorful and more tender than chicken, to which it is often compared, though in taste and texture it is more like the best veal. It takes to a variety of simple cooking techniques.

We begin with a classic rustic preparation that includes thyme, shallots, and mushrooms; the second dish starts the same way, but finishes under the broiler, with a mustard coating. Next up is rabbit curry, a popular dish that has been on the menu at Vong since it opened, followed by the supremely tender rabbit confit, served with an arugula salad. Finally, there is rabbit pho—our take on the ubiquitous Vietnamese soup.

KEYS TO SUCCESS

Rabbit is similar to chicken in structure, but it is not the same. Cut it into 10 pieces—the rack, saddle, flaps, and rear and front legs each providing 2 pieces.

Don't overcook; rabbit should be well done but not at all dry.

All of these recipes will work equally well for cut-up chicken; the first three will work well for veal chunks also.

Rabbit chasseur

2 tablespoons extra-virgin olive oil

3 tablespoons butter (or use all oil)

One 2- to 3-pound rabbit, cut into 10 pieces

8 cloves garlic, peeled and lightly crushed

4 sprigs thyme

Salt and freshly ground black pepper

15 small shallots, or pearl onions, peeled

8 ounces mushrooms, any type you like, trimmed and sliced
(remove and discard stems of shiitakes)

½ cup dry white wine

¼ cup minced chives

A simple, rustic dish that is a perfect introduction to the pleasures of rabbit.

1 Preheat the oven to 400°F. Put the oil and 2 tablespoons of the butter in a large ovenproof skillet and turn the heat to medium-high. When the butter melts, add the rabbit pieces and turn the heat to high. When the rabbit begins to brown, turn the heat to medium and add the garlic, thyme, and salt and pepper to taste. When the rabbit is nicely browned, stir in the shallots and mushrooms and put the skillet in the oven for 15 minutes.

2 Remove all but the legs from the skillet and keep warm. Add the wine, stir, and return to the oven for another 10 minutes.

3 Put the skillet on top of the stove and remove the legs, adding them to the other meat. Add the remaining 1 tablespoon butter to the cooking liquid and stir until melted, then taste and add more salt and pepper if necessary.

4 Spoon the sauce and vegetables over the rabbit and serve, garnished with the chives.

MAKES 4 SERVINGS   TIME: 40 MINUTES

Rabbit with mustard

2 tablespoons extra-virgin olive oil

3 tablespoons butter (or use all oil)

One 2- to 3-pound rabbit, cut into 10 pieces

8 cloves garlic, peeled and lightly crushed

4 sprigs thyme

Salt and freshly ground black pepper

15 small shallots or pearl onions, peeled

½ cup dry white wine

½ cup Dijon mustard

2 cups fresh bread crumbs, more or less

1 tablespoon sherry vinegar

Minced parsley for garnish

Similar to the first presentation, but finished with a coating of Dijon mustard and bread crumbs—you might call this devilled rabbit. Serve with a salad and sautéed potatoes.

1 Preheat the oven to 400°F. Put the oil and 2 tablespoons of the butter in a large ovenproof skillet and turn the heat to medium-high. When the butter melts, add the rabbit pieces and turn the heat to high. When the rabbit begins to brown, turn the heat to medium and add the garlic, thyme, and salt and pepper to taste. When the rabbit is nicely browned, stir in the shallots and put the skillet in the oven for 15 minutes.

2 Remove all but the legs from the skillet and put on a baking sheet. Add the wine to the skillet, stir, and return to the oven for another 10 minutes.

3 Put the skillet on top of the stove and remove the legs, adding them to the other meat. Turn on the broiler; set the rack a good 4 or even 6 inches from the heat source. Smear the meat all over with the mustard, then dip it in the bread crumbs to coat; set aside. Strain the rabbit cooking liquid, then put it in a small saucepan over low heat; stir in the remaining butter and 1 tablespoon sherry vinegar and keep warm.

4 Broil the rabbit until lightly browned on both sides, just a couple of minutes, turning only once. Spoon some of the sauce onto each of four plates and top with the rabbit; garnish with parsley and serve.

MAKES 4 SERVINGS   TIME: 45 MINUTES

Curried **rabbit**

7 stalks lemongrass

2 ounces galangal or ginger

7 small chiles

6 lime leaves, chopped

1 teaspoon cumin seeds, lightly toasted in a skillet until fragrant

¾ cup cilantro stems (include the roots if possible), chopped

2 cloves garlic, peeled and chopped

3 shallots, peeled and minced

½ cup nam pla (Thai fish sauce)

3 tablespoons sugar

1 tablespoon Thai yellow curry paste (sold in most Asian markets)

One 2- to 3-pound rabbit, cut into 10 pieces

2 tablespoons peanut or neutral oil, such as canola or grapeseed

1 large onion, peeled and chopped

Salt and freshly ground black pepper

2 cups One-Hour Chicken Stock (page 3), or other chicken stock

1 can (about 12 ounces) unsweetened coconut milk

1 cup cilantro leaves

Juice of 1 lime

The actual work time for this dish is less than for any other dish in this section, but it is spread out over 24 hours; and you probably will have to do some shopping for special ingredients. The result is a super curry, best served with Steamed Sticky Rice (page 103), or jasmine rice cooked in coconut milk.

1   Trim, peel, and roughly chop 5 of the lemongrass stalks. Chop half the galangal or ginger. Stem and chop 5 of the chiles. Combine the chopped lemongrass, galangal, and chiles, 3 of the lime leaves, the cumin, cilantro stems, garlic, shallots, nam pla, sugar, and curry paste in a blender and puree. Rub this all over the rabbit and marinate, covered and refrigerated, overnight. (You will not need all of the mixture for marinating the rabbit—refrigerate the remainder separately.)

2   Put the oil in a deep skillet or casserole and turn the heat to medium-high. Add the onion and stir; add salt and pepper to taste and ½ cup of the remaining curry mix. When the onion is soft, add the rabbit and stock. Stir, then add the coconut milk, along with any remaining curry mix, including the marinade. Roughly

chop the remaining 2 stalks lemongrass, galangal or ginger, 2 chiles, and 3 lime leaves, and wrap them in cheesecloth; add them to the pan and bring to a boil. Turn the heat to low, partly cover, and simmer for about an hour.

3 When the rabbit is tender, transfer it to a warm platter. Remove the cheesecloth and carefully puree the sauce in a blender, with the cilantro. Blend in the lime juice, pour over the rabbit, and serve.

MAKES 4 SERVINGS   TIME: 90 MINUTES, PLUS OVERNIGHT MARINATING

Rabbit confit

One 2- to 3-pound rabbit, cut into 10 pieces, bones reserved

11 cloves garlic, peeled and lightly crushed

15 branches thyme

Coarse salt

3 cups duck fat or extra-virgin olive oil

1 tablespoon butter

¼ cup extra-virgin olive oil

1 carrot, peeled and chopped

1 onion, peeled and chopped

1 stalk celery, chopped

3 cloves

2 tablespoons sherry vinegar

Salt and freshly ground black pepper

6 to 8 cups arugula, trimmed, washed, and dried

This is also a perfect recipe for chicken or duck; it helps to have a thermometer so you can maintain the right temperature during the cooking. The best thing to round out the meal here is potatoes cut into chunks and sautéed in the fat you used for confiting; when they're crisp, finish them with a little minced garlic and some parsley.

1 Set aside the rabbit front legs and bones in the refrigerator. Mix the remaining rabbit with 10 cloves of the garlic, 10 branches of the thyme, and a few pinches of coarse salt and marinate, refrigerated, overnight.

2 Put the duck fat or olive oil in a saucepan large enough to accommodate it and the rabbit and turn the heat to medium. When the fat melts or the oil reaches about 200°F, add the marinated rabbit and the garlic from the marinade. Cook, never letting the heat exceed 200°F, until the meat is perfectly tender, about 1½ hours. Let cool in the fat if you have the time.

3 While the rabbit is cooking, combine the butter and 1 tablespoon of the oil in a skillet and turn the heat to medium-high. When the butter melts, add the rabbit front legs and bones and turn the heat to high. Brown well on both sides, then add the remaining garlic clove and 5 thyme branches, the carrot, onion, and celery. Cook until the vegetables begin to brown, around 10 minutes, then add 3 cups water and the cloves. Cook over high heat until only about ½ cup

liquid remains; strain, discard the solids, then transfer the liquid to a small saucepan and reduce over high heat to 3 tablespoons.

4 Combine the remaining 3 tablespoons olive oil and the sherry vinegar in a small bowl, along with salt and pepper to taste. Whisk to combine, then whisk in the reduced rabbit stock. Serve the cooled confit (including the garlic, if you like) on a bed of arugula, with the vinaigrette drizzled over all.

MAKES 4 TO 6 SERVINGS   TIME: 24 HOURS, LARGELY UNATTENDED

Rabbit pho

4 stalks lemongrass, bruised with the back of a knife and cut in half the long way

1 large knob ginger (about 6 ounces), cut in half the long way

1 large onion, cut in half (don't bother to peel it)

2 cinnamon sticks

3 star anise

2 small dried chiles

6 cloves garlic, peeled

One 2- to 3-pound rabbit, cut into 10 pieces

4 ounces rice vermicelli

2 cups broccoli florets (or use any assortment of vegetables you like)

1 tablespoon peeled and minced or julienned ginger

2 tablespoons soy sauce, or to taste

½ cup roughly chopped cilantro

½ cup roughly chopped basil leaves, preferably Thai

A fine meal-in-a-bowl, dark and rich with exotic flavors. Make sure you really blacken the seasonings in Step 1.

1 Char the lemongrass, halved ginger, and onion in a large dry skillet over high heat—really blacken these seasonings on both sides. Transfer them to a pot or casserole.

2 Combine the cinnamon, star anise, and chiles in a small skillet and turn the heat to medium. Toast, shaking the skillet periodically, until the spices are fragrant, just a minute or two. Add them to the pot, along with the garlic, rabbit, and water to cover. Bring to a boil, then turn the heat to medium and cook for about 1½ hours, or until the rabbit is very tender.

3 When the rabbit is just about done, soak the rice noodles in hot water to cover for at least 15 minutes. Cook the broccoli in boiling salted water until tender, about 5 minutes; drain and set aside.

4 When the rabbit is done, remove it and keep it warm. Strain the broth and return it to low heat. Add the minced ginger and soy sauce to taste. Drain the noodles and combine them with the rabbit and vegetables in a large terrine. Pour the broth over all and serve, garnished with the herbs.

MAKES 4 TO 6 SERVINGS   TIME: ABOUT 2 HOURS, SOMEWHAT UNATTENDED

Simple to Spectacular

Seasonings and sauces

THESE are simple salt mixtures, easily put together, that can make a big difference in almost any food, regardless of cooking method. They're also convenient when making spice rubs, mixed drinks, or anything else where you want "salt-plus."

We begin with a spicy salt that contains the not exactly secret ingredient of pepper; it's a no-brainer, but it's convenient and simple. Our celery salt will be a revelation, one that has nothing whatsoever in common with commercial celery salt. Ginger salt has been a staple for Jean-Georges for years; he always dries ginger peels to make it. The last two mixtures are more exotic, really salt-based spice rubs—both are great to have around.

KEYS TO SUCCESS

Use coarse salt, either kosher or sea.

Start with fresh spices whenever you can.

Don't think these last forever; they do not. Store in a covered container and use them as quickly as you can. Once ground, dried peels begin to lose potency within days.

Spicy **salt**

1 tablespoon peppercorns

1 tablespoon kosher salt

Think of this as a strong, convenient, and interesting salt. Leave it on the table and use it within a few days.

1 Crack the pepper in a spice grinder or coffee mill; it should not be too fine.

2 Combine with the salt.

MAKES 2 TABLESPOONS   TIME: 5 MINUTES

Celery **salt**

1 knob celeriac (celery root)

1 tablespoon kosher salt

This is incredible when added to a Bloody Mary, or sprinkled on simply grilled or roasted fish. Celeriac, or celery root, can be found in most supermarkets.

1 Wash and scrub the celeriac. Use a paring knife to remove 2 tablespoons of the peel; discard the hairy parts. Reserve the root itself for another use.

2 Set the peels on a pan in one layer in a warm, dry place and let sit until dry, 12 to 24 hours.

3 Combine the peels and salt in a spice grinder or coffee mill; grind until fairly fine. Store in a covered container; this will keep for a few weeks but will gradually decrease in intensity.

MAKES 2 TABLESPOONS   TIME: A FEW MINUTES, PLUS 12 TO 24 HOURS DRYING TIME

Simple to Spectacular

Ginger **salt**

1 large piece ginger

1 tablespoon kosher salt

This is nice in a saltshaker; it's perfect for most Asian dishes, great as a dry rub for grilled meat, wonderful on steamed fish or shellfish. If you like, add a teaspoon of black sesame seeds, which lend a lovely color and a slightly more complex flavor.

1 Wash and scrub the ginger. Use a paring knife to remove 2 tablespoons of the peel. Reserve the ginger itself for another use.

2 Set the peels on a pan in one layer in a warm, dry place and let sit until dry, 12 to 24 hours.

3 Combine the peels and salt in a spice grinder or coffee mill; grind until fairly fine. Store in a covered container; this will keep for a few weeks but will gradually decrease in intensity.

MAKES 2 TABLESPOONS   TIME: A FEW MINUTES, PLUS 12 TO 24 HOURS DRYING TIME

Exotic **salt**

½ star anise

1 clove

¼ teaspoon nutmeg, preferably in one piece rather than ground

1 teaspoon coriander seeds

½ teaspoon red pepper flakes

½ teaspoon cumin seeds

1½ tablespoons kosher salt

Sprinkle this on fish or chicken just before grilling or roasting, then add a little bit more after the cooking is done. Also good on lamb and game birds.

1 Combine all the spices except the salt in a small skillet and turn the heat to medium (if any of the spices are already ground, hold them aside with the salt). Toast, shaking the skillet occasionally, until fragrant, just a minute or two.

2 Combine the spices in a spice grinder or coffee mill; grind until fairly fine. Add the salt and any reserved spices and store in a covered container; this will keep for a few weeks but will gradually decrease in intensity.

MAKES ABOUT 2 TABLESPOONS   TIME: 15 MINUTES

Citrus **salt**

Zest of 1 orange, removed in strips with a peeler or paring knife

Zest of 1 lemon, removed in strips with a peeler or paring knife

Zest of 1 lime, removed in strips with a peeler or paring knife

¼ cup sugar

1 tablespoon kosher salt

Another mix that is perfect for fish, especially shrimp and scallops, and chicken. Or sprinkle some of it on Salmon Seviche with Green Peppercorns (page 203). Remove as much of the white pith from the inside of the zest as you can before cooking them.

1 Preheat the oven to 300°F. Combine the zest and sugar in a small saucepan with 1 cup water. Cook over medium heat, stirring only occasionally, until there is only about ¼ cup liquid left, about 15 minutes.

2 Drain the zest and put it on a foil-lined baking sheet. Bake for 35 minutes, or until dry; if the zest threatens to brown, turn down the heat. Let the zest cool to room temperature; it will crisp up in about 5 minutes.

3 Combine the zest in a spice grinder or coffee mill; grind until fairly fine. Add the salt and store in a covered container; this will keep for a few weeks but will gradually decrease in intensity.

MAKES ABOUT ¼ CUP   TIME: ABOUT 1 HOUR, SOMEWHAT UNATTENDED

Spice mixes

LIKE the seasoned salts on the preceding pages, these blends can be used before, during, or after cooking. The difference is that these are spice-, not salt-based, and therefore far more assertive. Some—chile and curry powder—are familiar to you, though you may not know how to make them from scratch. Others are Jean-Georges' creations, and he uses them in a variety of ways; see the individual mixes for suggestions.

KEYS TO SUCCESS

Use fresh, preferably whole, spices whenever possible. Whole spices retain their flavor much better than ground ones and can be toasted before grinding, which brings out their flavor even more.

Store these in closed opaque containers. They will last for weeks, even months, before losing a noticeable amount of flavor.

Chile **powder**

2 tablespoons dried oregano, preferably Mexican

1 to 2 teaspoons dried chiles, stemmed and crumbled, or to taste

1 tablespoon cumin seeds

If you use 1 teaspoon of chiles, this will be hot; 2 will make it fiery. Of course, this also depends on the type of chile.

1 Combine all the ingredients in a small dry skillet and turn the heat to medium. Toast, shaking the skillet periodically, until fragrant, just a minute or two.

2 Grind in a mortar and pestle or a spice or coffee grinder. Store, covered, for up to several months.

MAKES ABOUT ¼ CUP   TIME: 10 MINUTES

Curry **powder**

1 star anise

6 cardamom pods

3 cloves

½ teaspoon cumin seeds

2 teaspoons coriander seeds

½ teaspoon mace pieces or ground mace

½ teaspoon fenugreek, in one piece or ground

1 teaspoon white peppercorns

¼ teaspoon cayenne pepper

2 teaspoons turmeric

This is a good, fragrant, basic curry powder; infinite variations are possible, and you can easily make it hotter simply by adding more cayenne. Combine this with coconut milk, and you can make a quick curry of almost anything.

1 Combine the whole spices in a small dry skillet and turn the heat to medium. Toast, shaking the skillet periodically, until the spices are fragrant, just a minute or two.

2 Combine with the ground spices and grind in a mortar and pestle or a spice or coffee grinder. Store, covered, for up to several months.

MAKES ABOUT ¼ CUP   TIME: 10 MINUTES

Simple to Spectacular

Meat spice mix

2 teaspoons cardamom seeds, removed from the pods
(pods discarded)

1 clove

1 teaspoon dried red chile flakes

2 teaspoons sesame seeds

1 cinnamon stick

2 teaspoons cumin seeds

2 teaspoons fenugreek seeds or ground fenugreek

2 teaspoons mace pieces or ground mace

This is great rubbed on lamb, beef, or pork before roasting.

1 Combine the whole spices in a small dry skillet and turn the heat to medium.
Toast, shaking the skillet periodically, until the spices are fragrant, just a minute
or two.

2 Combine with the ground spices and grind in a mortar and pestle or a spice or
coffee grinder. Store, covered, for up to several months.

MAKES ABOUT ¼ CUP   TIME: 10 MINUTES

Mint-licorice **spice mix**

Finely grated zest of 1 lime

Finely grated zest of 1 orange

8 big or 12 small mint leaves

½ vanilla bean, minced (with the seeds)

½ licorice stick, roughly chopped

Real licorice comes in stick form, and it is not always easy to find—try a health food store, or an Asian market. It's very woody, so use a heavy knife to chop it.

Rub this on cod, scallops, or other fish before roasting.

1 Combine all ingredients on a sheet of waxed paper and microwave at half power for 30-second intervals, pinching and crumbling between each interval until dry. Or let sit in a warm place overnight.

2 Grind in a mortar and pestle or a spice or coffee grinder. Store, covered, for up to several months.

MAKES ABOUT ¼ CUP   TIME: 20 MINUTES (OR OVERNIGHT, LARGELY UNATTENDED)

Simple to Spectacular

Fish spice mix

1 tablespoon coriander seeds

1½ teaspoons cumin seeds

1 tablespoon star anise

1 whole nutmeg, broken into a few pieces

1 tablespoon red pepper flakes

4 cloves

Jean-Georges calls this "cod spice" because he uses it on cod all the time, but it's great on any white-fleshed fish that you're planning to roast, grill, or even steam.

1 Combine the spices in a small dry skillet and turn the heat to medium. Toast, shaking the skillet periodically, until the spices are fragrant, just a minute or two.

2 Grind in a mortar and pestle or a spice or coffee grinder. Store, covered, for up to several months.

MAKES ABOUT ¼ CUP   TIME: 10 MINUTES

Tapenade

TRADITIONAL tapenade is an olive puree, made with black olives, anchovies, and capers. We make it both simpler and more complicated—our basic tapenade is little more than olives. But we also create one with Moroccan spices, one with green olives and ginger, and a lovely combination of olive puree and Meyer lemons. All make wonderful dips for raw or cooked vegetables, condiments for simple grilled or broiled foods, or pre-roasting rubs for chicken or fish.

KEYS TO SUCCESS

Use brined, not oil-cured, olives. Although there are good olives produced in California, it's easiest to stick to those sold in bulk from France, Greece, Italy, or Spain.

Note that olives vary by weight depending on the relative size of pit and meat; measure after pitting.

To pit the olives, put a few at a time on a cutting board and press on them with the bottom of a pot to split them. Or press the side of a knife blade onto them, one at a time; lean on the knife until the olive splits. Then pull out and discard the pits. (Some olives are sold already split, which makes them easier to pit.)

Do not make the tapenades too fine—even if you use a blender or food processor, they should have the same coarse texture they would if you used a mortar and pestle.

Simplest tapenade

4 ounces pitted brined black olives (about 1 cup)

2 tablespoons extra-virgin olive oil

Salt and freshly ground black pepper

This will thin when first made, but once refrigerated, it will thicken and you can use it as a dip or a spread for bread. Or spread it on fish after cooking.

1 Combine the olives and oil with 1 tablespoon water in a blender or small food processor and blend until pureed, but not too fine. Add more water if necessary.

2 Season with salt and pepper and serve or refrigerate. Use within a couple of days.

MAKES ABOUT ¾ CUP   TIME: 10 MINUTES

Traditional **tapenade**

4 ounces pitted black olives (about 1 cup)

1 anchovy fillet

1 tablespoon capers, drained

1 teaspoon sherry vinegar

2 tablespoons extra-virgin olive oil

8 big leaves basil

Salt and freshly ground black pepper

This is the classic, a great dip for carrots, celery, fennel, or other raw vegetables, or for bread.

1 Combine the olives, anchovy, capers, vinegar, oil, basil, and 1 tablespoon water in a blender or small food processor and blend until pureed, but not too fine. Add more water if necessary.

2 Season with salt and pepper and serve or refrigerate. Use within a couple of days.

MAKES ABOUT ¾ CUP   TIME: 15 MINUTES

Tapenade with Moroccan spices

Seeds from 4 cardamom pods (discard the husks)

½ inch cinnamon stick

1 teaspoon coriander seeds

½ teaspoon cumin seeds

4 ounces pitted brined black olives (about 1 cup)

2 tablespoons extra-virgin olive oil

Salt and freshly ground black pepper

This is an unusual tapenade to start with, but the taste of cinnamon makes it unforgettable. Serve it with roasted or grilled chicken, or braise some chicken with this in the cooking mix.

1 Combine the spices in a small dry skillet and turn the heat to medium. Toast, shaking the skillet periodically, until the spices are fragrant, just a minute or two. Use a mortar and pestle or a coffee or spice grinder to grind the spices to a powder.

2 Combine the olives, oil, spice mix, and 1 tablespoon water in a blender or small food processor and blend until pureed, but not too fine. Add more water if necessary.

3 Season with salt and pepper and serve or refrigerate. Use within a couple of days.

MAKES ABOUT ¾ CUP   TIME: 15 MINUTES

Green olive tapenade with ginger and coriander

1 head garlic

2 tablespoons extra-virgin olive oil

¼ cup unpeeled almonds

1 lemon

4 ounces pitted brined green olives (about 1 cup)

½ ounce ginger (about a 1-inch piece), peeled and cut
into chunks

Salt and freshly ground black pepper

Begin with roasted garlic, then add almonds, lemon, ginger, and green olives, and you have an assertive but elegant tapenade, unlike any other. Use less salt in this tapenade, since green olives are generally saltier than black.

1 Preheat the oven to 350°F. Cut the head of garlic in half and place flesh side down in a small ovenproof skillet or pan. Drizzle the olive oil over the garlic. Roast for 40 minutes, or until nicely browned on the bottom. Cool, then squeeze out the pulp and mix with the oil.

2 Meanwhile, put the almonds in a small ovenproof skillet or pan and roast, shaking occasionally, until fragrant, about 15 minutes. Cool, then roughly chop.

3 Cut the lemon in half and segment it as you would a grapefruit, discarding the seeds. Combine the lemon pulp, olives, ginger, garlic and oil, and 1 tablespoon water in a blender or small food processor and blend until pureed, but not too fine. Add more water if necessary (it probably will not be).

4 Season with salt and pepper and serve or refrigerate; use within a couple of days. Just before serving, garnish with the chopped almonds.

MAKES ABOUT ¾ CUP   TIME: ABOUT 1 HOUR, LARGELY UNATTENDED

Simple to Spectacular

Meyer lemons stuffed with **tapenade**

2 Meyer or other lemons, washed

Salt and freshly ground black pepper

1 teaspoon sugar

4 ounces pitted brined black olives (about 1 cup)

2 tablespoons extra-virgin olive oil

Here, we fill lemon shells—Meyer lemons are best, but you can use regular lemons—with half lemon puree and half tapenade. The result is starkly beautiful, black and yellow, and delicious; you can even eat the shells. Serve with roast chicken, shrimp, or anything else you like.

1 Preheat the oven to 400°F. Wrap the lemons in two layers of foil and bake for about 1½ hours—they will shrivel and collapse.

2 Cut the lemons in half and scrape the pulp into a bowl; save the shells. Press the pulp through a coarse sieve, using a rubber spatula to push it through. Season it well with salt and pepper and add the sugar.

3 Combine ¾ cup of the olives with the oil and 1 tablespoon water in a blender or small food processor and blend until pureed, but not too fine.

4 Fill the lemon shells with half lemon puree, half tapenade. Chop the remaining olives and use for garnish.

MAKES 4 SERVINGS   TIME: ABOUT 2 HOURS, LARGELY UNATTENDED

VINAIGRETTE is any combination of oil, acid—usually vinegar—and seasonings. Within those boundaries, there are countless possibilities. We explore five, using a couple of unusual techniques, and hope that they inspire you to experiment further with this, the most versatile of all sauces.

We start with a basic vinaigrette, just olive oil and lemon juice. Next, another fairly standard vinaigrette, and one that happens to be one of Jean-Georges' favorites, spiked with honey, garlic, and balsamic vinegar. The next three are unusual and quite super: one based on beurre noisette, another loaded with chopped vegetables—this will turn any simple grilled or broiled food into a great dish—and, finally, truffle vinaigrette, a magnificent treat.

KEYS TO SUCCESS

We make these all in the blender, using hot water to lighten the emulsion without breaking it. You can also whisk together the ingredients, though the results will not be as creamy.

Use a lot of pepper and sufficient salt to make sure the flavor is strong and bright.

Some vinaigrettes retain their flavor longer than others; see the individual recipes for details.

Basic vinaigrette

½ cup fresh lemon juice

½ cup extra-virgin olive oil

Salt and freshly ground black pepper to taste

Make this fast, simple vinaigrette at the last possible minute for best flavor; be sure to use sufficient salt and pepper. This is great on grilled chicken.

1 Combine the ingredients in a blender and turn on the machine. While it's running, add 2 tablespoons hot water and blend until smooth.

2 Taste and adjust the seasoning, then serve.

MAKES ABOUT 1 CUP   TIME: 5 MINUTES

Simple to Spectacular

Jean-Georges' classic **vinaigrette**

1 small clove garlic, peeled

¼ cup balsamic vinegar

2 teaspoons honey

Salt and freshly ground black pepper to taste

6 tablespoons neutral oil, such as canola or grapeseed

Creamy, butterscotch-colored, and slightly sweet—an ideal salad dressing. This will keep for up to 3 days in the refrigerator, but bring it back to room temperature before serving.

1 Combine the ingredients in a blender and turn on the machine. While it's running, add 1 tablespoon hot water and blend until smooth.

2 Taste and adjust the seasoning, then serve or refrigerate.

MAKES ABOUT 1 CUP   TIME: 5 MINUTES

Beurre noisette **vinaigrette**

4 tablespoons butter

2 tablespoons sherry vinegar

2 tablespoons balsamic vinegar

½ cup extra-virgin olive oil

Salt and freshly ground black pepper to taste

This butter-based vinaigrette will convert any salad—including grain-based salads—into a luxury dish. It's also a simple dressing for fish. You can use a blender for this or simply beat it lightly with a fork and leave it "broken"—it will look and taste great either way.

Store this in the refrigerator for a few days, but rewarm it gently before using.

1 Put the butter in a small saucepan over medium heat. Stir, scraping down the sides with a rubber spatula, until the butter foam subsides and the butter turns nut-brown. Immerse the bottom of the pan in cold water to stop the cooking.

2 Combine the butter with the remaining ingredients in a blender and puree, or blend with a fork. Taste and adjust the seasoning, then serve or refrigerate.

MAKES ABOUT 1 CUP   TIME: 15 MINUTES

Simple to Spectacular

Vegetable **vinaigrette**

¼ cup sherry vinegar

½ cup extra-virgin olive oil

2 tablespoons soy sauce

Salt and freshly ground black pepper to taste

2 tablespoons minced shallots

2 tablespoons minced zucchini

2 tablespoons minced beet

2 tablespoons minced fennel

2 tablespoons peeled, seeded, and minced tomato

1 tablespoon minced chives

This contains so many vegetables that it is almost a side dish, good with chicken or fish. Consider our list of vegetables a guideline rather than a requirement, and substitute freely; just make sure you don't overcook them—they should retain some crunch. And make this only at the last minute so the vegetables stay that way.

1 Combine the first 4 ingredients in the container of a blender and turn on the machine. Add 2 tablespoons hot water and puree. Pour into a bowl and stir in the shallots; set aside.

2 Bring a small pot of water to a boil and salt it. Put a bowl of ice water next to it. Blanch the vegetables (except the tomato), one at a time, for about 30 seconds in the boiling water, then remove with a strainer or slotted spoon and put in the cold water to stop the cooking.

3 Just before serving, stir all the vegetables into the vinaigrette, along with the chives. Use immediately.

MAKES ABOUT 2 CUPS   TIME: 30 MINUTES

Truffle vinaigrette

¼ cup canned truffle juice

Juice of 1 lemon

2 teaspoons sherry vinegar

½ cup extra-virgin olive oil

Salt and freshly ground black pepper to taste

2 ounces black truffle, minced

This is made with less acid than most vinaigrettes because the truffle flavor is so delicate. If time allows, let it sit for an hour so the flavors meld before serving. You can store this in the refrigerator for a few days with no loss of flavor. Serve it on a salad or on hearty meats like beef or sweetbreads.

1 Combine the first 5 ingredients in a blender and turn on the machine. Add 2 tablespoons hot water and puree until smooth. Add the minced truffles and, if time allows, let rest for an hour.

2 Taste and adjust the seasoning, and serve.

MAKES ABOUT 1 CUP   TIME: 10 MINUTES, PLUS RESTING TIME

Mayonnaise

LIKE vinaigrette, mayonnaise is a basic, all-purpose sauce that is quickly made—at least in its simpler forms—and infinitely varied. Like vinaigrette, it is easily produced in a blender (although it will emulsify perfectly well if you use a wire whisk and a bowl). And, like vinaigrette, the homemade version is far superior to the store-bought variety.

We do a basic mayonnaise, which you can vary by adding almost any herbs or spices you like; an anchovy-saffron version, whose strong flavor and brilliant color smacks of the Mediterranean; an unusual Asian mayonnaise, which has specific but unique uses; a mayonnaise based on a soft-cooked egg, essentially a perfect tartar sauce; and one based on lobster oil, which has incredible flavor.

KEYS TO SUCCESS

If you're beating by hand, use a squeeze bottle to add the oil slowly until you get the hang of it. Eventually, you can just pour from a measuring cup. It's not as tricky as it looks, or as some people would have you believe.

We like to use grapeseed oil, at least most of the time, because it has a clean, neutral flavor. There are times, though, when good olive oil is preferable.

Vinegar is classic in mayonnaise, but lemon juice gives a cleaner flavor; try both.

Mayonnaise

1 egg yolk

2 teaspoons Dijon mustard

1 cup neutral oil, such as grapeseed or canola

Salt and freshly ground black pepper

1 tablespoon fresh lemon juice

The all-purpose mayonnaise, good for tuna fish or sandwiches, but also for plain cooked fish, hot or cold, or cold chicken or meats.

1 *To make by hand,* use a wire whisk to beat together the egg yolk and mustard in a bowl. Begin to add the oil, a little at a time, as you beat, adding more as each bit is incorporated. Once a thick emulsion forms—you'll know it—you can add the oil a little faster. Depending on how fast you beat, the whole process will take 2 to 5 minutes.

To make by machine, put the egg yolk and mustard in the container of a blender or food processor and turn on the machine. While it's running, add the oil in a slow, steady stream. Once an emulsion forms, you can add it a little faster. Transfer to a bowl.

2 Add salt and pepper to taste, then stir in the lemon juice.

MAKES 1 CUP   TIME: 10 MINUTES

Simple to Spectacular

Saffron-anchovy **mayonnaise**

1 egg yolk

1 teaspoon Dijon mustard

¼ teaspoon saffron threads

½ teaspoon finely minced garlic

1 cup extra-virgin olive oil

Salt and freshly ground black pepper

1 tablespoon fresh lemon juice

2 anchovy fillets, minced

Best made in advance so the saffron has time to bloom and the garlic to mellow. Use for fish soup or any boiled or steamed fish dish.

1 *To make by hand,* use a wire whisk to beat together the egg yolk, mustard, saffron, and garlic in a bowl. Begin to add the oil, a little at a time, as you beat, adding more as each bit is incorporated. Once a thick emulsion forms—you'll know it—you can add the oil a little faster. Depending on how fast you beat, the whole process will take 2 to 5 minutes.

To make by machine, put the egg yolk, mustard, saffron, and garlic in the container of a blender or food processor and turn on the machine. While it's running, add the oil in a slow, steady stream. Once an emulsion forms, you can add it a little faster. Transfer to a bowl.

2 Add salt and pepper to taste, then stir in the lemon juice and anchovies.

MAKES 1 CUP   TIME: 10 MINUTES, PLUS OPTIONAL RESTING TIME

Asian **mayonnaise**

1 egg yolk

1 teaspoon grainy mustard

1 tablespoon peeled and finely grated ginger

¼ cup roasted sesame oil

¾ cup neutral oil, such as grapeseed or canola

1 tablespoon soy sauce

1 teaspoon fresh lime juice

1 teaspoon minced chile

1 tablespoon sesame seeds

This is great on top of fried fish, especially garnished with a few more toasted sesame seeds. Or with plain grilled fish, garnished with cilantro.

1 *To make by hand,* use a wire whisk to beat together the egg yolk, mustard, and ginger in a bowl. Combine the oils. Begin to add the oil, a little at a time, as you beat, adding more as each bit is incorporated. Once a thick emulsion forms—you'll know it—you can add the oil a little faster. Depending on how fast you beat, the whole process will take 2 to 5 minutes.

To make by machine, put the egg yolk, mustard, and ginger in the container of a blender or food processor and turn on the machine. While it's running, add the oils in a slow steady stream. Once an emulsion forms, you can add the oil a little faster. Transfer to a bowl.

2 Add the soy sauce, lime juice, chile, and sesame seeds and stir.

MAKES 1 CUP   TIME: 10 MINUTES

Simple to Spectacular

Soft-boiled **sauce tartare**

1 egg

1 tablespoon Dijon mustard

½ cup neutral oil, such as grapeseed or canola

2 tablespoons chopped cornichons

2 tablespoons chopped capers

2 tablespoons chopped parsley

1 teaspoon white wine vinegar

Salt and freshly ground black pepper to taste

The half-cooked egg gives this mayonnaise a richer "mouth-feel," and is a perfect base for capers and cornichons, traditional ingredients in tartar sauce. The sauce is almost like a salad, and it makes a good accompaniment for fried, roasted, or steamed fish. Use a little less salt than usual to compensate for the capers and cornichons.

1 Bring a small pot of water to a boil and boil the egg for 6 minutes; drain and immediately run under cold water to stop the cooking.

2 Peel the egg, then mash it in a bowl with a fork. Beat in the mustard. Begin to add the oil, a little at a time, as you beat, adding more as each bit is incorporated. Once a thick emulsion forms—you'll know it—you can add the oil a little faster. Depending on how fast you beat, the whole process will take 2 to 5 minutes.

3 Stir in the remaining ingredients, adjust the seasoning, and serve.

MAKES ABOUT 1 CUP   TIME: 20 MINUTES

Lobster-oil **mayonnaise**

Bodies from two 1- to 1½-pound lobsters, back shells removed and discarded

2 cups plus 1 tablespoon neutral oil, such as grapeseed or canola

1 medium carrot, peeled and chopped

1 medium onion, peeled and chopped

1 stalk celery, chopped

1 head garlic, cut in half

3 branches thyme

1 bay leaf

1 tablespoon tomato paste

1 egg yolk

1 teaspoon Dijon mustard

Salt and freshly ground black pepper

1 tablespoon chopped tarragon, chervil, or parsley

1 tablespoon fresh lemon juice

Making lobster oil is a fair amount of work, but you'll have a cup left after making the mayo and the oil keeps forever (refrigerated). It is great also in vinaigrettes and even on its own, as a dressing in lobster or other salads or for sautéing crabcakes or fish cakes. Lobster bodies are free at most fish markets.

1 Cut the lobster bodies into 5 or 6 pieces. Place the 1 tablespoon oil in a deep skillet or casserole and turn the heat to high. Add the bodies and cook, stirring, for about 5 minutes. Add the carrot, onion, celery, garlic, thyme, bay leaf, and tomato paste. Cook, stirring, for 2 minutes, then add the 2 cups oil.

2 Stir, then turn the heat to very low and simmer for 2 hours, stirring only occasionally. Turn off the heat and let cool to room temperature. Strain through a cloth and refrigerate until ready to use.

3 *To make the mayonnaise by hand:* Use a wire whisk to beat together the egg yolk and mustard in a bowl. Measure 1 cup of the lobster oil and begin to add it, a little at a time, as you beat, adding more as each bit is incorporated. Once a thick emulsion forms—you'll know it—you can add the oil a little faster. Depending on how fast you beat, the whole process will take 2 to 5 minutes.
To make by machine, put the egg yolk and mustard in the container of a blender or food processor and turn on the machine. While it's running, add the 1 cup oil in a slow steady stream. Once an emulsion forms, you can add it a little faster. Transfer to a bowl.

4 Add salt and pepper to taste, then stir in herb and lemon juice.

MAKES ABOUT 2 CUPS   TIME: ABOUT 4 HOURS, LARGELY UNATTENDED

Desserts

SIMPLE frozen desserts are easy as long as you have an ice cream machine. This group features intense flavors, presented, with the exception of the last one, in straightforward fashion. They're even better when accompanied by a slice of pound cake or a cookie.

Here, the character of strawberries is enhanced by the addition of red wine, and raspberries are augmented by chiles. Tamarind, a sour flavor reminiscent of plums, is given a rare center-stage role. We add dairy to one sorbet to produce a simple ice cream–like rum-raisin concoction. And we offer a dessert that has long been popular at Jean Georges, orange sorbet in candied orange rinds.

KEYS TO SUCCESS

Freeze sorbet as close to serving time as you can; if it becomes rock-hard in the freezer, let it soften slightly before serving. Sorbets are really best when freshly made and straight from the machine. The best strategy for ideal sorbet is to make the mix ahead and keep it refrigerated, for up to a day, before freezing, then freeze it while you are eating the main course so that the sorbet is freshly made for dessert.

You do not need a $500 machine for sorbets and ice creams. The kind that sits in your freezer, with an electric churn, is perfectly adequate and will set you back about $60.

Strawberry–red wine **sorbet**

1 pound strawberries, hulled and halved or quartered, depending on size

½ cup dry red wine

1 cup sugar

1 vanilla bean

Juice of 1 lemon

This requires no cooking and no straining; it is best, however, if you let the mixture rest for a little while before freezing.

1 Combine the strawberries, red wine, and sugar in a bowl and stir. Split the vanilla bean lengthwise in half and scrape out the seeds. Add them, along with the pod and the lemon juice, to the strawberries and stir; let sit for about 45 minutes. Remove the vanilla pod.

2 Puree the mixture in a blender. Freeze in an ice cream maker according to the manufacturer's directions. Serve as soon after freezing as possible, or store in the freezer and allow to soften slightly before serving.

MAKES 4 SERVINGS, ABOUT 1 PINT

TIME: 60 MINUTES, LARGELY UNATTENDED, PLUS FREEZING TIME

Raspberry-chile **sorbet**

1½ pounds raspberries

1 Thai chile, stemmed, seeded, and roughly chopped

½ cup sugar

Juice of 2 lemons

One chile will do the trick here; if you want just a hint of heat, start with half—you can always add more before churning the sorbet.

1 Combine all the ingredients with 1 cup water in the container of a blender and puree. Pass through a fine strainer to remove the seeds.

2 Freeze in an ice cream maker according to the manufacturer's directions. Serve as soon after freezing as possible, or store in the freezer and allow to soften slightly before serving.

MAKES 4 SERVINGS, ABOUT 1 PINT   TIME: 10 MINUTES, PLUS FREEZING TIME

Tamarind **sorbet**

One 1-pound package tamarind pulp

½ cup sugar

An unusual sorbet, and an unusual role for tamarind, a tropical fruit whose pulp is sold in many Asian markets (you can sometimes find tamarind puree, in which case you can omit Step 1). The dark pulp is sold in small blocks. This tastes much like a sorbet made from tart plums.

1 Place the tamarind pulp in a saucepan with 1 cup water and turn the heat to medium. Cook, whisking lightly, breaking up the lumps, and adding more water whenever the mixture becomes dry, until you've added a total of about 2 cups. The process will take about 10 minutes; the result should still be quite thick, but fairly smooth.

2 Meanwhile, combine the sugar with ½ cup water in a small saucepan and bring to a boil, stirring; cool.

3 Put the tamarind through a food mill; you will have about 1 cup of smooth pulp. Whisk it together with the sugar syrup and 1½ cups water (sparkling water makes a lighter sorbet). Freeze in an ice cream maker according to the manufacturer's directions. Serve as soon after freezing as possible, or store in the freezer and allow to soften slightly before serving.

MAKES 4 SERVINGS, ABOUT 1 PINT   TIME: 30 MINUTES, PLUS FREEZING TIME

Rum-raisin fromage blanc (or yogurt) **sorbet**

½ cup raisins or currants

¼ cup light or dark rum

½ cup sugar

2 cups fromage blanc or yogurt, preferably full fat

Juice of 1 lemon

Fromage blanc, a fresh cheese, is much like sour cream. Yogurt is a perfect substitute. Either adds great creaminess to this sorbet.

1 Combine the raisins or currants and rum and set aside to soak. Combine the sugar and ½ cup water in a saucepan and bring to a boil, stirring. Cool.

2 Mix together the sugar syrup, fromage blanc or yogurt, lemon juice, and 1 cup water. Freeze in an ice cream maker according to the manufacturer's directions; when the mixture is nearly frozen, add the soaked raisins and their liquid. Serve as soon after freezing as possible, or store in the freezer and allow to soften slightly before serving.

MAKES 4 SERVINGS   TIME: 15 MINUTES, PLUS COOLING AND FREEZING TIME

Simple to Spectacular

Orange sorbet in oranges

2 navel oranges

2½ cups sugar

2½ cups orange juice, preferably fresh

16 to 20 pignoli nuts or sunflower seeds

You need not limit this lovely presentation to oranges; the same procedure will work equally well with grapefruit, lemon, and lime—though with any of those, you will need more sugar in the sorbet mixture.

1 Cut both of the ends off the oranges so they will sit flat, then cut them in half. Cut around the inside of the rind to remove all the pulp (discard or eat); then use a paring knife to carefully remove as much of the white pith as possible.

2 Combine 2 cups of the sugar with 4 cups water in a saucepan and bring to a boil. Add the orange shells, lower the heat, and simmer for 1½ hours. Cool.

3 Meanwhile, combine the remaining ½ cup sugar with ½ cup water in a small saucepan. Bring to a boil, stirring, then cool slightly and stir into the orange juice. Freeze in an ice cream maker according to the manufacturer's directions.

4 Spread the sorbet into the orange shells and freeze on a tray for 30 minutes before serving. Decorate with the nuts or seeds as if they were pits and serve.

MAKES 4 SERVINGS   TIME: ABOUT 2 HOURS, LARGELY UNATTENDED

Simple to Spectacular

Ice cream

MOST of what is true for sorbet is also true for ice cream, especially this: It is best made at the last minute, because once it sits in a zero-degree freezer for any length of time, its texture will never be the same. In fact, the way some restaurants ensure that their ice cream is creamy and smooth is to freeze it just before service; what is left over after service is then often not frozen at all, but simply refrigerated, and the mixture is refrozen the next day.

Ice cream, as everyone knows, takes well to a wide variety of flavors. We start with a basic but very, very rich vanilla ice cream, and add to it in novel but not childish ways: citrus and rice, roasted almonds, glazed chestnuts, and a very bitter caramel. All of these are what you might call "adult" flavors—sophisticated, delicious, and complex rather than syrupy-sweet.

KEYS TO SUCCESS

Freeze ice cream as close to serving time as you can; the best strategy is to make the mix ahead and keep it refrigerated, for up to a day, before freezing, then freeze while you are eating the main course so that the ice cream is freshly made for dessert.

If you are in a hurry, chill the custard by placing the bowl in a larger bowl of ice water.

You do not need a $500 machine for sorbets and ice creams. The kind that sits in your freezer, with an electric churn, is perfectly adequate and will set you back about $60.

Vanilla ice cream

10 egg yolks

½ cup sugar

1 quart (4 cups) half-and-half

2 vanilla beans

The richest, purest vanilla ice cream you've ever had. Not especially sweet, either.

1 Use a whisk or electric mixer to beat the egg yolks and sugar until light yellow and thick.

2 Put the half-and-half in a saucepan. Split the vanilla beans in half the long way and scrape the tiny seeds into the half-and-half; add the pods as well. Bring to a boil over medium heat. Pour about a third of the half-and-half into the egg mixture and stir, then pour that mixture back into the remaining half-and-half.

3 Cook over medium-low heat, stirring almost constantly, until the mixture reaches 175° to 180°F, or is slightly thickened; do not boil. (There will be a thick coating on the back of a spoon, one that will hold the outline of your finger after you pass it through.)

4 Cool in the refrigerator (or over a bowl of ice, which is faster), then pass through a fine strainer and freeze in an ice cream machine. Serve immediately or transfer to the freezer; be sure to allow the ice cream to soften slightly before serving.

MAKES ABOUT 1 QUART; 6 TO 8 SERVINGS

TIME: ABOUT 30 MINUTES, PLUS CHILLING AND FREEZING TIME

Citrus-rice ice cream

⅓ cup basmati rice

2 cups milk

⅓ cup plus 2 tablespoons sugar

Pinch of salt

5 egg yolks

2 cups half-and-half

Finely minced zest of 1 orange

Finely minced zest of 1 lemon

Finely minced zest of 1 lime

A brightly flavored ice cream with a little of the texture of rice pudding.

1 In a medium saucepan, bring the rice, milk, 2 tablespoons of the sugar, and the salt to a boil, then lower the heat and cover. Cook for about 20 minutes, or until the milk is mostly absorbed.

2 Meanwhile, use a whisk or electric mixer to beat the egg yolks and the remaining ⅓ cup sugar until light yellow and thick. Bring the half-and-half to a boil over medium heat. Pour about a third of the half-and-half into the egg mixture and stir, then pour that mixture back into the remaining half-and-half.

3 Cook over medium-low heat, stirring almost constantly, until the mixture reaches 175° to 180°F, or is slightly thickened; do not boil. (There will be a thick coating on the back of a spoon, one that will hold the outline of your finger after you pass it through.) Combine with the cooked rice mixture and the zest.

4 Cool in the refrigerator (or over a bowl of ice, which is faster), then freeze in an ice cream machine. Serve immediately or transfer to the freezer; be sure to allow the ice cream to soften slightly before serving.

MAKES A LITTLE MORE THAN 1 QUART; 6 TO 8 SERVINGS

TIME: ABOUT 30 MINUTES, PLUS CHILLING AND FREEZING TIME

Roasted almond **ice cream**

3 cups skinned almonds, coarsely chopped

1 quart milk

10 egg yolks

¾ cup sugar

The key here is darkly roasted almonds. These are infused in milk, which in turn absorbs their flavor. The process is simple.

1 Preheat the oven to 400°F. Place the almonds on a baking sheet and roast them, shaking occasionally, until they are quite dark in color, 10 to 15 minutes.

2 Bring the milk to a boil and add the almonds; let sit, refrigerated, for at least 12 and up to 36 hours. Strain the milk and discard the almonds.

3 Use a whisk or electric mixer to beat the egg yolks and sugar until light yellow and thick. Bring the milk to a boil over medium heat. Pour about a third of the milk into the egg mixture and stir, then pour that mixture back into the remaining milk.

4 Cook over medium-low heat, stirring almost constantly, until the mixture reaches 175° to 180°F, or is slightly thickened; do not boil. (There will be a thick coating on the back of a spoon, one that will hold the outline of your finger after you pass it through.)

5 Cool in the refrigerator (or over a bowl of ice, which is faster), then pass through a fine strainer and freeze in an ice cream machine. Serve immediately or transfer to the freezer; be sure to allow the ice cream to soften slightly before serving.

MAKES ABOUT 1 QUART: 6 TO 8 SERVINGS

TIME: ABOUT 30 MINUTES, PLUS 24 HOURS RESTING TIME AND FREEZING TIME

Simple to Spectacular

Glazed chestnut **ice cream**

1 cup peeled and chopped chestnuts (see page 98 for peeling instructions)

1¾ cups sugar

10 egg yolks

1 quart (4 cups) half-and-half

½ cup rum

Here you will be making marrons glacés, candied chestnuts. The soft texture and rich flavor of chestnuts are perfect in ice cream, and they go especially well with rum. It's very important not to hold this ice cream for too long after freezing.

1 Combine the chestnuts with 1 cup of the sugar and 1 cup water in a saucepan. Bring to a boil and cook, stirring occasionally, until the chestnuts are tender, about 30 minutes. Drain off any remaining liquid.

2 Meanwhile, use a whisk or electric mixer to beat the egg yolks and the remaining ¾ cup sugar until light yellow and thick. Bring the half-and-half to a boil over medium heat. Pour about a third of the half-and-half into the egg mixture and stir, then pour that mixture back into the remaining half-and-half.

3 Cook over medium-low heat, stirring almost constantly, until the mixture reaches 175° to 180°F, or is slightly thickened; do not boil. (There will be a thick coating on the back of a spoon, one that will hold the outline of your finger after you pass it through.) Stir in the chestnuts and rum.

4 Cool in the refrigerator (or over a bowl of ice, which is faster), then freeze in an ice cream machine. Serve immediately or transfer to the freezer; be sure to allow the ice cream to soften slightly before serving.

MAKES ABOUT 1 QUART: 6 TO 8 SERVINGS

TIME: ABOUT 45 MINUTES, PLUS COOLING AND FREEZING TIME

Caramel ice cream with crunchy sesame

2¼ cups sugar

1 quart milk

12 egg yolks

1 cup sesame seeds

Neutral oil, such as canola or grapeseed, as needed

Our favorite: This one is bitter, hardly sweet at all, despite all the sugar, because when sugar is cooked to the dark-brown stage, it loses its sweetness. Use a heavy saucepan to make the caramel and you should have no trouble at all.

1 Put 1¼ cups of the sugar in a large heavy-bottomed saucepan and turn the heat to medium. Cook, occasionally shaking the pan but not stirring (you can scrape down the sides with a rubber spatula, but do not stir the sugar itself) until the sugar liquefies, bubbles, and turns dark brown, at least 10 minutes. Turn off the heat, then carefully add the milk—very carefully, as it will bubble up, and this mixture is hot and sticky. Turn the heat back to medium and cook, stirring with a wire whisk, until the sugar dissolves; remove from the heat.

2 Use a whisk or electric mixer to beat the egg yolks until they are light yellow and thick. Pour about a third of the milk mixture into the egg mixture and stir, then pour that mixture back into the remaining milk mixture.

3 Cook over medium-low heat, stirring almost constantly, until the mixture reaches 175° to 180°F, or is slightly thickened; do not boil. (There will be a thick coating on the back of a spoon, one that will hold the outline of your finger after you pass it through.) Cool in the refrigerator (or over a bowl of ice, which is faster).

4 Meanwhile, oil a cookie sheet or baking pan. Cook the remaining 1 cup sugar to caramel in the same fashion as in Step 1. Stir in the sesame seeds and spread on the cookie sheet. When it is cool, place the hard sheet of caramel between several sheets of plastic wrap and beat with a rolling pin or pot bottom until you have rather fine crumbs.

5 Freeze the caramel custard in an ice cream machine; add the sesame crumbs when the ice cream is just about done. Serve immediately or transfer to the freezer; be sure to allow the ice cream to soften slightly before serving.

MAKES ABOUT 1 QUART; 6 TO 8 SERVINGS

TIME: ABOUT 1 HOUR, PLUS COOLING AND FREEZING TIME

Simple to Spectacular

Crème brûlée

ONE of the simplest desserts ever, crème brûlée became a symbol of classy restaurants in the 80s, largely because home cooks couldn't figure out how to create the crunchy burnt-sugar topping that gives the dish its name. If you have a good hot broiler, though, you can do it easily. But if you don't—as is the case for most of us—you can do what the restaurants do and buy a small propane torch for caramelizing the dusting of sugar.

Our crème brûlées begin with the basic version (note that it has only four ingredients, and can be put together in about 10 minutes). We then add a couple of different flavors—green tea and lime in one instance, chocolate and anise in another—to give you a sense of how easy it is to vary this classic. Finally, we abandon familiar crème brûlée altogether, creating what amounts to crème brûlée pie and crème brûlée napoleon—a couple of innovations that will shock if not alienate the traditionalists, but are really delicious.

KEYS TO SUCCESS

Varying flavors in crème brûlée is easy: just infuse the dairy base with spices like cinnamon or ginger, or citrus zest, or coffee beans—there's almost nothing you can think of that won't work.

Cooking the custards in a covered water bath (called a bain-marie) provides more even heat and reduces the chance of overcooking.

The hardest part of making crème brûlée is judging the doneness of the custard, and the chances are good that the first couple of times you make it, you will in fact overcook it. That's because it's hard to believe how much residual heat there is in the custard and its container, and how much cooking will take place after the custards are removed from the oven. But custards are almost always done when the center portion is still quite jiggly, and should be removed then. Begin checking these after 30 minutes, and believe us—they're done before you think they are.

The custards themselves can be cooked well in advance, up to a day or more, but the burnt topping must be executed at the last minute.

Vanilla **crème brûlée**

2 cups cream

2 vanilla beans, split the long way

5 egg yolks

½ cup sugar, plus more for topping

The basic, classic crème brûlée, and hard to beat. Make the custard a day in advance if you like.

1 Preheat the oven to 325°F. Combine the cream and vanilla in a saucepan and cook over medium-high heat until a few bubbles rise to the surface. Cool for about 5 minutes.

2 Meanwhile, beat the egg yolks and sugar together until light yellow. Pour about a quarter of the cream into this mixture, then pour the sugar-egg mixture back into the cream and stir. Pour into four 6-ounce ramekins, or six 4-ounce ramekins, and place the ramekins in a baking dish; fill the dish with water to come halfway up the sides of the dishes and cover with foil.

3 Bake for 30 to 45 minutes, or until the center is barely set. Cool or chill.

4 When you're ready to serve, cover the top of each custard with a thin layer of sugar and heat it with the flame of a propane torch, until the sugar bubbles, browns, and begins to burn (or run it under a broiler).

MAKES 4 TO 6 SERVINGS   TIME: ABOUT 1 HOUR, PLUS TIME TO CHILL

Green tea **crème brûlée**

1 cup milk

1 tablespoon green tea powder (macha), found at Japanese markets

Minced zest of 2 limes

5 egg yolks

½ cup sugar, plus more for topping

1 cup heavy cream

Just one of the many unusual flavor variations for crème brûlée. You could make a coffee-orange crème brûlée following the same pattern, simply by using crushed coffee beans (about ¼ cup) in place of the green tea powder (strain them out after the infusion) and orange instead of lime.

1 Heat the milk in a small saucepan over medium-high heat until a few bubbles rise to the surface. Stir in the macha and the lime zest and let cool for about 5 minutes.

2 Meanwhile, beat together the egg yolks and sugar until light yellow. Pour about a quarter of the milk into this mixture, then pour the sugar-egg mixture back into the milk and stir. Add the cream and let stand, refrigerated, overnight.

3 Preheat the oven to 325°F. Pour the cream mixture into four 6-ounce ramekins, or six 4-ounce ramekins, and place the ramekins in a baking dish; fill the dish with water to come halfway up the sides of the dishes and cover with foil.

4 Bake for 30 to 45 minutes, or until the center is barely set. Cool or chill.

5 When you're ready to serve, cover the top of each custard with a thin layer of sugar and heat it with the flame of a propane torch, until the sugar bubbles, browns, and begins to burn (or run it under a broiler). Serve immediately.

MAKES 4 TO 6 SERVINGS   TIME: 24 HOURS, LARGELY UNATTENDED

Simple to Spectacular

Chocolate-anise **crème brûlée**

2 cups heavy cream

1 vanilla bean, split the long way

6 star anise

5 egg yolks

½ cup sugar, plus more for topping

1 tablespoon unsweetened cocoa powder

4 ounces semisweet chocolate, chopped into bits

The anise flavor is very, very subtle here, but it is noticeable. If you prefer a straight chocolate flavor, simply omit the star anise (you can then skip the infusion time in Step 2 as well).

1 Combine the cream, vanilla, and star anise in a saucepan and cook over medium-high heat until a few bubbles rise to the surface. Cool for about 5 minutes.

2 Meanwhile, beat the egg yolks and sugar together until light yellow. Stir in the cocoa and chocolate. Pour about a quarter of the cream into this mixture, then pour the sugar-egg mixture back into the cream and stir until the chocolate is completely melted. Let sit for an hour at room temperature, or overnight, refrigerated.

3 Preheat the oven to 325°F. Strain the chocolate mixture and pour it into four 6-ounce ramekins, or six 4-ounce ramekins, and place the ramekins in a baking dish; fill the dish with water to come halfway up the sides of the dishes and cover with foil.

4 Bake for 30 to 45 minutes, or until the center is barely set. Cool or chill.

5 When you're ready to serve, cover the top of each custard with a thin layer of sugar and heat it with the flame of a propane torch, until the sugar bubbles, browns, and begins to burn (or run it under a broiler). Serve immediately.

MAKES 4 TO 6 SERVINGS   TIME: ABOUT 2 HOURS, SOMEWHAT UNATTENDED

Squash-spice **crème brûlée pie**

¼ teaspoon cardamom seeds

1 inch cinnamon stick, broken up

1 clove

½ star anise

½ teaspoon ground ginger

2 pounds butternut squash, more or less

⅓ cup plus 2 tablespoons sugar, plus more for topping

2 tablespoons maple syrup

1 cup heavy cream

4 egg yolks

Butter as needed

2 cups cake crumbs, preferably from pound cake (see head-note)

This is a crème brûlée "pie," not a far cry from a traditional American custard-cream pie. You can make it in a regular piecrust, but we use pound cake crumbs (actually those from Sableuse; see our first book), which actually makes things easier and tastier.

Note that there is no bain-marie used for this dish.

1 Preheat the oven to 400°F. Combine the first 4 ingredients in a small saucepan over medium heat. Toast, shaking the pan occasionally, until the spices are fragrant, just a minute or two. Add the ginger and grind to a powder in a coffee grinder or spice mill.

2 Peel and seed the squash and cut it into chunks. Put 1 cup water and the squash in the bottom of a baking pan lined with foil. Sprinkle with 2 tablespoons of the sugar and all but ½ teaspoon of the spice mix. Cover with foil and bake for about 1 hour, or until the squash is very tender. Puree the squash in a blender with the maple syrup and a little bit of the cooking liquid if necessary; measure out 1 cup.

3 Turn the oven to 325°F. Put the cream in a small saucepan and cook over medium-high heat until a few bubbles rise to the surface. Cool for about 5 minutes.

4 Meanwhile, beat the egg yolks and the remaining ⅓ cup sugar together until light yellow. Pour about a quarter of the cream into this mixture, then pour the sugar-egg mixture back into the cream and stir; add the squash puree and stir again to combine.

5 Butter the bottom and sides of a 9-inch tart pan and press the cake crumbs into it, making sure there are no cracks or holes. Pour in the cream mixture and bake for about 30 minutes, or until the center is barely set. Cool or chill.

6 When you're ready to serve, cover the top of the pie with a thin layer of sugar mixed with the reserved spice mix and heat it with the flame of a propane torch until the sugar bubbles, browns, and begins to burn (or run it under a broiler). Serve immediately, straight from the pan.

MAKES 6 TO 8 SERVINGS   TIME: ABOUT 2 HOURS, PLUS COOLING TIME

Coconut crème brûlée napoleons

1 cup unsweetened grated coconut

2 cups canned unsweetened coconut milk

2 vanilla beans, split the long way

5 egg yolks

½ cup sugar

1 sheet of phyllo dough

Melted butter

Powdered sugar as needed

Another crème brûlée that doesn't meet the strict definition of the dessert, but about which no one will complain. Coconut lovers will go wild over this, as we do.

1 Preheat the oven to 325°F. Put the coconut in a small skillet and turn the heat to medium. Toast, shaking the pan occasionally, until it's fragrant, just a minute or two. Combine the coconut milk, vanilla, and half the toasted coconut in a saucepan and cook over medium-high heat until a few bubbles rise to the surface. Cool for about 5 minutes.

2 Meanwhile, beat the egg yolks and sugar together until light yellow. Pour about a quarter of the coconut milk into this mixture, then pour the sugar-egg mixture back into the coconut milk and stir. Line an 8-inch-square baking pan with plastic wrap; pour the mixture into it.

3 Bake for 30 to 45 minutes, or until the center is barely set; chill. Cut into eight squares.

4 Preheat the oven to 350°F. Brush the phyllo strips lightly with butter. Cut each strip into 4 pieces, about the same size as the squares of crème brûlée. Sprinkle 12 of the pieces with the remaining coconut and top with the remaining 12 pieces; dust with powdered sugar. Bake on a baking sheet for 6 to 8 minutes, or until lightly browned.

5 To make the napoleons, top 4 of the pieces with a square of crème brûlée; top each with a square of phyllo, another layer of crème brûlée, and finally a square of phyllo. Serve immediately.

MAKES 4 SERVINGS   TIME: ABOUT 1 HOUR, PLUS CHILLING TIME

Simple to Spectacular

Bananas cooked in butter

AT its most basic, a fine, quick dessert that can be made at the last minute with three ingredients you undoubtedly have in the house—bananas, butter, and brown sugar. At its most complex, this becomes a four-star dessert of smooth, creamy banana and coconut cream in a crisp spring roll. In between, we do bananas with a caramel sauce, bananas with a kind of cashew brittle, and bananas with French toast, this last a brilliant brunch dish.

KEYS TO SUCCESS

What's a ripe banana? One that is completely yellow, with dark spots just beginning to appear. Those are best for these recipes.

Use a nonstick skillet for cooking the bananas, handle them carefully, and they will not break apart.

Bananas with butter and brown sugar

4 tablespoons butter

4 ripe bananas, peeled

2 tablespoons brown sugar

Fast, easy, and good.

1 Preheat the oven to 450°F. Place an ovenproof nonstick skillet over medium-high heat and add the butter. When the butter melts and its foam subsides, add the bananas. Quickly turn once, then sprinkle with half the brown sugar and turn again; sprinkle with the remaining sugar. Place in the oven.

2 Roast for 5 minutes, or until browned on one side. Turn and cook for another 5 minutes or so. Carefully remove and serve with the pan juices.

MAKES 4 SERVINGS   TIME: 20 MINUTES

Simple to Spectacular

Bananas with caramel sauce

1 cup sugar

1 vanilla bean

½ cup heavy cream

4 tablespoons butter

4 ripe bananas, peeled

2 tablespoons brown sugar

A quickly and easily made caramel sauce turns the roasted bananas into a rich and luxurious dessert.

1 Preheat the oven to 450°F. Put the sugar in a small heavy saucepan and cook over medium heat, without stirring. As it heats, split the vanilla bean the long way and scrape the seeds into the sugar; discard the pod. When the sugar has melted, swirl the pan and continue to do so occasionally until the sugar turns dark brown. Turn off the heat and carefully add the cream (it will bubble up). Over low heat, stir until most of the lumps dissolve, then whisk until smooth and remove from the heat. (*You can store this caramel sauce in the refrigerator for up to 2 days and reheat it gently with a little cream or water before using.*)

2 Place an ovenproof nonstick skillet over medium-high heat and add the butter. When the butter melts and its foam subsides, add the bananas. Quickly turn once, then sprinkle with half the brown sugar and turn again; sprinkle with the remaining sugar. Place in the oven.

3 Roast for 5 minutes, or until browned on one side. Turn and cook for another 5 minutes or so. Carefully remove and serve with the caramel sauce.

MAKES 4 SERVINGS   TIME: 30 MINUTES

Bananas with cashew craquelin

Butter, as needed

1 cup sugar

1 cup chopped cashews

4 tablespoons butter

4 ripe bananas, peeled

2 tablespoons brown sugar

Vanilla ice cream, lightly whipped heavy cream, or
crème anglaise

This begins with a caramel sauce, like the preceding recipe, but the sauce is then used to enclose cashews. The result is cashew brittle, or *craquelin*, as the French call it, which gives the bananas crunch and loads of extra flavor.

1 Use the butter to grease a baking sheet with a rim. Place the sugar in a large heavy skillet and turn the heat to low. Cook without stirring until the sugar turns liquid. Then stir constantly until it turns golden but not brown.

2 Stir in the cashews and immediately pour the mixture onto the greased baking sheet. Cool completely, then break into large pieces and put in a plastic bag and smash into pieces about the size of granola. *(You can make the craquelin days in advance if you like. Store in a sealed container in a dry place.)*

3 Preheat the oven to 450°F. Place an ovenproof nonstick skillet over medium-high heat and add the butter. When the butter melts and its foam subsides, add the bananas. Quickly turn once, then sprinkle with half the brown sugar and turn again; sprinkle with the remaining sugar. Place in the oven.

4 Roast for 5 minutes, or until browned on one side. Turn and cook for another 5 minutes or so. Carefully remove and turn in the craquelin. Serve with ice cream, whipped cream, or crème anglaise.

MAKES 4 SERVINGS   TIME: ABOUT 1 HOUR

French toast with **bananas**

1 egg

1 egg yolk

½ teaspoon vanilla extract

1 teaspoon light or dark rum

¼ cup sugar

1 cup half-and-half

4 tablespoons butter

4 slices good white bread, preferably sourdough

4 bananas, peeled and cut into ¾-inch rounds

2 tablespoons brown sugar

Confectioners' sugar

This is a good French toast recipe, and really splendid with the baked bananas.

1 Mix together the egg, yolk, vanilla, rum, sugar, and half-and-half in a broad, shallow bowl. Put 2 tablespoons of the butter in a large nonstick skillet and turn the heat to medium-high. Put each slice of the bread in the batter and, when the butter foam subsides, cook the bread until nicely browned on both sides, in batches if necessary.

2 Meanwhile, put the remaining 2 tablespoons butter in another nonstick skillet over medium heat. When the foam subsides, cook the banana pieces, turning frequently and sprinkling them with the brown sugar, until lightly browned, 5 to 10 minutes.

3 Cover each piece of French toast with a portion of the bananas and sprinkle with confectioners' sugar. Serve hot.

MAKES 4 SERVINGS   TIME: 30 MINUTES

Caramelized banana spring roll

¼ cup unsweetened dried coconut

¼ cup sugar, or more to taste

6 tablespoons butter

2 tablespoons flour

1 egg

4 ripe bananas, peeled

1 tablespoon brown sugar

8 spring roll wrappers, 8 inches square

1 egg yolk, beaten

Oil for deep-frying

Confectioners' sugar

A super-dessert, and not all that complicated. It begins with a coconut frangipane—a creamy mixture of dried coconut, sugar, and butter—combined with bananas cooked as in the other recipes here. Then they're combined in a spring roll wrapper and deep-fried to make a sweet, crisp, creamy, hot dessert.

1 Combine the coconut, sugar, 4 tablespoons of the butter, the flour, and egg and beat with a whisk or electric mixer until quite white, about 5 minutes. Taste and add more sugar if necessary; it should be slightly sweet.

2 Cut the bananas in half the long way, then cut each half into 4 pieces. Place the remaining 2 tablespoons butter in a nonstick skillet and turn the heat to medium. When the butter foam subsides, cook the bananas, turning frequently and sprinkling them with the brown sugar, until they are lightly browned all over. Remove the bananas from the heat and cool for a few minutes.

3 Place 1 of the spring roll wrappers on a counter, with a point facing you. Lay a portion of the bananas across the center of the wrapper, making a 4-inch strip from left to right. Spoon some of the coconut mixture over it. Fold over the left and right corners of the wrapper so that they overlap in the middle. Brush a bit of the egg yolk over the top half of the wrapper. Fold the bottom half up, then roll up tightly; the yolk will seal the spring roll. *(You can prepare the spring rolls in advance up to this point; refrigerate, well wrapped or in a covered container, for up to 2 hours.)*

4 Heat the oil in a deep pot to 365°F. Deep-fry the spring rolls, 3 or 4 at a time, for 2 minutes or less, or until an appealing shade of brown. Drain on paper towels, then sprinkle with confectioners' sugar and serve.

MAKES 4 SERVINGS   TIME: 45 MINUTES

Simple to Spectacular

Poached pears

A classic dessert, largely because a good pear is one of the great fruits, and it takes so well to cooking—its flavor becomes more intense, its texture even creamier than when eaten out of hand.

And pears go so well with other flavors. We take poached pears to the limit, beginning with vanilla and moving on to chocolate. Then we poach a pear with Asian spices, something Jean-Georges made popular years ago. A red wine caramel makes a splendid finish to another dessert, and finally, we stuff the pears with a classic praline before poaching.

KEYS TO SUCCESS

The pears should be large and just about perfectly ripe before cooking. To judge ripeness, gently squeeze their "shoulders," which should yield to your touch.

The easiest way to core a pear is with a small melon baller, digging up from the bottom. An ordinary teaspoon works almost as well.

If you are not going to cook the pears right away, once they are peeled and cored, drop them into a bowl of cold water mixed with the juice of a lemon to keep them from turning brown.

Vanilla-poached pears

4 pears (about 6 ounces each), preferably Anjou

2½ cups sugar

2 vanilla beans

These easy poached pears have great flavor as long as you use fresh vanilla beans. Make them just before dinner and they'll be ready to serve at dessert time.

1 Peel and core the pears. Combine the sugar and 5 cups water in a saucepan large enough to hold the pears. Split the vanilla beans the long way and scrape out the seeds; add both seeds and pods to the water. Turn the heat to medium-high and bring to a boil.

2 Add the pears and adjust the heat so that the mixture bubbles, but not too vigorously. Cook for 8 minutes, or until a thin-bladed knife inserted into the pears meets with little resistance.

3 Let the pears cool in the liquid for 30 to 60 minutes (an hour longer is okay too; do not refrigerate). Serve with a little of the poaching liquid spooned over.

MAKES 4 SERVINGS   TIME: 15 MINUTES, PLUS COOLING TIME

Simple to Spectacular

Poached pears with chocolate sauce

4 pears (about 6 ounces each), preferably Anjou

3¼ cups sugar

2 vanilla beans

½ cup unsweetened cocoa powder, such as Valrhona or Hershey's

½ cup heavy cream

Here are poached pears teamed with a fast, fudgy, not-too-sweet chocolate sauce.

1 Peel and core the pears. Combine 2½ cups of the sugar and 5 cups water in a saucepan large enough to hold the pears. Split the vanilla beans the long way and scrape out the seeds; add both seeds and pods to the water. Turn the heat to medium-high and bring to a boil.

2 Add the pears and adjust the heat so that the mixture bubbles, but not too vigorously. Cook for 8 minutes, or until a thin-bladed knife inserted into the pears meets with little resistance. Let the pears cool in the liquid for 30 to 60 minutes (do not refrigerate).

3 Meanwhile, combine 1 cup water with the remaining ¾ cup sugar in a small saucepan; bring to a boil, stirring to dissolve the sugar. Turn off the heat and whisk in the cocoa, along with the cream. Return to very low heat and cook, stirring, just until thickened slightly. (*This can be made several hours in advance; keep at room temperature, then rewarm gently.*)

4 Serve the pears with the warm chocolate sauce spooned over them.

MAKES 4 SERVINGS   TIME: 20 MINUTES, PLUS COOLING TIME

Poached pears with star anise and ginger crème anglaise

4 pears (about 6 ounces each), preferably Anjou

2½ cups plus 2 tablespoons sugar

2 pieces star anise

1 cinnamon stick

2 cloves

1 teaspoon mace pieces or ½ teaspoon ground mace

1 vanilla bean

¾ cup milk

⅓ cup heavy cream

1 tablespoon grated ginger (don't bother to peel it)

3 egg yolks

Poached pears, accompanied by a gorgeous pale yellow sauce flecked with vanilla. Asian flavors make this lovely dish a surprising one as well.

1 Peel and core the pears. Combine 2½ cups of the sugar and 5 cups water in a saucepan large enough to hold the pears; add the star anise, cinnamon stick, cloves, and mace. Turn the heat to medium-high and bring to a boil.

2 Add the pears and adjust the heat so that the mixture bubbles, but not too vigorously. Cook for 8 minutes, or until a thin-bladed knife inserted into the pears meets with little resistance.

3 Let the pears cool in the liquid for 30 to 60 minutes (do not refrigerate).

4 Meanwhile, split the vanilla bean the long way and scrape out the seeds; combine the seeds and pod in a saucepan with the milk, cream, and ginger. Turn the heat to medium and cook until tiny bubbles appear at the sides; turn off the heat.

5 Beat the egg yolks and the remaining 2 tablespoons sugar until light yellow and thick. Pour some of the hot milk into this mixture, then stir. Stir the egg-milk mixture into the hot milk and cook over medium-low heat, stirring almost constantly, until the mixture reaches 175° to 180°F, or is slightly thickened; do not boil. (There will be a thick coating on the back of a spoon, one that will hold the outline of your finger after you pass it through.)

6 Strain the crème anglaise. Put a portion of it into each of four bowls, reserving a little bit of it. Top with the pears and the remaining sauce and serve.

MAKES 4 SERVINGS   TIME: 40 MINUTES, PLUS COOLING TIME

Roasted poached pears with red wine caramel

4 pears (about 6 ounces each), preferably Anjou

1 tablespoon butter, for the pan

1 vanilla bean

4 strips lemon zest (removed from the lemon with a vegetable peeler)

1 cup plus 4 teaspoons sugar

Juice of 1 lemon

⅔ cup red wine

1 teaspoon good balsamic vinegar

¼ cup crème fraîche or sour cream

These are "poached" in the oven, a slightly different technique than in the preceding recipes. They're first baked by themselves, then returned to the oven with an intense tart caramel sauce. This dessert, which is definitely for grownups, was inspired by the River Café in London.

1 Preheat the oven to 400°F. Core the pears. Butter the bottom of an ovenproof saucepan just large enough to hold the pears; stand the pears upside down in the saucepan. Split the vanilla bean the long way and scrape out the seeds. Place a strip of lemon zest in the cavity of each pear, along with a teaspoon of sugar and one-quarter of the vanilla seeds; discard the pod. Stand the pears right side up and drizzle with the lemon juice. Cover the pears with foil and bake for 10 minutes; they will shrivel slightly, and their skin will darken nicely.

2 Put the remaining 1 cup sugar in a heavy saucepan and turn the heat to medium. Cook, shaking the pan and scraping down the sides occasionally (do not stir the melting sugar), until the sugar is liquefied and quite dark, about 10 minutes. Turn off the heat. Mix the wine with ⅓ cup water. Stand back from the pan, and add the liquid to the caramel. Return to medium-high heat and cook, stirring, until the caramel dissolves. Pour this liquid over the pears and return to the oven, this time uncovered, for 40 minutes.

3 Carefully remove the pears from the pan and place on 4 plates. Cook the liquid over high heat until just about 2 tablespoons remain. Drizzle each pear with a little of the syrup and ¼ teaspoon of the balsamic vinegar. Top each with a tablespoon of crème fraîche or sour cream and serve.

MAKES 4 SERVINGS   TIME: ABOUT 1 HOUR, SOMEWHAT UNATTENDED

Simple to Spectacular

Butter-poached pears with praline

8 tablespoons (1 stick) plus 3 tablespoons butter

3 cups sugar

2 vanilla beans

4 pears (about 6 ounces each), preferably Anjou

¾ cup pecans or walnuts

¾ cup blanched almonds

1 egg

1 tablespoon flour

An elaborate recipe, in which you first poach the pears in beurre noisette, and then fill them with a freshly made praline. Finally, you reheat them and serve them warm. Beautiful.

1 Prepare a bowl of ice water and set aside. Put the stick of butter in a small saucepan and turn the heat to medium. Cook, swirling the butter occasionally, until the foam subsides and the butter turns nut-brown. Dip the bottom of the saucepan in the ice water to stop the cooking and set aside.

2 Combine 2½ cups of the sugar and 5 cups water in a saucepan large enough to hold the pears. Split the vanilla beans the long way and scrape out the seeds; add both seeds and pods to the water. Turn the heat to medium-high, add the browned butter, and bring to a boil.

3 Add the pears and adjust the heat so that the mixture bubbles, but not too vigorously. Cook for 8 minutes, or until a thin-bladed knife inserted into the pears meets with little resistance. Remove the pears from the liquid; discard all but ¼ cup of the liquid. Set the saucepan aside.

4 Combine the remaining ½ cup sugar with a scant ½ cup each of the pecans and almonds in a small food processor and process to a powder. Cream with the remaining 3 tablespoons butter in a small bowl, then beat in the egg and flour. (You can do this all in the food processor if you prefer.) Refrigerate until thickened (or chill the mixture over another bowl of ice water, stirring frequently; it will thicken quickly.)

5 Peel the pears. Cut off the top of each pear, right above the core, and set the top aside. Use a spoon or melon baller to core the pears, but leave the bottoms intact. Stuff with the nut mixture and cover with the tops of the pears.

6 Return the pears to the saucepan and spoon the reserved poaching liquid over them. Turn the heat to medium and cook for about 10 minutes, basting once with the liquid. Meanwhile, chop the remaining nuts and toast them in a dry skillet over medium heat, shaking occasionally, just until fragrant, about 2 minutes.

7 Serve the pears with the juice and filling (most of which will have fallen out) spooned over them, garnished with the toasted nuts.

MAKES 4 SERVINGS   TIME: ABOUT 1 HOUR

TARTS can be made with a variety of crusts. They can be filled with fruit, nuts, pastry cream, chocolate, wine, a combination of these, or practically nothing.

Starting with a filling of almost nothing (wait until you try this one, a classic popularized by the great Fredy Girardet, for years considered the best chef in Europe), we move on to a nearly-as-simple tart filled with clafouti, a pancake-like mixture that works when used as a tart filling, even though it's rarely done. Then we offer Jean-Georges' wonderfully bitter chocolate tart in a chocolate crust, and a fabulous caramelized walnut tart in an almond crust. Finally, there is an unusual tart of pastry cream flavored with sweet wine, very sophisticated and quite delicious.

KEYS TO SUCCESS

The best tart pans are those with removable bottoms; these recipes will work with pans that are 9 or 10 inches across.

If you have difficulty rolling out any pastry doughs, chances are that the dough is too warm. The best thing to do is to refrigerate the dough for 30 minutes, then start again; that usually does the trick.

Tart vaudoise

1 cup plus 2 tablespoons flour, plus a pinch

Pinch of salt

½ cup plus 1 teaspoon sugar

¼ teaspoon baking powder

3 tablespoons butter

2 to 4 tablespoons milk

1½ cups crème fraîche or sour cream

1 teaspoon cinnamon

A crust with a little cream in it—doesn't sound like much, does it? But it's magic, especially for people who prefer just a little sweet after a meal.

1 Combine the 1 cup plus 2 tablespoons flour with the salt, 1 teaspoon sugar, and the baking powder in a bowl or food processor. Add the butter and cut it in or process until the mixture is crumbly. Add 2 tablespoons of the milk and, using your hands, begin to gather the mixture into a ball; if it is still a little dry, add some or all of the remaining milk. Wrap in plastic and refrigerate for 30 minutes.

2 Roll out the dough on a lightly floured surface to a thickness of ¼ inch or less and line a 10-inch tart pan with it, pressing the dough into the bottom and sides and trimming the excess. Refrigerate for 15 to 30 minutes.

3 Preheat the oven to 450°F. Prick the bottom of the dough all over with a fork. Mix together the remaining ½ cup sugar and the pinch of flour with the crème fraîche or sour cream. Spread over the bottom of the tart shell, then dust with the cinnamon. Bake until the crust is golden brown, 10 to 15 minutes; cool completely before serving.

MAKES ONE 10-INCH TART, ABOUT 8 SERVINGS

TIME: ABOUT 1½ HOURS, LARGELY UNATTENDED

Simple to Spectacular

Clafouti **tart**

1 vanilla bean or 1 teaspoon vanilla extract	Pinch of salt
8 tablespoons (1 stick) cold butter, cut into bits	1½ cups flour
1¼ cups confectioners' sugar, plus some for dusting	2 eggs
	5 tablespoons sugar
4 egg yolks	2 tablespoons cornstarch
⅓ cup almond powder	1¼ cups cream
	1½ pounds cherries, pitted

This dough is called *paté sablé*, because it is "sandy"—crumbly and almost slightly gritty. You can buy almond powder, but you can also make it: Crush ½ cup slivered almonds (put them in a heavy plastic bag and hit them repeatedly with a pot or rolling pin), then grind them with 1 tablespoon confectioners' sugar in a food processor, making sure to stop the grinding before the mixture becomes oily.

1   If using a vanilla bean, split it the long way and scrape out the seeds. Combine the butter, ¾ cup of the confectioners' sugar, 2 egg yolks, and the vanilla seeds or extract in a food processor and mix. Add the almond powder, salt, the remaining ½ cup confectioners' sugar, and the flour and process until the mixture begins to come together. Transfer to a lightly floured surface and begin to knead—this dough will be gritty (that's where the name came from), but it will hold together, barely, as you work it. You may be tempted to add some liquid, but avoid it; that will rob the crust of its fragile, crumbly texture, which is what you want. When the dough holds together, wrap it in plastic and refrigerate for about 1 hour.

2   Gently roll the dough out on a floured surface, adding flour as necessary to keep it from sticking. If the dough becomes very sticky, refrigerate it again for a few minutes. When you have made a circle large enough to line a 9- or 10-inch tart pan with, do so; if it cracks, just patch the holes—the dough will press together easily. Refrigerate the crust, for 15 minutes or so.

3   Preheat the oven to 400°F. Bake the crust for about 10 minutes, or until it just begins to turn brown. Cool slightly.

4 Whisk together the remaining 2 egg yolks, the eggs, sugar, cornstarch, and cream. Arrange the cherries on the crust, then pour most of the batter over them. Bake for 5 minutes; the batter will settle a little bit. Add the remaining batter and bake until nicely browned on top and a skewer or thin blade inserted into the batter comes out clean, 15 to 25 minutes. Cool.

5 Dust the tart with confectioners' sugar, and serve.

MAKES ONE 9- OR 10-INCH TART, ABOUT 8 SERVINGS

TIME: ABOUT 1½ HOURS, SOMEWHAT UNATTENDED

Chocolate tart in a chocolate crust

Scant 1 cup flour

¼ cup unsweetened cocoa powder, plus some for dusting

Pinch of salt

5 tablespoons sugar

½ pound (2 sticks) cold butter

1 tablespoon milk

6 ounces good bittersweet chocolate, roughly chopped

1 egg

2 egg yolks

This is an easy crust to work with, yet it's extremely tender and delicate when baked. The filling is the work of a moment.

1 Combine the flour, cocoa, salt, and 2 tablespoons of the sugar in a bowl or food processor. Add half the butter and cut it in or process until the mixture is crumbly. Add the milk and, by hand, knead the mixture into a smooth ball; if it is too moist, add a little more flour. Wrap in plastic and refrigerate for 30 minutes.

2 Roll out the dough on a lightly floured surface. Line a 9- or 10-inch tart pan with it. Refrigerate the crust, for 15 minutes or so.

3 Preheat the oven to 400°F. Prick the bottom of the crust all over with a fork, then bake for 10 minutes, until firm.

4 Meanwhile, melt together the remaining butter and chocolate over low heat, stirring occasionally. Cool slightly. Whisk together the egg, the yolks, and the remaining 3 tablespoons sugar, then whisk into the chocolate mixture.

5 Fill the hot crust and bake for 3 minutes, no more. Remove from the oven and cool, then dust with cocoa and serve.

MAKES ONE 9- OR 10-INCH TART, ABOUT 8 SERVINGS

TIME: ABOUT 1½ HOURS, LARGELY UNATTENDED

Caramelized walnut **tart**

1½ cups plus 2 tablespoons flour	2 cups sugar
¾ cup almond powder	½ cup cream
13 tablespoons butter, softened	1½ cups walnuts

To make almond powder, see the headnote for the Clafouti Tart (page 407). This is a rich, gooey filling that appeals to those of us who have always loved caramel, yet it isn't too too sweet. The crust is a variation on Petit Beurre, an unusual cookie we featured in our first book. Be sure to refrigerate the tart for at least an hour before serving.

1 Preheat the oven to 400°F. In a bowl, mix together the flour, almond powder, 4 tablespoons of the butter, and ½ cup of the sugar, squeezing the mixture between your fingers. It will hold together, but barely. Press the dough onto a nonstick baking sheet, in a rectangle about ½ inch thick. Bake for 15 minutes, or until pale brown and cracking at the edges. Cool.

2 As soon as the pastry is cool—it will harden—use your fingers to crumble it into the container of a standing mixer with a paddle attachment. Add 5 tablespoons of the butter and mix for about 5 minutes, or until the butter is completely incorporated and you can press the dough together with your hand; again, it will be crumbly. Press the crumbs into the bottom and up the sides of a 9-inch tart pan to form a shell; refrigerate for 1 hour, or more.

3 Preheat the oven to 400°F. Bake the crust for 10 minutes, or until lightly browned. Remove and cool on a rack.

4 Put the remaining 1½ cups sugar in a heavy saucepan or skillet about 6 or 8 inches across. Turn the heat to medium and cook, shaking the pan gently from time to time but not stirring, until the sugar melts and turns quite brown, about 10 minutes. Turn the heat off, then carefully (it will bubble up) add the cream and the remaining 4 tablespoons butter all at once. Turn the heat to low and cook, stirring, until the butter melts, then cook for another 2 minutes or so. Stir in the walnuts until they are well coated; the mixture will be very sticky. Cool slightly.

5 Spread the filling in the baked shell; refrigerate for at least 1 hour before serving.

Simple to Spectacular

MAKES ONE 9-INCH TART   TIME: ABOUT 2 HOURS, LARGELY UNATTENDED

Tarte au vin

8 tablespoons (1 stick) butter, softened

1 cup confectioners' sugar

5 egg yolks

1¼ cups plus 1 tablespoon flour

One ½-bottle Sauternes or other sweet wine

Juice of 1 lemon

4 eggs

1 cup plus 2 tablespoons sugar, plus more for topping

3 tablespoons cornstarch

This unusual tart begins with a sweet crust that is offset by an almost sour filling, reminiscent of lemons but made with sweet wine. It's given a little crunch by caramelizing sugar on its top at the last moment as if it were crème brûlée.

1 Cream the butter and confectioners' sugar together in a bowl; add the egg yolks and whisk until creamy. Stir in 1 cup plus 2 tablespoons of the flour; the dough will be moist. Scoop it out of the bowl onto a piece of plastic wrap and refrigerate for 30 minutes.

2 Roll out the dough on a lightly floured surface to a thickness of ¼ inch or less. Line a 9- or 10-inch tart pan with it and trim the excess dough. Refrigerate for 15 to 30 minutes. Preheat the oven to 450°F. Bake the crust for about 10 minutes, or until it is nicely browned; cool completely before filling.

3 Combine the wine, lemon juice, and ½ cup water in a small saucepan; bring to a boil and turn off the heat. Separate the eggs. Beat the yolks with the 1 cup sugar, the cornstarch, and the remaining 3 tablespoons flour. Slowly pour about one-third of the wine mixture into the yolks, whisking all the while. Then pour the yolks back into the saucepan with the wine. Return to medium heat and cook, stirring almost constantly, until the mixture is thick and a few bubbles rise to the surface. Cool for about 5 minutes, stirring occasionally.

4 Whisk the whites until they hold stiff peaks, gradually adding the remaining 2 tablespoons sugar. Fold in the hot wine pastry cream. Pour into the cooled crust and refrigerate at least 2 hours. When you're ready to serve, cover the top of the tart with a thin layer of sugar and caramelize it with a propane torch (or run it under a broiler). Serve immediately.

MAKES ONE 9- OR 10-INCH TART   TIME: 45 MINUTES, PLUS CHILLING TIME

Index

413

Simple to Spectacular

Simple to Spectacular